SHARED SPACE : DIVIDED SPACE

TITLES OF RELATED INTEREST

SHARED SPACE: DIVIDED SPACE

Essays on Conflict and Territorial Organization

EDITED BY

Michael Chisholm
University of Cambridge

David M. Smith
University of London

London
UNWIN HYMAN
Boston   Sydney   Wellington

Published by the Academic Division of
Unwin Hyman Ltd
15/17 Broadwick Street, London W1V 1FP, UK

Unwin Hyman Inc.,
8 Winchester Place, Winchester, Mass. 01890, USA

Allen & Unwin (Australia) Ltd,
8 Napier Street, North Sydney, NSW 2060, Australia

Allen & Unwin (New Zealand) Ltd in association with the
Port Nicholson Press Ltd,
Compusales Building, 75 Ghuznee Street, Wellington 1, New Zealand

First published in 1990

British Library Cataloguing in Publication Data

Shared space / divided space: essays on conflict and territorial
organisation.
    1. Human. Geography. Spatial aspects.
    I. Chisholm, Michael. II. Smith, David M. (David Marshall),
1936–   .
304.238
ISBN 0-04-445153-9   ISBN 0-04-445714-6

Library of Congress Cataloging in Publication Data

Shared space / divided space: essays on conflict and territorial
organization / edited by Michael Chisholm and David M. Smith.
        p.   cm.
Includes bibliographical references.
    ISBN 0-04-445153-9   ISBN 0-04-445714-6
    1. Ethnic relations. 2. Human territoriality. 3. Nationalism.
I. Chisholm, Michael, 1931–   . II. Smith, David Marshall,
1936–   .
GN496.S53 1990
305.8–dc20   89-70554 CIP

Typeset in 10 on 12 point Bembo by Computape (Pickering) Ltd,
North Yorkshire
and printed in Great Britain by the University Press, Cambridge

Preface

When we speak of a nation or a state, we generally assume that it is cohesive and that its citizens share a 'national interest' which transcends class, language, race or creed. In practice, many countries experience deep internal divisions based on distinctive group identities, which often have a geographical expression. The manner in which the use of space is controlled, including the temporal rhythm of life in the spatial domain, has an important bearing on the control of conflict among individuals and groups, and on the extent to which divisions and differences within the population are reinforced or ameliorated. The organization of territory may contribute to social cohesion or it may exacerbate divisions, and consequently affects in an intimate way the survival and reproduction of society, or its demise. The ongoing interaction between the structure of society and its spatial form is a theme of critical importance in contemporary human geography and also in the work of social analysts more generally.

The idea for this book originated on a flight from Tel Aviv to London in 1986. The editors were returning from their first visit to Israel (as members of a group of British geographers invited under the auspices of the Academic Study Group for Israel and the Middle East). Experience in the field with Israeli colleagues opened our eyes and minds to the reality of life in shared yet divided space in a particularly volatile part of the world. As we shared our observations, it occurred to us that there is no up-to-date collection of case studies which conveys the extraordinary variety of such conflict situations in the contemporary world, and the similarly varied responses to the problem of how space can be organized. The territorial conflicts within Israel, Northern Ireland and South Africa are well known. Less familiar, perhaps, are the tensions which exist within the Indian sub-continent, within Australia and Canada, in parts of the Soviet Union, and elsewhere. And often unrecognized are the echoes of these problems which can be found in most societies, including Great Britain.

We have assembled a collection of essays, each of which addresses the theme of conflict and territorial organization in the context of specific contemporary societies. We attempt to show the diversity of the human experience and of the ways in which societies have actually responded to problems they face in sharing and dividing space. In this sense, the volume is descriptive of the world as it is and makes no claim to prescribe. As editors, we have encouraged our contributors to link their case material to the general themes they consider

vii

appropriate, but we have deliberately refrained from suggesting a common theoretical perspective, confident that reality must inform theory just as much as reality requires some theoretical framework for its interpretation.

We are grateful to our contributors for their help and co-operation. We hope that this volume is some compensation for their labours, though of course we accept responsibility for any defects there may be in its overall structure.

MICHAEL CHISHOLM
DAVID M. SMITH
Cambridge and London
June 1989

Contents

ix

List of tables

List of figures

Contributors

James Anderson Faculty of Social Sciences, The Open University.

Graham Chapman Department of Geography, School of Oriental and African Studies, University of London.

Michael Chisholm St Catharine's College and Department of Geography, University of Cambridge.

John Eyles Department of Geography, McMaster University.

Fay Gale Department of Geography, The University of Adelaide.

Roger Lee Department of Geography, Queen Mary and Westfield College, University of London.

Anthony Lemon Mansfield College and School of Geography, University of Oxford.

Dennis Pringle Department of Geography, St Patrick's College, Maynooth.

David M. Smith Department of Geography, Queen Mary and Westfield College, University of London.

Graham Smith Sidney Sussex College and Department of Geography, University of Cambridge.

Peter Slowe Department of Geography, West Sussex Institute of Higher Education.

Stanley Waterman Department of Geography, University of Haifa.

1

Introduction: the sharing and dividing of geographical space

DAVID M. SMITH

It is a matter of surpassing remark, when you come to think about it, what a change in the landscape occurs when you have made a place of your own. (Robert Ardrey 1971, 326).

Good fences make good neighbours. (Dominee Koot Vorster, quoted in Harrison 1981, 157).

The occupation of territory is fundamental to human existence. To survive even at the most 'primitive' level of social organization and technology requires access to natural resources of the land, sometimes supplemented by the sea but never wholly independent of *terra firma*. Whether perpetually on the move, as hunters and gatherers, or in fixed and permanent settlements, access to particular territory or to the product thereof is a necessary condition of life. And this may require exclusive access if the means of subsistence are to be assured: a place of their own may become their own place.

Some sharing of space is, of course, implicit in any group's occupation or control of a particular piece of territory. Individual membership of the group will be based on a shared identity, or understanding of entitlement to some of what is produced or appropriated collectively. A place may be found for individuals or subgroups who are, in certain respects, different, or do not 'fit in' to the predominant group. But exclusive command over territory also implies inability to share with some others, and their exclusion by various means. Hence the central paradox: people come together in space to facilitate survival (or human betterment, even prosperity), yet may also be obliged to exclude. The space accessible to humankind is continuous, yet there is a need to control access and hence create partitions, as Gottmann (1973) recognized in his classic work on territoriality. Geographical space must simultaneously be shared and divided.

Conflict is an inevitable outcome of this paradox, especially in a world with finite natural resources and other desirable attributes of territory. Such conflict can range from trivial incursions by others into the space we have made our own – our home, garden or neighbourhood – to warfare and the kind of global

1

conflict which threatens human survival. Good fences may keep out intruders at one spatial scale, and even make for better relations with others, but the wider resolution of conflict with a territorial basis challenges human wisdom to its limits.

This chapter provides an introduction to some general themes to be addressed in the case studies that follow. A review of the concept of territoriality leads to the significance of nationalism and its expression in the modern nation-state. Consideration of the exclusion or segregation of some members of society is followed by recognition of the circumstances in which formal separation or partition of territory may occur, and by brief reference to supranational integration. The individual case studies can then be set in context. Fuller discussion of the more general themes can be found in the literature cited and in modern political geography textbooks (e.g. Johnston 1982, Mellor 1989), as well as in some of the contributions to this collection.

Human territoriality

The human occupation and control of territory is more complex than is reflected in the traditional concerns of political geography with frontiers and boundaries, and the disputes to which they can give rise. It is also more subtle than the assertion of a 'territorial imperative' analagous to that of the animal kingdom. Humankind establishes an identity with pieces of geographical space, and a sense of place, comparable with the deepest of emotional ties and feelings. Such identity can be expressed at a variety of different scales, which are by no means mutually exclusive; they may in fact satisfy rather different needs. Just as home and (for some) garden may provide sources of security, privacy and recreation, being and feeling a Londoner or Liverpudlian, or standing on 'the Kop' on a Saturday afternoon supporting the local football team, can bestow a sense of belonging to and affiliation with something beyond self and family. Some people find their primary territorial identification at the regional rather than local scale, as Geordie, Northerner or New Englander; for many it is nationality and patriotism, while an increasing number may seek and actually feel international, perhaps European.

Territorial identity may require and be reinforced by symbols, like the American 'stars and stripes', the British lion (or bulldog) and the Welsh leek. Liverpool and Everton fans will be distinguished by their scarves and other emblems of affiliation, proudly and on occasions aggressively displayed, just as national chauvinists may flaunt their flag. Symbols can also play a part in territorial demarcation. Landowners post signs to 'keep out' of 'private property'. Graffiti may distinguish the 'turf' of rival city gangs as clearly, for those involved, as the limits of national territories may be identified by border posts. Such potent elements of the landscape as the white cliffs of Dover are a reminder of the role of conspicuous physical features in marking and deliminating space. Particular rivers, mountains and the like can take on deep, even mystical or religious significance in expressing what may have been the harrowing historical experience of surviving the struggle with nature or some hostile competitors for territory; hence the significance of Ayer's Rock to Australian Aboriginals, for example, or of Blood River to Afrikaner South Africans as a reminder of their victory over the Zulus.

But is is easy to overemphasize territory as a source of human identity, abstracting from the broader context in which such sentiments arise and are reproduced or changed. The two meanings of the word 'land', prefixed alternatively by 'a' and 'the', are suggestive of the association of different ways in which it is experienced: a reminder that the territory with which we identify may alse be the soil that we cultivate, as the source of material existence. The occupancy of land is purposeful and societal: the private ownership of land and its resources arises in a particular social milieu, as do urban gangs, and when white South Africans refer to 'their land' they make a political assertion which implicitly excludes blacks, backed by what the whites view as virtually divine right of occupancy. And to some, such as the indigenous peoples of America and Australia, the land is (or was) sacred, to be both utilized and respected collectively, with private ownership of the kind introduced by settlers from elsewhere an incomprehensible concept.

Territoriality is, therefore, not some innate human trait but a social construct. It can take different forms in different geographical and historical circumstances, and its specific manifestations must be contextualized. It is not sufficient to see territoriality simply as a normal and necessary characteristic of human existence, or an imperative as Ardrey (1971) put it. Territoriality and its various expressions must be recognized as means to some end, such as material survival, political control or xenophobia.

Something of this conception of territoriality is captured by Sack (1986, 19) as: 'the attempt by an individual or group to affect, influence or control people, phenomena and relationships by delimiting and asserting control over a geographical area'. Central to this practice will be the exercise of *claim* over territory, as opposed merely to its occupation, though the latter may assist and be a prerequisite for the former. To give effect to a claim, in the sense of delimiting and asserting control, may involve undisputed tribal right of occupancy, modern property rights backed by legal protection, or national state sovereignty. These all give legitimacy to the particular claim on territory, as externally recognized with its autonomy respected, though such recognition and respect may have had to be fought for, literally as well as figuratively, and may remain to some extent subject to dispute and possible conflict.

Hitler's Germany provides a frightening instance of the use of territoriality for political purposes. The concept of *Lebensraum* (literally, living space) was used to justify the territorial expansion thought necessary to secure for the German people enough food and raw materials for a vigorous and healthy population. An ideology of racial superiority was used to legitimize the

3

occupation of land of the Slavs to the east, and then to eliminate the Jews to achieve the ultimate homogenization and fusion of people and territory. Human history provides few more eloquent illustrations of the awful power of territoriality, and of its eventual limitations as German expansion came into conflict with the capacity of others to defend their historic homelands.

That the use of territoriality to achieve particular ends can be indirect is illustrated by the conflict between Britain and Argentina over the Falkland or Malvinas Islands in the South Atlantic, which erupted in warfare in 1983. Whatever the merits of the competing national claims, that these small islands achieved such significance at this particular time was related to a wider political context. The internal popularity of the Galtieri government in Argentina had much to gain from the capture of 'their' Malvinas, just as the Thatcher government in Britain increased its popularity at home by repulsing the invasion of 'our' Falklands. In different circumstances and at different times, control of this territory would not have been an issue or would have been resolved peacefully, as was the case for many years.

The identification with territory can substitute, or be substituted for, other possible affiliations. Thus *patriotism* as a form of territoriality may transcend religious, ethnic or class identity, and can be used to focus a people's loyalty. It may be easier to persuade people to fight for the territorial integrity of Britain (including the Falklands) than for the Church of England, the 'ruling class', or a particular economic order such as capitalism. Calls to patriotism can thus obscure other interests. As Johnston, Knight & Kofman (1988, 5) suggest:

> territoriality ... reifies power, identifying it with a place rather than with social relations. In other words, territoriality can be used ideologically, to promote certain interests which require social control by associating them with a place within which that control is recognised.

This emphasizes the importance of not necessarily taking territoriality at face value, but understanding its specific manifestations in their broader political, economic and social context.

Nations and states

The relationship between territoriality and political organization is of such recent concern in geography that Knight (1982, 514) could comment that:

> In some general works by political geographers lip service is given to the emotional bonds of groups to politico-territorial identities, generally defined loosely as the nation or nation-state, but remarkably little has been done beyond this. Rather than quickly bypassing such bonds of group as being of little importance, we should focus further attention on the theme

4

for, by doing so, we come into touch with one of mankind's continuing problems, that of how best to give political recognition to these identities.

Subsequently, considerable attention has been given to the links between territorial identity, nationalism (or regionalism) and the state, as forces promoting integration and also making for instability or political conflict.

It is important at the outset to distinguish between nations and states, as the modern nationalist ideal that they should be geographically coincident as *nation-states* can otherwise lead to confusion (Anderson 1988, 21). The term *nation* is usually applied to a population group, or a *people*, with certain unifying characteristics. A *state* is a particular political unit with territorial delimitation, possessing *sovereignty* in the sense of being recognized by others and its autonomy within its boundaries generally respected. The territory of a state in its usual 'national' sense is sometimes referred to as a *country*. Another meaning of the word 'state' has come into common usage in social science in recent years, as the body or apparatus performing functions of government, national or local (as in the 'local state'). The concept of the nation-state expresses identity between a people and their sovereign geographical space. And as Williams (1986, 196) reminds us, 'the quest for national congruence, defined as the attempt to make both national community and territorial state into coextensive entities, has been a major feature of modern history, particularly in Europe'. Living in a world now organized into nation-states, it is easy to overlook the relatively recent origin of the idea of congruence between a people with shared characteristics and the spatial expression of their political organization. The modern conception of the nation-state emerged from monarchies such as England, France and Spain in late feudal times and became codified as nationalist doctrine only at the time of the French Revolution. Anderson (1989, 36) quotes John Stuart Mill's *Considerations of Representative Government* (1872) as indicative of the authority which this view had achieved by the latter part of the 19th century:

> It is, in general, a necessary condition of free institutions that the boundaries of government should coincide in the main with those of nationality ... Where the sentiment of nationality exists in any force, there is a *prima facie* case for uniting all the members of the nationality under the same government, and a government to themselves apart.

The problem is, of course, that the historical disposition of national groups involves spatial mingling, making geographical coincidence difficult to achieve and its pursuit laden with conflict.

Nationalism is a complex phenomenon, and subject of a growing literature in political geography and beyond (e.g. Knight 1982, Williams & Smith 1983, Johnston, Knight & Kofman 1988, Williams & Kofman 1989). The common association with statehood is reflected in many definitions; for example, Wusten (1988, 189) descibes nationalism as, 'a doctrine proposing some measure of political autonomy for and in the name of a social collectivity assumed to be homogeneous and cohesive'. It can arise initially from a people's perceived common identity, be it cultural, ethnic or religious. It can also be strengthened or promoted by the creation of a state and the subsequent process of internal homogenization: 'The nationalism of the state thus reinforces and reproduces the collective sense of identity of its citizens, an identity that attempts to transcend alternative allegiances' (Johnston, Knight & Kofman 1988, 8). Nationalism has a strong intellectual as well as emotive appeal, which assists its power as an instrument in political mobilization and territorial organization, for it enables something to be imposed upon individual differences and class cleavages, as well as on the internal cultural diversity which is the reality of most 'national' populations.

Class is perhaps the most important of the allegiances which can conflict with nationalism. Just as an emphasis on territoriality may obscure underlying social relations of power, so nationalism and its implicit unity of purpose may distract attention from class divisions and social disunity. This is captured by Anderson (1989, 36) in his emphasis on the role of culture in the formation of nations:

Nationalisms are territorially-based forms of ideology and politics; they link historically and culturally defined 'nations' to political statehood, either as a reality or an aspiration. Nationalists typically find their unifying symbols and criteria of 'belonging' in the particular history and geography of their territory – its culture, language, landscape, and so forth – and, despite antagonistic class relations within the nation, geographical proximity in particular territory can also provide at least an illusion of a common economic interest.

Hence the widely accepted notion of a 'national economy' which, like the 'national interest', can be promoted without explicit reference to the class interests which will gain (or lose) unequally from its operation. The focus on nationalism as a state-building force should not obscure the economic significance of the rise of the modern nation-state. The emergence and spatial expansion of capitalism generated needs for an infrastructure of transport and communications as well as the regulation of trade and elements of social services, all of which could most conveniently be satisfied at a national scale through a taxation system which ensured a degree of uniformity of provision as well as facilitated the externalization of some costs of production on the part of capital. If a form of nationalism was harnessed to the creation of nation-states in 19th-century Europe, then specific historical circumstances rather than a natural and universal human trait were involved. As Agnew (1989, 173–4) remarks:

6

The coming of the nation-state in the nineteenth century was an important component in the growth of industrial capitalism. But it rose to importance in a very special set of circumstances and commitments to it in the form of nationalism were incomplete or often absent. Nationalism was never something inscribed on the hearts of men or a natural human characteristic. Rather, it was the political product of a particular set of circumstances that waxed and waned in content and support as circumstances changed. More significantly, perhaps, it was moulded by the experiences and expectations of everyday life. To the extent that nationalism takes hold of a population it is from the bottom up rather than from the top down. Nationalism, therefore, *can be* a response to practical conditions. It cannot be an autonomous force.

We will return to this issue later, for it is central to current debates on group and place identity.

The role that nationalism may play in the process of territorial political organization can thus vary considerably. The most common may be in connection with the aspirations of a relatively homogeneous cultural group, broadly defined, but even this may involve the unification of a population more or less diverse in certain respects. But nationalism can also be harnessed to the domination of one group by another, involving the imposition of what may be an alien or oppressive economic and social order. South Africa is a case in point: Afrikaner nationalism has assisted the domination and subordination of the black population, and also to some extent marginalized those whites who identify as English South Africans.

It will be clear from the above that nationalism and its outcomes are subject to both positive and negative interpretations (Knight 1982, 521). It may help to achieve group identity and cohesion, facilitated by territorial security. But it also implies, and often requires in practice, the domination of others, and possibly their exclusion and spatial separation.

Exclusion and segregation

One of the apparent paradoxes of the nation-state is that, whereas it customarily bestows certain rights of citizenship equally among the population, its institutions also permit and indeed legitimize unequal treatment in other respects. The democratic principle of one-person-one-vote, equal treatment under the law, and so on, do not entail equal access to property under capitalism, or indeed to privilege under socialism, never mind all the other inequalities built into markets or whatever mechanisms distribute society's benefits and burdens. Unequal access to the national territory, and indeed exclusion of some people from parts of it, is the rule rather than the exception.

7

Nation-states almost invariably incorporate 'minorities', distinct from the dominant population in some way that is held to justify different and usually unequal treatment. The sources of minority identity are principally racial, ethnic or religious, but they can also relate to role in the social relations of production. For example, in some societies there are slaves, who do not enjoy the same formal rights as the rest of the population, serfs are not treated as landowners, and the franchise may be conditional on property ownership – as in Britain not so very long ago. Gender may also be a source of inequality with respect to what may otherwise be regarded as basic rights of citizenship: the full female franchise was achieved within living memory in Britain. The deprived 'minorities' may actually be majorities in some societies, whether 'natives' in colonial countries, blacks in contemporary South Africa or women in the Muslim world and in Victorian Britain.

The formal social exclusion of individuals or distinctive groups of people is a long-established practice. It may be related to the imperative of *physical survival*, as for example in the case of lepers or other carriers of infectious illness which could threaten the entire population. One response to the AIDS epidemic in Britain has been to suggest that a system of exclusion may be required, whereby AIDS sufferers would be confined to separate living areas (*The Times*, 18 November 1987). The containment of others posing a physical threat, such as violent criminals or the mentally deranged, is a universally recognized necessity.

Exclusion may also be related to *social reproduction*, or the perpetuation of a particular kind of society. That this may not always be easy to distinguish from physical threat can be illustrated by the case of AIDS referred to above, a condition which raises moral issues concerning 'proper' sexual conduct as well as endangering public health. If ever implemented, the spatial exclusion of those with AIDS could be construed not only as a response to society's physical survival imperative, but also to the 'moral panic' raised by increasingly public affiliation with homosexuality. Spatial exclusion would reinforce a view of heterosexuality as the norm, as well as exaggerating the extent to which AIDS is infectious and its sufferers a physical threat to others.

Anthropologists have identified various forms of exclusion of particular people at particular times, as part of the rituals of small agrarian or hunter-gatherer societies which bind them together and assist their reproduction. Examples relate to puberty, rites of passage such as coming of age or bereavement, and fertility, as well as to individuals whose appearance or behaviour fails to fit some prescribed norm. That such practices are by no means confined to preindustrial societies is illustrated by the treatment of those identified or labelled as 'deviants' today. As Sibley (1988, 410) has remarked: 'there are many recent instances of collective action against groups who appear to threaten the perceived spatial and social homogeneity of localities, whether the threat comes from ethnicity, sexual orientation, disability or life-style'. He sees this process as similar to the purification and cleansing rituals of more 'primitive' societies. While there are links with the notions of racial purity propagated in Hitler's Germany and, less extremely, among white South Africans, this form of exclusion is part of a broader impulse to seek conformity and uniformity with specified spatial limits. And it may be self-reinforcing; as Philo (1989, 259) recognizes:

> once initiated, the many 'mainstream' fears and prejudices regarding certain 'outsider' groups often feed into concrete social practices through which distinctions between these 'mainstream' and 'outsider' peoples are *reproduced* and even rendered more acute. And these concrete practices commonly boast a *spatial* dimension, as when society seeks to exclude their 'outsiders' from normal places of living and working.

Philo had in mind in particular those classified as lunatics in 19th-century Britain and incarcerated in asylums as a result; their deviation from normal conduct may have been far from madness in any clinical sense, just as those political dissidents in the Soviet Union once sent for psychiatric treatment may have been guilty merely of publicizing their sanity. The message is clear: that there is a particular conception of normal and acceptable conduct, conformity to which assists its reproduction.

Geographical space is deeply implicated in social exclusion. Social inter-action generally implies physical propinquity (modern means of communicating over long distances notwithstanding) and to separate people spatially if in no other way can be an effective means of exclusion and control. The prison, asylum and leper colony are examples of total spatial exclusion of people seen to threaten society in various ways, while the ghetto within which Jews were once confined, for much if not all of the time in some European cities, was almost as rigid a form of containment *de facto* if not always *de jure*. Few ghetto walls survive today, but in Berlin one such structure conspicuously divides people speaking the same language but living under different political ideologies; its complete removal would symbolize much more than the possible reunification of Germany.

Racial segregation in urban residential space is a repetitive feature of the contemporary city, notably in the United States, and if no longer maintained by custom of quasi-legal authority, many blacks still 'know their place'. Groups distinguished by ethnicity or religion may also be subject to a not entirely voluntary form of spatial congregation. Less formal still is the residential sorting and grouping of similar people which can be observed to some extent in the socialist cities of Eastern Europe where accommodation is assigned according to need (in principle if not always in practice), as well as under capitalism, where unequal incomes brought to the housing market make for socio-economic differentiation with a strong spatial expression.

Of course, the spatial sorting of groups within a nation-state or its cities may to some extent reflect an unproblematic, even healthy, diversity of a population making choices among alternative living environments. The term *pluralistic* society is sometimes used to describe this kind of situation. Politically, the diverse groups are able to hold one another in check, so that none achieves a dominance which would enable them to impose their will on others. However, the assertion of pluralism can be used to mask cleavage and conflict, serving an ideological role in conveying a false sense of harmony and implying that particular institutional arrangements somehow resolve conflict satisfactorily.

If marked spatial segregation exists, it is often most evidently experienced by immigrants. They may have come from the countryside to the city, and find particular localities congenial or convenient (perhaps because of cheap housing or neighbours of a similar origin), while other areas are inaccessible on financial grounds. They may be from another country and culture, differentiated by language and skin colour. Their social and spatial history may be one of initial segregation and exclusion from much of the mainstream of what is sometimes referred to as the 'host' society, followed by attempts to integrate involving assimilation into the indigenous society through a process of acculturation which involves abandoning some imported attitudes and values. Spatial integration, or a reduction in segregation, may then take place. There can also be a subsequent retrenchment, involving the reassertion of traditional values, perhaps accompanied by voluntary (re)segregation and the establishment of the group's own institutions, such as the schools for Muslim children now appearing in some British cities. Much depends on the historical and local circumstances of the group in question, and on the response of the indigenous people and institutions.

As race is the most common criterion of social exclusion and spatial segregation in the contemporary world, it is easy to bestow some autonomous causal power on race, racism and racial discrimination in the patterning of cities and societies. But just as territoriality and nationalism are social constructs, the nature and operation of which will depend very much on the prevailing geographical and societal context, so it is with race(ism). Hence (Smith 1989, 153):

> Segregationism may be regarded as a system of beliefs which seeks justification for racial exclusivity *within* national boundaries, one which helps politicians justify not only overtly separatist practices, but also the inadvertently segregationist outcomes of ostensibly aracial policy.

Thus, most public housing projects in American cities and some (usually inferior quality) council blocks in British cities may be occupied exclusively by blacks, despite supposedly 'colour-blind' housing allocation policies, the outcome being accepted within an ideology or commonsense understanding in which race is a relevant criterion in the differential treatment of people. Racism is thereby reproduced, in the spatial form of the city as well as in people's consciousness and social practice.

A further aspect of the internal division of space is the way this may be used for the purpose of political control of a diverse population, elements of which may challenge the majority or dominant group. Williams & Kofman (1989, 5) explain this as follows:

> The sovereign control of territory by the state ensures that the dominant culture can circulate freely throughout the space . . . within its boundaries. It can divide and rule its territory so as to hinder or prevent attempts by subordinate cultures from developing a solid base from which to reproduce their own culture.

A national education system, perhaps with a centrally determined core curriculum, can assist homogeneity, discouraging the use and preservation of regional languages or dialects. This strategy implies central control and a minimum of barriers (including political boundaries) to the dissemination of a common culture. Groups which might form alliances against the state can be split up into different political jurisdictions, as with the black 'homelands' in South Africa, which emphasize tribal identity as against racial solidarity. Reservations can be designated for particular peoples, to help preserve their identity as well as the homogeneity of the rest of the population. Some degree of local or regional autonomy can be given to those within specific areas, as a concession to their differences, while preventing the break-up of the state.

Political jurisdictions can be defined so as to internalize certain benefits while perhaps externalizing some of the costs. For example, the benefits from a new public facility such as an electricity generating station may be confined to residents of a particular city, while some of the air pollution generated may spill over into other areas. Suburban commuters may be the main beneficiaries from the facilities provided by rates or taxes paid by inner-city residents. Another aspect of this subdivision of space is *gerrymandering*, or the deliberate (re)drawing of political boundaries to achieve political advantage, used in some American cities to deprive blacks and Hispanics of representation in proportion to their numbers in the population, and in South Africa to give disproportionate weight to the rural conservative vote. Such measures are often indicative of an insecure territorial hold on the part of the dominant group, and of the danger of loss of control, which can then lead to demands for separation.

Separation and partition

The presence of dissatisfied or nonconforming groups can be a serious source of tension and conflict within a society. They may threaten the (perhaps superficial) unity of culture achieved in the building of a nation-state, exposing

11

an underlying diversity which calls into question the predominant nationalistic basis of territorial integration and control. The central state authorities are impelled to respond. As Knight (1988, 118) puts it:

> Dissenting minorities exist in many states. For some sub-state regional minorities the struggle against state oppression is constant, difficult and, indeed, at times severe, for tyrannical governments (of the left and of the right) aggressively seek to control, subdue, and even eradicate those who do not conform to what is held to be the societal norm.

An understandable reaction on the part of the minorities is to seek political independence. And this can imply spatial separation, in the sense of a people seeking a sovereign territory of their own.

Just as nationalism is a potent force for territorial integration, as in the formation of nation-states, it can also be marshalled behind separatism or territorial disintegration. Indeed, 'in recent years the major growth of nationalism has been in the form of separatist or autonomist movements aimed at the break-up of existing states rather than in the form of a nationalism of existing states' (Agnew 1989, 167). The recognition and resurgence of nationalist sentiments can provide a source of collective identity conspicuously opposed to that of the dominant group, challenging it in the same kind of terms as those used to legitimize the existing state, and offering a rationale for some alternative political/territorial organization. To quote Williams & Kofman (1989, 2):

> Thus linguistic, religious and territorial affiliations are pressed into service to liberate subject peoples from the bondage of being ruled by those perceived as being non-nationals. Self-determination is the *sine qua non* of the modern nationalist movement. So profound has been the nationali-zation of modern political culture that the nation-state is taken to be the natural locus of modern political affiliation.

This suggests that the process of formation of nation-states over the past few centuries somehow failed to take account of important and enduring national identities. Or could it be that circumstances have changed, to resurrect latent nationalisms or even create new ones?

The changing significance and expression of nationalism poses difficulties for those seeking generalization: it is an enigma for theorists (Agnew 1989, 167). The assertion that nationalism is a global phenomenon and an autono-mous force which somehow transcends other affiliations, from individualism to class consciousness, is contradicted by the reality that it is time and place specific in its incidence in support of separatism, just as in support of national spatial integration.

The fact that modern separatist movements often occur in peripheral and relatively underdeveloped regions may suggest a link with the process of uneven development under capitalism, with the core somehow exploiting the periphery which is thereby stimulated to respond. The thesis of *internal colonialism* is an influential derivative of this perspective (Johnston 1982, 124–6; Anderson 1985, 23–4). However, by no means all poor peripheral regions exhibit separatist tendencies driven by nationalism, and some such movements focus on relatively prosperous regions such as the Basque country in Spain. Furthermore, it is within the peripheral republics, rich (Baltic) and poor (Asiatic), that nationalism is currently being asserted in the socialist Soviet Union. These observations make it hard to accept national separatism as the inevitable outcome of the operation of a particular mode of production.

A less deterministic approach is to recognize certain necessary conditions for separatism, along with some 'trigger mechanism' to set a movement in motion. The necessary conditions may include real or perceived material deprivation, cultural domination, political inequality, and some ethnic basis reflecting a failure of the homogenization process; they may appear largely local in origin, or arise from changing positions in the national or international economy. The crucial additional ingredient could be mobilization of intellectuals capable of articulating a nationalist ideology, a charismatic leader, an act of brutal state repression, or simply someone throwing a bomb. Human agency, through the power of individuals, may be the crucial ingredient in making an active social movement out of the necessary but not sufficient structural conditions. There is much conviction to the argument that nationalism in its separatist role is a matter of practical politics (Agnew 1989), of what is found effective in a particular context.

The range of possible considerations in specific circumstances, and indeed the very complexity of the issue, is explained as follows by Johnston, Knight & Kofman (1988, 12):

> If we wish to achieve a more contextual and historically rooted understanding of nationalism, we shall have to undertake an analysis that incorporates the relationship between the state and civil society (national and regional), the economic, social and cultural transformation these societies have undergone, the different responses of the social classes and groups to these changes, and finally the internal geographical divisions of the territory claimed by nationalist movements. It is only with a rounded understanding of nationalism that we can appreciate that nationalism is not an inevitable strategy, but rather that it emerges as one amongst several possible territorial and political responses to a changing world.

A catalogue of modern separatist movements would embrace many parts of the world. Anderson (1985, 5) identifies 17 instances of 'regional resurgence' in Europe, including the familiar Scottish, Welsh and Irish nationalist movements and the perhaps less well known cases of Alsace and the South Tyrole.

Kidron & Segal (1981) provide a more comprehensive picture. But rather than repeat cases here it is more useful to recognize the different spatial forms which such *secessionist* movements can take (Johnston 1982, 140). The most common is when part of a state claims separate nationhood and the right to a separate territory, as with the establishment of the state of Eire (the Irish Republic) in Ireland and the aspiration of some Scottish nationalists. Another form is the unfication of nations which are split up but make a claim to their own state, as the Jews achieved with the formation of Israel and to which the Kurds in parts of Iraq, Iran, Syria, the USSR and Turkey aspire. A third form is *irredentism*, under which people living in part of one state assert that they and their territory should be part of another, or the claiming of part of another state on this basis, the Armenians of Nagorno-Karabakh in the Azerbaijan Republic of the Soviet Union being a highly publicized recent case.

The response of the central state to separatist claims (if not to ignore or repress them) can be to make some concessions in the form of *devolution*. This involves allowing certain recognized territorial sub-units a degree of political autonomy short of complete independence. For example, the Spanish government has conceded considerable autonomy to the Basques, Catalans and Andalusians. In Britain the possibility of devolution is a continuing element in the process of coming to terms with Welsh and Scottish nationalism. The outcome may be *federalism*, under which the nation is divided into relatively autonomous units, as in Belgium, which is now a federation of the Flemish and Walloon sections of the country. However, most federal states are not the result of concessions to nationalistic separatism (e.g. Australia, the Soviet Union and the United States), though they may assist the accommodation of different identities, as in Canada.

A more extreme response is *partition*, or national territorial disintegration. As Waterman (1989, 122) remarks, 'partition is often understood to be a geographical solution of last resort, in contrast to federalism which is sometimes referred to as the "ideal geographical solution" to the problem of ethnic minorities within states'. Partition is thus proposed or implemented when tension or hostility between groups has reached the point of potential or actual conflict and the use the force against one another. Stultz (1979) has distinguished various kinds of partition, such as that following international conflict (e.g. the divisions of Germany and Korea), the breaking away of one state from another (as with Norway from Sweden, Bangladesh from Pakistan), the creation of entirely new national entities (in, e.g. Ireland, India and Palestine), and *de facto* but otherwise unrecognized partition as in the case of Cyprus.

There is a distinction between *divided nations* such as Germany and Korea, where separate states have been created for part of the same national group, and *partitioned states* where the internal heterogeneity of the original state has been recognized in its break-up, as with former British India. In so far as the original basis for nationality continues to be a potent force, then pressures for reuniting the divided states will arise, whereas this is unlikely in the case of partitioned states where the earlier basis for territorial integration may have been externally imposed (by colonization, for example), with little regard for the pre-existing human geography. Where the current unifying element within the parts of divided nations is political ideology, i.e. capitalism or communism, the prospects for reunification may be remote; the future of 'East' and 'West' Germany will provide an interesting test of the capacity of nationalism to overcome almost half a century of political division.

Supranationalism and localism

These observations lead to the question of whether there are allegiances that transcend those of nation and state, encouraging broader spatial integration (or otherwise). The obvious case is that of the *empire*, which was able to unite large tracts of the 'known' world more than 2000 years ago and much of the entire world under British imperialism, albeit with some coercive force. That such organizations were transient is a matter of history. Capitalism as a mode of production is intrinsically expansionary and now unifies much of the con-temporary world through economic interdependence and shared social rela-tions which overlay local or national culture. Indeed, there is an increasing internationalization of culture promoted by product homogenization, the consumption imperative of capitalism, and the power of mass communication to convey messages and lifestyles almost instantaneously from one part of the world to another. Communism is supposed to unite the workers of the world; more obviously it has promoted economic collaboration and integration among certain nations (members of COMECON) while remaining open to some influences from the capitalist world – not least its culture of conspicuous consumption. Another supranational force is religion, once pre-eminent, then eclipsed by other forces, and now ascendant again in the form of Islam.

Any supranational movement will generate some tension with existing territorially based affinities. As the best known of these movements in recent years, the European Economic Community (EEC) has been remarkably successful, in its own terms, in working towards a common market in 1992. However, the possible conflict with national sovereignty is seldom far beneath the surface and periodically erupts as the British government, for example, reacts against standardization of product description, monetary union or a charter of workers' rights, thought somehow to threaten the 'national interest'. Nationalism can still be harnessed, selectively, in chauvinistic displays of independence, and often with considerable regard to politics at home.

The prospects of world government, truly united nations and even a 'global village' figure large in some contemporary rhetoric. The truth is still of a sharply divided world, whether by political ideology, religion, ethnicity or nationalism. And there are signs in some places of a renewed localism, as people seek and find identity in the close and familiar rather than in remote and possibly debased political doctrines, the mass culture of consumerism, or ethnic and religious movements which at times seem to make a virtue out of violence. This can be back to the countryside in some idealistic rejection of urban life, the development of neighbourhood exclusivity, or seeking to preserve ethnic/cultural distinction brought from elsewhere or resurrected from the past. Insularity, the assertion of local distinction and the privatization of life about home and family are not unnatural reactions to a wider world over which people may feel little if any control. More than ever before, perhaps, people feel a need for a place of their own, and to build good fences.

The case studies

The cases in the chapters that follow may now be set briefly in context. They have been grouped so as to correspond roughly with the main topics introduced above, though they do not follow quite the same sequence. Some are rather specific in focus while others address a number of related issues.

First (Ch. 2), Michael Chisholm takes the case of Britain as a 'plural' society, with what is usually regarded as a strongly homogeneous population and in which overt conflict has been slight. The subdivision of space is seldom so rigid as in the 'Cutteslowe walls', which still separated two neighbourhoods in Oxford in the late 1950s, yet residential segregation on the basis of ethnicity, religion and class clearly exists, both as a historical legacy and associated with 'New Commonwealth' immigration. This raises the question of the extent to which such divisions are voluntary or enforced, and whether they are a good or bad thing. While there may be sound reasons for groups congregating voluntarily, the housing market acts as a constraint on dispersal, especially for immigrants, while continuing spatial concentration limits the capacity of the education system to facilitate a process of cultural homogenization and integration – which is itself being increasingly resisted by some groups, e.g. Muslims seeking their own schools. Chisholm concludes with observations at the broader scale, expressed in the resurgence of Welsh and Scottish nationalism which have thus far failed to pose much of a threat to the unity of Great Britain.

John Eyles (Ch. 3) concentrates on the division of urban residential space, familiar subject matter for social geography where there is a long tradition of viewing the spatial organization of the city as patterned by population characteristics. Eyles' focus is on the American city, where segregation on racial and ethnic grounds is a repetitive feature. He stresses the shifting, socially constructed (negotiated and contingent) nature and meaning of race, ethnicity and racism. He also shows that trends in racial segregation and inequality depend on the indicators and methods of measurement used. Typologies of different patterns of segregation can be identified, with different implications for group organization and identity. The blacks have been uniquely constrained from assimilation and remain isolated spatially, victims of economic marginalization and prejudice shared by no other group: race and place remain closely interwined. For others, ethnicity can be an important source of positive identity, but not necessarily associated with place.

The significance of ethnicity and nationalism in nation-building is examined in Canada by Peter Slowe (Ch. 4). He considers nationalism to be a form of ethnicity reinforced by state power, which has been strong enough to bind the competing ethnicities of English and French Canadians. English Canadian identity and Anglophone hegemony were maintained for a long time by political association with Britain; its retention was subsequently assisted by a shared history, mythology and language as well as by political, cultural and social integration. French Canadian identity was originally dependent on mythical association with what Slowe describes as a rural idyll of seigneurs and priests, as well as on language. Its subsequent reconstruction as a new French Canadian culture recognizing the reality of a modern industrial society, has been assisted by the room found for this group within the wider nation of Canada which accepts the dualistic nature of its population. Thus the French separatist movement based on Quebec turned out to be merely a transient expression of a changing identity.

A rather different form of nation-building is described next by Graham Smith (Ch. 5). The Union of Soviet Socialist Republics (USSR) has political ideology as its unifying element. This vast state incorporates 15 republics with some degree of autonomy in principle if not prominent in actual practice, and a larger number of nationalities distinguished by history, culture and language. There is a longstanding tension between the centralized Russian-dominated state and its incorporated nationalities, which is now being expressed in a resurgence of nationalisms posing a challenge to the broader union and its political ideology. The so-called national question has emerged as a major threat to the process of *perestroika* (restructuring) initiated by President Gorbachev, the ultimate success of which may depend on the extent to which reform from above (and from the centre) and ethno-regional interests (in the periphery) can accommodate one another.

The Indian sub-continent or South Asia is another major part of the world with tension between diversity and political integration. Graham Chapman (Ch. 6) points to the divisions of language, religion, culture and economy within what might otherwise be recognized as a natural geographical region on which political unification could be based. Attempts to unify this territory culminated in the British Raj, but this was unable to survive the religious forces making for spatial separation; hence the creation of Pakistan. The spatial discontinuity of the original Pakistan soon led to the separation of Bangladesh. The present geopolitical subdivision of South Asia represents the prioritization of religious homogeneity over both local diversity and natural geographical cohesion at a broader sub-continental scale. The outcome is instability, within the existing states and in the relations between them.

Israel provides another example of what might be regarded as an unstable geo-political situation (Ch. 7). Here, as Stanley Waterman explains, two peoples claim sovereignty over the same territory, the one (Palestinian Arabs) having been involuntarily incorporated into the new state of the other (Israeli Jews). The existence of Israel is itself a potent territorial expression of the nationalism which united a people who had for centuries been scattered across the globe, and whose identity and need for security was heightened by the Holocaust of the Second World War. The Palestinians themselves belong to the broader external grouping of the Arab peoples, who have at times threatened the survival of Israel, but they have developed their own form of nationalism to underpin an increasingly strident and violent threat from within. Waterman reveals the importance of the occupation and settlement of land in the Jewish control of Israeli territory as well as of the occupied 'West Bank' area.

Next, James Anderson (Ch. 8) examines the separatist movement associated with Basque nationalism in Spain, which has led to devolved government for three provinces. Basque nationalism arose from the incomplete nature of the unification of the Spanish state, which enabled the region to retain some of its own institutions and a language different from any other in Europe. It was strengthened by a process of industrialization which was seen to be introducing into the region an alien creed (socialism) as well as an unfamiliar population (migrants seeking work). Anderson argues that the rise of nationalism and separatism in this peripheral region is not convincingly explained by uneven development and subordination to the centre, but by a more complex interplay of economic, social and political processes in which geography is closely implicated, although the concept of internal colonialism has been effectively marshalled behind the Basque cause.

The case of Ireland, considered by Dennis Pringle (Ch. 9), is in some respects similar to that of the Basque country: a 'peripheral' yet integral part of an established state with separatist aspirations. Here it is religion added to national identity which differentiates the population. Partial separation was accomplished by partition at one spatial scale (between Northern Ireland and the Republic of Ireland, and between both of these and Britain), but with the result that significant numbers of people of one religous group live within a state dominated by the other. In Northern Ireland there has been bitter conflict between the alternative nationalisms of Catholicism/Irish republicanism and Protestantism/British unionism. Residential segregation in these circumstances is unsurprising, with territoriality reinforcing other aspects of separation and group identity, and hence the potential for further conflict. In the Irish Republic, however, a greater degree of spatial and social integration of the (smaller, Protestant) minority has been achieved, and overt conflict largely avoided. This does not suggest that integration is the solution to Northern

Ireland's problems, however, for here the (Catholic) minority is much larger and part of an all-Ireland Catholic (and possibly republican) majority.

For the next case (Ch. 10) we move to the rigidly imposed racial separation of apartheid in South Africa. Separation takes place at three spatial scales: individual (or 'petty apartheid'), within urban residential space via race 'group areas', and nationally through the creation of independent states for the black majority (the 'homeland' or 'Bantustan' policy at one time referred to as 'separate development' and later as 'multi-nationalism'). This extreme response on the part of a threatened (white) minority has involved large-scale population movement to create race-space homogeneity. Anthony Lemon explains how residential segregation reinforces as well as reflects the social formation, limiting change to more open pluralism. However, rigid separation is now breaking down, as the contradiction between a divided society and polity and an increasingly integrated economy generate tensions that the imposed spatial structure cannot accommodate, either within the cities or at the national scale. But it will not be easy to dismantle the urban and political geography which apartheid has created. And while it is no easier to envisage a solution to conflict in South Africa, some form of spatial reorganization must be a central strategy.

The land set aside under apartheid for the emergence of black states was originally referred to as 'reserves'. The reservation of land for an indigenous population is more commonly associated with what have become distinct minorities marginalized by occupation and settlement by people from elsewhere. Fay Gale (Ch. 11) looks at the spatial 'solution' arrived at by European settlers to the 'problem' of the Aboriginal people, which required legitimizing the appropriation of most of the land they occupied. The answer was the designation of reserves. While there are shameful aspects of the way the Aboriginals were treated, confinement to reserves helped to preserve their culture, and, to an extent, their physical characteristics; even those Aboriginals who have become urbanized derive their identity from their reserve backgrounds. Gale explains how the contemporary movement for Aboriginal land rights (in the sense of legal ownership and title) is an attempt to consolidate spatial separation as a means of ethnic and cultural survival. There is also an increasingly voluntary element in the spatial separation of Aboriginals in the cities, including the introduction of schools with Aboriginal cultural material in the curriculum. Thus, imposed segregation is being replaced by voluntary separation, opposed by most of the white majority, but uniting what is actually a diverse Aboriginal people. The division of space may now be rebounding, to the advantage of the Aboriginals.

Finally, we move to the supranational scale, as Roger Lee (Ch. 12) considers the various meanings attached to Europe in the context of integration. He stresses the limitations of an institutional interpretation, which concentrates on the imposition of a European community or common market upon the pre-existing pattern of nation-states. It was the emergence of capitalism which transformed an interconnected Europe into one of interdependence and growing *de facto* integration, from the Industrial Revolution onwards, albeit with a geographical unevenness which has persisted to the present. And it is capitalist social relations which bind together the EEC as the nearest thing yet to European unity, yet in a Europe divided since the Second World War on the basis of political ideology. However, moves towards completion of formal economic integration implicit in monetary union, for example, threaten national sovereignty in part of the world where nation-states have a long and potent history. But it is not simply a case of integration promoting uniformity, for the process of economic and social development will continue to be uneven in its geographical consequences: regional distinction will thus be maintained, even if national identity becomes increasingly blurred.

Roger Lee's concluding description of a funeral in the Chianti region of Italy, with its evocation of the everyday routinized practices of social reproduction, brings us back from the political economy of supranationalism to the local level of the experience of ordinary people. No matter how logical the formal division or integration of geographical space may be to those in power, who seek to resolve conflict as they understand it or to take advantage of the sharing of territory, their relevance to the lives of local populations may be more problematic. National boundaries may be an inconvenience, for example to work-seekers like the Mexicans crossing into California each day, even more so to families and ethnic groups separated by political diktat, and a brutal constraint akin to prison for those wanting what they see as freedom from some oppressive regime. However, the relaxation or removal of boundaries may mean little to the vast majority of people, for example Britons for whom the full realization of the European market in 1992 may affect some supermarket prices, even the coins in their pocket, but not their established routines of work, home and packaged tour to the Costa del Sol and its familiar distinctly un-Spanish cuisine. The supranational ideals of Europeanism are essentially those of the self-interested and intellectual: most people will not become international workers, nor necessarily less chauvinistically Brummy, Geordie or Scouse. The locale will continue to be the focus of life, for most of their lives. They will not, however, be oblivious to the broader territorial definitions, identities and processes, nor lacking in some sense of their meaning, for it is they who experience the consequences, including the conflicts. Awareness of the world beyond may be expanding, but everyday life continues to be largely local. The paradox of geographical space is as intense as ever, its annihilation by time only partial, its division as much part of life as its sharing.

References

Agnew, J. 1989. Nationalism: autonomous force or practical politics? Place and nationalism in Scotland. In C. H. Williams & E. Kofman (eds), 167–93.

Anderson, J. 1985. *Regions against the state*. Unit 26 course D205. Milton Keynes: Open University Press.

Anderson, J. 1988. Nationalist ideology and territory. In R. J. Johnston, D. B. Knight & E. Kofman (eds), 18–39.

Anderson, J. 1989. Nationalism in a disunited kingdom. In *The political geography of contemporary Britain*, J. Mohan (ed.), 35–50. London: Macmillan.

Ardrey, R. 1971. *The territorial imperative*. New York: Dell.

Gottmann, J. 1973. *The significance of territory*. Charlottesville: University Press of Virginia.

Harrison, D. 1981. *The white tribe of Africa*. London: BBC Publications and Ariel.

Johnston, R. J. 1982. *Geography and the state*. London: Macmillan.

Johnston, R. J., D. B. Knight & E. Kofman (eds) 1988. *Nationalism, self-determination and political geography*. London: Croom Helm.

Kidron, M. & R. Segal 1981. *The state of the world atlas*. London: Pluto and Heinemann.

Knight, D. B. 1982. Identity and territory: geographical perspectives on nationalism and regionalism. *Annals of the Association of American Geographers* **72**, 514–31.

Mellor, R. E. H. 1989. *Nation, state and territory*. London: Routledge.

Philo, C. 1989. 'Enough to drive one mad': the organization of space in the 19th-century lunatic asylum. In *The power of geography*, J. Wolch & M. Dear (eds), 258–90. London: Unwin Hyman.

Sack, R. 1986. *Human territoriality*. Cambridge: Cambridge University Press.

Sibley, D. 1988. Purification of space. *Environment and Planning D: Society and Space* **6**, 409–21.

Smith, S. 1989. The politics of race and a new segregationalism. In *The political geography of contemporary Britain*, J. Mohan (ed.), 151–71. London: Macmillan.

Stultz, N. M. 1979. On partition. *Social Dynamics* **5**, 1–13.

Waterman, S. 1989. Partition and modern nationalism. In C. H. Williams & E. Kofman (eds), 117–32.

Williams, C. H. 1986. The question of national congruence. In *A world in crisis?*, R. J. Johnston & P. J. Taylor (eds), Oxford: Basil Blackwell, 196–230.

Williams, C. & A. D. Smith 1983. The national construction of social space. *Progress in Human Geography* **7**, 502–18.

Williams, C. H. & E. Kofman (eds) 1989. *Community conflict, partition and nationalism*. London: Routledge.

Wusten, H. van der 1988. The occurrence of successful and unsuccessful nationalisms. In R. J. Johnston, D. B. Knight & E. Kofman (eds), 203–21.

2

Britain as a plural society

MICHAEL CHISHOLM

The wall itself was a substantial structure. Some seven feet tall it was supported at intervals by buttresses, and it was topped by a set of formidable revolving iron spikes which ran its entire length. The wall extended right across the road, across the footpaths at each side of the road and into the front gardens of the adjacent houses where it was linked to the garden fences by a tangle of barbed wire. It provided a completely impassable barrier. (Collison 1963, 13–14).

Is that a description of the Berlin Wall in its early years, or even of the 'peace lines' in Belfast? No, it is an account of the Cutteslowe walls in Oxford in the late 1950s. They were erected in 1934, separating two residential developments, one built slightly before the other. The first was a council estate built to rehouse people displaced by slum clearance; the second was a private development. As Figure 2.1 shows, the effect of the walls was to prevent council tenants obtaining direct access to Banbury Road and hence to local shops and the city centre. The walls were not finally demolished until March 1959, barely 30 years ago.

The walls, although highly unusual, were not unique. Collison records two other examples, one in Cardiff (1955) and another in Dartford, Kent (1958). They represent extreme cases of *forcible* separation, dividing residential areas on the basis of class in situations which, in every other respect, could be regarded as peaceful. While we are not accustomed to such overt separation by *force majeure*, we are habituated to the idea of class distinctions and the geographical expression of these distinctions in the patterning of residential areas, however much we may deplore this feature of society and fear for the exaggeration of the social divides occasioned by such separation, and worry about the permanence of social stratification from one generation to the next (Kerckhoff, Campbell & Winfield-Laird 1985). More important, though, our widespread concern with class obscures the fact that Great Britain is not an ethnically[1] homogeneous society and that the differences which do exist have, or may have, repercussions on the way that space is divided and shared, at various geographical scales. The problems in Ulster, therefore, are often regarded as a special (and extreme) case, for which we do not perceive parallels in mainland Britain. Indeed, by comparison with Ulster, and other parts of the world,

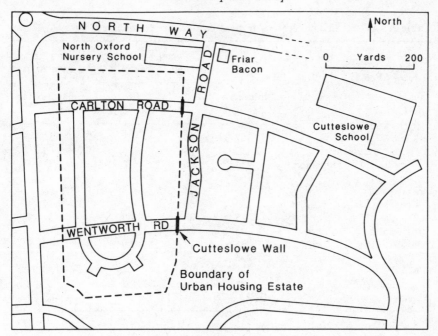

Figure 2.1 The Cutteslowe walls, Oxford.
Source: Collison 1963.

Great Britain is a mercifully peaceful place. Occasionally that peace is broken by riots, mostly urban and often loosely labelled 'race riots', but the concern which they generate is apt to evaporate with the subsequent quiescence. In any case, such disturbances directly affect only a very small number of persons, especially of the white host population. It is easy, therefore, to ignore such problems as there are, in the hope that they will go away of their own accord. On the other hand, to maintain the peaceful character of this country, it behoves us to consider carefully the plural nature of our society and the impact on that peace of the way in which space is shared and divided by class and by ethnic group.

Britain as a plural society

Net emigration has been a longstanding feature of Britain, and the immigrant flows used to be mainly from Europe, especially at times of political upheaval or economic disaster. Since the Second World War, both patterns have changed. Britain now experiences net immigration, and the inward movement originates in diverse countries, such that immigrants may now be distinguished by colour of skin as well as by language, religion and culture.

Table 2.1 Great Britain: ethnic composition of the population, 1984–6.

Ethnic group	Total number 000	Percentage 0–15	Percentage 60 or over	Percentage resident in English metropolitan areas
White	51 107	20	21	31
All ethnic minorities	2 432	34	4	69
West Indian or Guyanese	534	26	6	81
Indian	760	32	5	66
Pakistani	397	44	2	66
Bangladeshi	103	50	1	79
Chinese	115	28	5	52
African	103	26	4	75
Arab	66	17	5	62
Mixed	235	53	3	58
Other	119	28	4	63
Not stated	691	29	17	37
All ethnic groups	54 230	21	20	33

Source: Social Trends **18**, 1988, 26.

New Commonwealth immigration was on a very considerable scale in the 1950s and early 1960s, giving rise to widespread fears concerning the continued harmony of British society. These anxieties were heightened by riots in 1958 (Nottingham and Notting Hill) and translated into legislation which, since 1962, has sought to restrict the flow. With the tightening of restrictions, plus changes in the labour market, the inward movement is now quite small and likely so to remain for the foreseeable future. Nevertheless, as Table 2.1 shows, ethnic minorities now comprise 4.5 per cent of the population in Great Britain, and that proportion is almost certain to increase over the next 30 years on account of the relative youthfulness of these elements in the population. Note also that those of Irish birth comprise somewhat over 0.5 million, or about 1 per cent of the total.

Religious affiliation provides the second dimension along which the population divides. Table 2.2 shows that church membership totals some 8.63 million persons, and that this total is spread among several Protestant and non-Protestant denominations. Some of these are closely identified with ethnic minorities, most notably, perhaps, in the case of the Muslims, many of whom have Asiatic origins.

The third dimension or plurality relevant in the present context is social class. Notwithstanding that class and class conflict have been an important theme in much postwar literature, the practical definition of class remains elusive (Robertson 1984). Is class to be determined by relationship to the means of production (as Marxists assert), or by reference to specific criteria, of income,

Table 2.2   United Kingdom: adult membership of churches (millions).

	1975	1985
Anglican	2.27	1.98
Methodist	0.60	0.47
Baptist	0.27	0.24
Presbyterian	1.65	1.39
Other Protestant	0.54	0.57
Total Protestant	5.29	4.65
Roman Catholic	2.54	2.16
Non-Trinitarian	0.31	0.35
Muslim	0.40	0.85
Other churches and religions	0.41	0.62

Source: Social Trends **18**, 1988, 171.

housing, lifestyle and attitudes? Or should we take the self-assessment of individuals, subjective though that may be? If we take the last view, then approximately one-quarter of the population is 'middle class', almost one-fifth 'upper working class' and almost exactly half consider themselves to be 'working class' (Table 2.3). Note, however, that from one generation to the next, the proportion of 'working class' is declining, with a corresponding increase in the other two categories.

The fourth dimension is the existence in the United Kingdom of four territorial units which, in at least two cases, are often perceived as nations. By sheer size of population, England is the dominant partner, with 47.3 million inhabitants in 1986. Scotland is the second largest (5.1 million), followed by Wales (2.8 million) and Ulster with 1.6 million. Collectively, the three smaller components comprise 17 per cent of the total. Ulster will be considered in Chapter 8 and will not be further discussed in the present essay. In respect of both Wales and Scotland, nationalism has been and remains a political force with which to reckon.

Two fundamental points are implied in the above listing of the dimensions of differentiation. Problems concerned with the sharing and dividing of space may occur at various geographical scales – from the residential neighbourhood to the major regional divisions. In the second place, problems may arise in just one dimension but may also arise in two or more simultaneously. For example, some ethnic divisions intersect with income differences and hence with social class. The greater the degree of such intersection, the less tractable are the problems regarding the sharing and dividing of space. On the whole, the issues which surround these matters have been given comparatively little public attention in Britain, possibly because it is widely assumed either that this is a homogeneous population, or if it is not, that it should be. Thus Rex was moved to observe, in the context of ethnic segregation in the inner cities:

Table 2.3   Great Britain, 1984: self-rated social class (percentages).

Social class	Self	Parents
Upper middle	2	2
Middle	25	18
Upper working	19	10
Working	48	59
Poor	3	8
Do not know / no response	3	2
	100	99
Sample size	1675	1675

Source: Social Trends **16**, 1986, 23.

The idea of a multi-ethnic, multi-cultural society is not a very important element either in our political ideologies or in the professional ethos of planners . . . Creating and planning such an area is a considerable challenge to planners, but one they have hardly begun to consider. (Rex 1981, 38 and 41).

Separatism or integration: good or bad?

Britain emerged from the Second World War with a strongly imprinted class structure permeating social, economic and political institutions, visible in the separation of residential areas by the quality of housing and environment. Flushed by victory in a damaging war, it was optimistically believed that a 'new Jerusalem' could be built (Barnett 1986), in which, *inter alia*, social barriers would be broken down and integration across the class divide fostered, through education, social welfare arrangements and the like. The building of New Towns and the renewed onslaught on slums formed part of this programme. Integral to the New Town concept was the idea of neighbour-hood units, providing a reasonable social mix within a small area, in which the daily necessities of life were all close at hand. By mixing income and/or social groups geographically, it was held that access to public resources, such as schools, libraries, shops, etc., could be equalized. It was further believed that understanding and tolerance would be enhanced, so that even if differences of income and tastes persisted, harmony could be achieved.

That ideal contrasts with the considerable degree of spatial differentiation which occurs in British cities, as highlighted by Engels and others in the 19th century and confirmed by classic modern works such as Jones 1960 on Belfast and Robson 1969 on Sunderland. During the 1930s, the Chicago school of sociologists provided a theoretical basis to explain the fact of social segregation in urban areas. These and other studies, showing the sharpness of social segregation on class, religious and ethnic dimensions, have been summarized in several readily available works (e.g. Burtenshaw & Bateman 1981, Herbert & Johnston 1976a, Timms 1971, Peach 1975). The New Town ideal was thus in conflict with observed realities and our understanding of the relevant economic and social processes.

As the flow of New Commonwealth immigrants became established, they tended to congregate in a limited number of areas, such as Notting Hill in London (Peach 1966 and 1968, Robinson 1986). This spatial concentration was widely perceived to accentuate the differentiation of the urban mosaic, contrary to the expressed ideal of the time. Simultaneously, slum clearance and the building of large council estates, combined with the construction of large owner-occupied estates, were tending to create and reinforce the 'working-class'/'middle-class' divide in the housing market.

That there is considerable spatial separation of immigrant groups is not in doubt, with London the main focus. The 1981 census recorded the place of birth for all persons enumerated. In Great Britain, 6.3 per cent were born abroad, divided as:

Irish Republic	1.1%
New Commonwealth and Pakistan	2.8%
Other countries outside the UK	2.3%
	6.2%

(Note the rounding error.) Those born in the New Commonwealth and Pakistan accounted for 9.5 per cent of the total population within Greater London. At the borough level in London, concentrations exceed that level by a considerable margin, the five highest being:

Hackney	16.5%
Ealing	17.0%
Newham	17.1%
Haringey	18.7%
Brent	22.5%

Elsewhere in the country, the two most notable concentrations of New Commonwealth and Pakistani first-generation immigrants are Slough, at 13.5 per cent, and Leicester, at 15.3 per cent. Other sizable concentrations are to be found in Bradford, Luton and Wolverhampton (OPCS 1984). However, as Table 2.4 shows, these concentrations are the exception rather than the rule, in that ethnic minorities are found throughout the country.

Is segregation by class or ethnic group something to be deplored? Or is it something that might confer benefits? Or if neither the extreme of full integration or full separation is desirable or practicable, what should the balance be, and how might that balance shift over time? Hence, given that a

Table 2.4 Great Britain, 1981: percentage of the population born in the New Commonwealth and Pakistan.

Percentage range	Number of districts and boroughs
0.1–0.9	224
1.0–1.9	125
2.0–4.9	73
5.0–9.9	23
10.0–14.9	8
15.0–19.9	5
20.0 and over	1
	459

Source: OPCS 1984.

considerable degree of spatial segregation does exist, in which direction ought policy to be moving and how quickly? These are difficult questions for which, I believe, simple and clearcut answers do not exist. However, central to our thinking about these matters is one important question of fact: is the *de facto* separation which we observe to be attributed to some form or forms of coercion, or does it arise voluntarily? On the answer to that question will depend our attitude to two propositions which represent opposite points of view:

> One of the most-voiced fears about West Indian and other coloured immigration to Britain is that it might result in the formation of ghettos. There is a universal and probably correct assumption that ghettos are the geographical expression of social failure. The ideal distribution, from a social point of view, seems to be dispersal. (Peach 1968, 83).

> the orderly social geography of the city is the product of like individuals making like decisions on where to live within the framework of constraints which society imposes. (Herbert & Johnston 1976b, 2).

Segregation: voluntary or enforced?

This question may be posed in respect of both ethnic and class divisions of society. Although the two dimensions intersect, in the present context we will treat them separately, starting with ethnic segregation.

As the ethnic concentrations began to crystallize in the 1950s and early 1960s, many commentators believed that incipient 'ghettos' were arising from

28

the essentially involuntary behaviour of the recent immigrants. This viewpoint was persuasively argued by Rex & Moore in 1967 (see also Rex 1981). On the basis of detailed work in Sparkbrook, Birmingham, Rex & Moore concluded that it was the constraints imposed by the housing market which obliged recent immigrants to congregate. On the one hand, new immigrants, initially just one family member in many cases, either did not qualify for local authority housing or would have to wait an inordinate length of time. In practice, therefore, council housing was not initially available, except for quite small numbers. On the other hand, the mortgage market was not readily accessible either, given the low incomes that many immigrants earned and the attitude of building societies to the reliability of those earnings. Thus, the New Commonwealth immigrants were forced to turn to the private rented sector and, in due course, to purchase cheap older properties which would serve for multiple occupation. Consequently, the location of properties to rent provided the initial focus of settlement, especially where properties were available that could be used for multiple occupation.

The Rex & Moore thesis provides a plausible mechanism to explain why many initial footholds were established in particular places. It is less convincing as an account of the consolidation and persistence of urban segregation. Robinson (1979) has argued that in Blackburn the segregation of Asians conforms to a thesis which was advanced in the early 1970s, that Asian immigrants intend to return to their country of origin, and that segregation of a voluntary nature occurs because the immigrants do not regard themselves as permanent residents. However, the evidence which Robinson adduces for upward social mobility and changes in the areas of concentration suggests that the Asian inhabitants of Blackburn are in fact behaving like permanent, not transitory, residents, although that is not the construction which Robinson puts on the data. More generally, if the return migration thesis were valid, we would expect to see a rising flow of outward migration, given the large influx of the 1950s and early 1960s; of this there is no sign. Robinson now writes of the 'myth of return' (Robinson 1986).

Another explanation for segregation is that immigrants have come with the intention of settling permanently and that the segregation which does occur arises voluntarily. In the first place, chain migration is a common feature of migration streams, recognized by Torsten Hägerstrand in his studies of Swedish migration to North America which led to his classic theory of diffusion. Once a bridgehead has been established in an alien, and possibly hostile, environment, subsequent immigrants are likely to gravitate thereto. They know earlier migrants or have an introduction, they can expect to be given initial shelter and help in finding a job and they will not have to rely solely on their often limited knowledge of English. Subsequently, there may well be positive benefits for the immigrant groups staying in close proximity (Boal 1972 and 1976, Peach 1984, Rex 1981). Friendship and kinship networks are more easily maintained over short distances than long, especially for

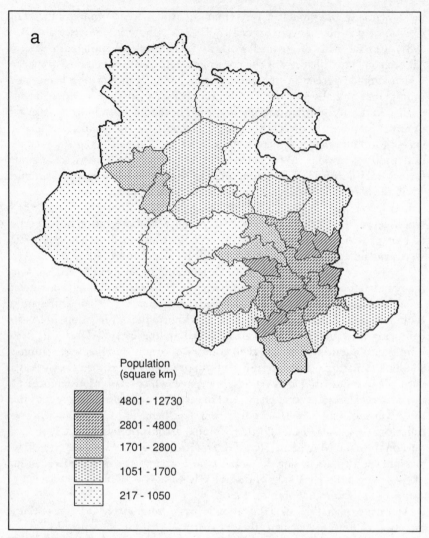

Figure 2.2a Ethnic segregation by ward, Bradford, 1981. Total population density.
Sources: Ram & Phillips 1985, Census of Population.

persons whose incomes are low. Concentration also means that certain facilities can be provided which a dispersed population would not warrant; for example, in the early 1960s one could buy green bananas and sweet potatoes in Shepherds Bush market (London), and other foodstuffs desired by the locally large population of West Indians. If there is hostility between the host and immigrant communities, then extreme segregation provides either for mini-

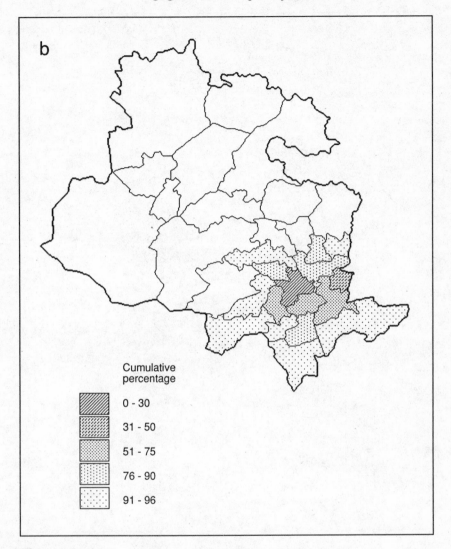

b

Cumulative
percentage

0 - 30

31 - 50

51 - 75

76 - 90

91 - 96

Figure 2.2 b Ethnic segregation by ward, Bradford, 1981.
Sixteen wards with most of the Indian electorate.

mizing contact or for defence against attack. Even in the absence of this
motive, people who maintain their own culture will wish to build their own
places of worship and assembly, even schools, the existence of which will then
provide a permanent incentive to maintain close proximity.

Immigrants do not form a homogeneous group. Those arriving from
different national origins form distinct communities, as the West Indians of
Notting Hill and the Asians of Bradford. Furthermore, these national
groupings are themselves clearly divided. The West Indians come from

31

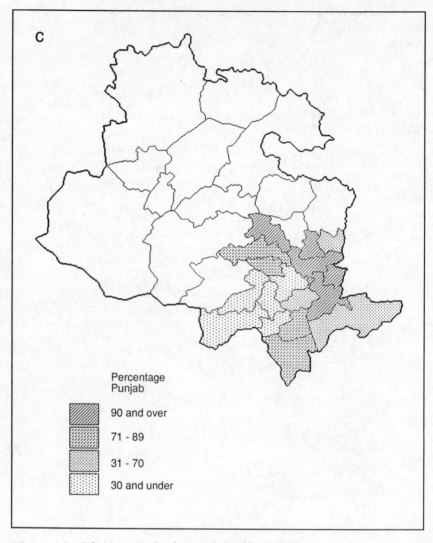

Figure 2.2 c Ethnic segregation by ward, Bradford, 1981.
Sixteen wards, proportion of Indian electorate from the Punjab.

distinct islands and their provenance is reflected in the geography of settlement in Britain (Peach 1966, 1968 and 1984). Similarly, within a city the Asian population dissolves into distinct groups – the Gujarati and Punjabi people, those who speak Urdu, etc. (Robinson 1979 and 1984, Ram & Rees 1985; see Figure 2.2). The separation of immigrants according to source regions, occurring within the general areas of immigrant concentration, suggests a strong element of voluntary behaviour. This impression is reinforced by the fact that the location of concentrations within cities has often changed quite noticeably over the last 20–30 years; concentrations are maintained but move geographically. Banton summed up the situation with these words:

> it is possible that even were discrimination in employment and housing successfully combated, the minority communities might prefer to remain separate in certain spheres of social life. (Banton 1967, 388).

However, we should not lose sight of the fact that New Commonwealth immigrants are widely distributed throughout Great Britain. The 1981 census records place of birth and tabulates for each district the proportion born abroad. Taking just those born in the New Commonwealth and Pakistan, the pattern shown in Table 2.4 is striking. They are represented in every single district but the number of districts in which the proportionate concentrations are large is remarkably small. Their wide dispersal and relatively small numbers, even though they may be (and usually are) geographically concentrated within the districts, suggests a substantial element of the voluntary in the overall pattern.

Thus it may be the case that the causes of ethnic segregation are changing over time. Initially, it seems likely that the involuntary mechanism postulated by Rex & Moore predominated, reinforced by the hostility of the host population. With the passage of time, the voluntary element may be becoming more important, albeit reinforced by continuing hostility and the limited choice available for those with low incomes and high rates of unemployment. At the same time, the host community has itself relaxed some of the drive toward homogeneity and is more willing to accept a diversity of speech and culture – for example, the BBC no longer insists on the use of a standard 'Queen's English' for news programmes and the like. Consequently, it has become easier to accept the desire of identifiable groups – whether immigrant or not – to maintain their separate identities.

At first sight, class segregation differs from ethnic segregation, in that individual and intergenerational mobility is possible between classes but not between racial groups, other than by intermarriage. Nevertheless, on one view of the social sorting process, class and ethnic divisions arise for essentially the same reasons. If we follow the Chicago branch of urban ecology on the one hand, and on the other accept the primacy of markets, we will expect spatial sorting according to income to be the norm. Since class and income are apt to be related, the effect will be segregation by social status. If, within a market economy, individuals are free to locate and relocate in a manner which reflects their circumstances, spatial differences within the city will be a mirror held to the range of social differences. The spatial pattern will be considered as problematic only if the social differences of which it is the mirror are themselves regarded as unacceptable, or if the fact of spatial sorting creates difficulties, as proponents of the 'cycle of deprivation' hold.

The British housing market is, however, segmented in a manner which impedes the free mobility of individuals and families and, for some at least, locks them into a situation in which they are conscious of curtailed freedom. Of all the dwellings in the United Kingdom in 1986, 63 per cent were owner-occupied, 27 per cent were rented from local authorities and New Towns, and only 10 per cent were available on private rental. Council dwellings are intended for those on low incomes, whose resources are inadequate for them to command on the open market the space they need for a civilized life. Notwithstanding the imperfect match between low income and council tenure, council estates are generally perceived to be 'working-class' in character. In constrast, owner-occupation is associated with the 'middle class'.

The distribution of dwellings among the tenure groups has changed dramatically over the years. In 1913/14, the private rented sector accounted for 90 per cent of the total, owner-occupiers 8 per cent and local authorities only 2 per cent (Balchin 1985). The private rented sector has been steadily squeezed out by rent and other controls, the increase in owner-occupation and, until 1978–80, by the local authority/New Town stock. However, new building by local authorities and New Towns has been cut back in the last decade, and the 1980 introduction of the 'right-to-buy' has sharply accelerated sales of publicly owned dwellings to sitting tenants; as a consequence, this sector declined from 32 per cent of the total to 27 per cent between 1978–80 and 1986. In the seven years from 1980 to 1986, almost 970 000 local authority and New Town dwellings were sold, or 14 per cent of the 1978–80 stock (*Social Trends* **18**, 1988, 132 and 136; see also Kleinman & Whitehead 1987).

In the early postwar period, there was urgent need for a large net addition to the national stock of dwellings as well as for the resumption of the prewar slum clearance programme. It was widely assumed that unit costs would be lower if individual developments were large. As a result, many council estates and private developments were conceived and executed on a large scale in and around the bigger cities, notwithstanding that this was contrary to the ideal of the socially mixed neighbourhood unit, on the basis of which the New Towns were simultaneously being built.

Opportunities for upward and downward mobility across the tenure divide are limited. In normal circumstances an owner-occupier cannot voluntarily relinquish his home and become a council tenant, since either he will not qualify for a tenancy or will score so few points that he will be far down the queue. Conversely, many council tenants were effectively trapped in the public rented sector, either because saving the requisite down payment for a mortgage would be beyond their financial means, or, were that hurdle successfully cleared, the variability of earnings might preclude the offer of an adequate mortgage. The fact that recently some 14 per cent of the publicly owned stock of dwellings has been sold under the generous terms available with the 'right-to-buy' provisions indicates that there was indeed a significant minority of council tenants who wished to change tenure but had been unable to do so. Although this legislation was enacted for patently political reasons by the Conservative government of Mrs Thatcher, as a means of breaking the electoral domination of Labour in many council estates, the policy touched a chord with many council tenants and has now been formally endorsed by the Labour Party. More recently, 'right-to-rent' legislation may take the process substantially further. While the overall effect should be to reduce the barriers to mobility between tenures for many present-day council tenants, there is a real concern that in the process the residual core of persons who genuinely need publicly provided shelter will be even further 'marginalized', or segregated. To set against that outcome is the undoubted fact that monolithic council estates now have significant numbers of owner-occupiers in their midst, which is a move, however small, towards the expressed ideal of integration across class divides.

Tenure has a measurable impact upon geographical mobility. Council tenants are relatively free to move within the dwelling stock of their housing authority, so that even if the initial allocation gives individuals accommodation which is regarded as inferior or badly located, subsequent spatial sorting does occur. But that sorting tends to create and then to perpetuate 'better' and 'worse' estates within the stock of each individual authority. On the other hand, migration between housing authorities is difficult and consequently limited in scope. Council tenants are 50 per cent more likely to move than are owner-occupiers, but of those who do move, owner-occupiers are 14 times more likely to move between standard regions than are council tenants. The overall effect is that owner-occupiers are much better able to adjust their residential location between the standard regions than are council tenants; in this sense, space is very unequally divided. In the conclusion to the study from which these data are taken, the authors remark:

we view our results as a comment on the lack of administrative and political determination to tackle the more difficult aspects of managing council houses ... rather than as a central issue in the debate concerning the desirability of reducing the council house stock. (Hughes & McCormick 1981, 936).

The division of the housing stock almost entirely between council tenancies and owner-occupiers has undoubtedly been a major source of long-term inequality between households over and above that which can be attributed to income differences alone. There is little doubt that, given the large scale of many estates in both the public and private sectors, the effect has been to emphasize the homogeneity of residential areas and the sharpness of the social divide which separates them.

Micro-scale divisions of space

Within urban areas, we are all familiar with the way in which 'natural' barriers separate social areas. Railways and canals are classic cases, with urban motorways a more recent additional barrier. It would be unduly expensive to build large numbers of bridges and tunnels to cross such barriers, which are generally accepted with little or no comment. In addition, though, most of us are familiar with suburban road systems which, lacking crucial connections, are disjointed and incomplete. That incompleteness may have arisen through the accidents of history, or may be due to conscious decisions by planners and others. Whatever the origin, the effect is to facilitate movement in certain directions and to inhibit it in others; some households are joined, maybe as a neighbourhood, but simultaneously they are separated from others.

Figure 2.3 illustrates this widespread phenomenon, showing a small area lying to the northwest of central Cambridge. As the city expanded, 19th-century development occurred in the Huntingdon Road/Halifax Road area, followed at the end of that century and early in the 20th by the construction of Richmond Road and Oxford Road. Windsor Road was built in the interwar period, while the areas leading off Tavistock Road were built after 1945. The Sherlock Road complex has the largest houses in this segment of Cambridge. Socially there are considerable differences between the small segments, associated with the age and style of the dwellings and the circumstances under which development occurred. The road pattern imposes a degree of separateness, which is only partially mitigated by some pedestrian ways. Residents accept the existence of the partial barriers to movement, because they self-evidently exist and the cost of providing road links would be high relative to any perceived gain. If we compare Figure 2.3 with Figure 2.1, however, we are entitled to speculate what might have happened if Carlton Road and Wentworth Road in Oxford had been built to form an enclave off Banbury Road, and with no connection to Jackson Road.

The situation exemplified from Cambridge is replicated in most if not all cities and towns, not as an occasional aberration but as a common pattern. The social engineering which is implied in such cases is accepted. At one level it is hardly noticed and never commented upon. On another, such partitioning of space may confer on the residents of each area a sense that they know their neighbours, and are aware of the presence of strangers whose intentions may be untoward. The control which one has over private space is in some degree extended to the immediately adjacent public space. It is the absence of such control which seems to be one of the great failures associated with gargantuan high-rise blocks of flats.

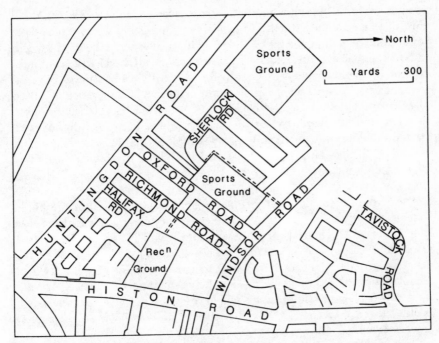

Figure 2.3 The limited connectivity of residential road systems, part of northwest Cambridge.

School, locality and choice

We have a confusing situation in Britain. From 1945 onwards, the prevailing ethos has been to break down class barriers in the education system, to provide better opportunities for those who come from 'working-class' backgrounds. The most effective means for achieving this aim has been perceived to be the abolition of selectivity, which in turn implies some form of comprehensive schooling. At the secondary level, the maintained sector is now dominated by comprehensive schools. At both the primary level and the secondary level it has been customary for each school in the public sector to have its own catchment area. As a result, all the children within a given catchment should go to the same school, with only limited exceptions. In general, it has been assumed that the absence of selectivity will enhance the opportunities for those from deprived backgrounds without adversely affecting the more fortunate ones, and that the mixture of social classes would help to ameliorate class divisions.

The most widely noted divergence from this ideal of social mixing is the existence of private schools, which educate about 7 per cent of the nation's children. However, there are other ways in which the school system makes separate provision, and though political controversy is absent, this should not cause us to ignore the existence of explicitly or implicitly separate provision. Some children with severe physical handicap, such as the deaf, attend special schools at public expense. Much larger numbers are affected by the continued existence of voluntary-aided schools, for which the public purse pays the greater part of the costs but in certain important respects the instruction reflects a particular religious belief. In 1986, about 23 per cent of all pupils in the public sector in England attended voluntary schools, which, in the majority of cases, are denominational. Church of England schools predominate at the primary level, Roman Catholic at the secondary level, while other voluntary schools of long standing include both Methodist and Jewish schools (*Social Trends* **18**, 1988, 53).

The second major departure from the homogenizing ideal in the public sector is the treatment of Welsh in the Principality's schools. It is already the language of instruction in some schools, and is widely taught as a 'second' language. That position will be reinforced with the introduction, in 1992, of a national curriculum. Thereafter, Welsh will be taught as a core subject in all schools designated as bilingual, and elsewhere as a foundation subject. The aim is that all 16-year-old school leavers will have 'a substantial degree of fluency in Welsh', thereby creating 'a bilingual society in Wales' (*Sunday Times*, 15 January 1989).

Because day schools draw their pupils from quite a small radius, the social mix within schools is determined by the social mix within their respective catchment areas – working-class council estate, middle-class suburb, etc. Only very exceptionally will a school draw its pupils from a representative cross-section of society. The absence of selective entry does not, therefore, guarantee the mixing of classes and the amelioration of class divisions. Indeed, existing spatial differences may be reinforced through the operation of the market for owner-occupied housing, in that parents may be willing to pay a premium price to live within the catchment of a school which is esteemed.

The homogenizing ideal of postwar education provision has, therefore, been significantly limited in practice for some considerable time. Nevertheless, it has been assumed that the children of immigrants from the West Indies, India, Pakistan and elsewhere should attend their local schools to receive an education in the official language of the host community and to absorb its religious faith and culture. However great the difficulties which the children might face, it was generally assumed that such a policy provided the best means for the integration of the immigrants.

The present Conservative administration takes the view that parents should be given greater choice in the education of their children and should be able to exercise greater control in the management of schools. Legislative provision has recently been made to give effect to these policy objectives, by easing the restrictive effects of school catchment areas, by working toward greater devolution of financial responsibility to individual schools and by providing the possibility of opting out of local authority control and so receive funding direct from the Department of Education and Science. This thrust of policy intersects with a potentially very important social phenomenon.

The marked concentration of postwar immigrants in a limited number of places, especially within London but also elsewhere, implies that some schools have a considerable proportion of their pupils drawn from ethnic minorities. For example, Inner London has 20 secondary schools in which ethnic minorities comprise 60 per cent or more of the enrolment (*Economist*, 12 September 1987, 32). Over the years, there have been rumblings of discontent from host-community parents, who believe that their children are obtaining an inferior education. The perception is that limited familiarity with English on the part of immigrants' children impedes normal instruction, and in some cases there are also anxieties about attitudes to work and achievement. These discontents came to widespread public notice in 1987, when the parents of 26 white children in Dewsbury protested that the Kirklees Education Authority would not permit them to attend the school of first choice (Overthorpe), offering the seven- and eight-year-old youngsters places at Headfield instead. Both schools are Church of England and both appear to have similar academic standards. However, about 85 per cent of the Headfield children were of Asian origin, whereas at Overthorpe more than 90 per cent were white (*Economist*, 12 September 1987, 32). The episode was unfortunate in several respects. The parents were anticipating by one year a general relaxation of the rules concerning school catchment areas. In addition, it now appears that the refusal to meet the parents' wishes was a decision taken by officials contrary to the policy of the education authority. In the event, after a year of private tuition in a pub and a High Court action, the council has agreed to meet parental wishes (*Independent*, 10 December 1988; see also Midgley 1988).

Some immigrants have also felt anxious about the assumption that their children should automatically attend the local school and become 'integrated' thereby. In particular, fundamental Muslims take the view that religious and secular life cannot be separated. If prayers are to be said five times each day, if pubescent girls are to be segregated from boys, if strict rules of clothing and diet are to be maintained, attendance at a maintained school run on the basis which is accepted by the host community is not regarded as fit and proper. To meet these special needs, 14 independent Muslim schools have been registered in England 'over the past 7 years' (*Social Trends* **18**, 1988, 53). The total number of pupils is very small – some 1500 – representing a tiny proportion even of Muslim children. However, the fact that such schools have been established suggests that Muslim immigrants are maintaining their cultural identity, despite the obstacles in their path.

Perhaps the most significant development, however, is the recent move to seek voluntary-aided status for independent Muslim schools. Two applications have been lodged, one for Zakaria Muslim Girls' High School in Batley, Yorkshire, and the other for Islamia Muslim School in Brent, London. Zakaria is a secondary school, whereas Islamia is primary (Midgley 1988). Following in the wake of the Dewsbury episode, these applications raise important issues. They cannot logically be turned down on the principle of restricting the denominational coverage of the voluntary-aided schools to the denominations already represented, even if such a course were legal. Indeed, in a rational policy context of widening parental choice, the *prima facie* case must be in favour of granting the status requested; the Labour Party has decided to accept this logic (*Independent*, 9 May 1989). The practical problem, however, is that these schools are small – only 127 pupils at Zakaria, which is a secondary school – which implies high unit costs and limited curriculum options.

Which is the lesser evil, to grant voluntary-aided status (perhaps with qualifications regarding the level of public funding to be provided) or to refuse it? If the status is granted, the way is open for other applications, and the effect may be to accentuate and perpetuate ethnic differences, with the long-term risks that this may imply. To refuse runs the risk that a concerted campaign may be waged, in which tempers may rise and a difficult situation be made worse. In any case, if voluntary-aided status is not granted, the privately financed separate schooling will be likely to continue, so that the problem will not go away. In facing this dilemma, it is unhelpful to mix emotive terms and to state, as Midgley (1988) has done, that the grant of voluntary-aided status would be 'another step along the road to racial apartheid in the nation's schools'. If we look across the North Sea to Sweden for a moment, we will observe that there is a legal right for 'all children of immigrants to be taught in their mother tongue, often in tiny classes' (*Economist*, 12 November 1988, 28). The Swedes would not appreciate their system being labelled 'racial apartheid', notwithstanding that the use of minority languages is a very radical apparent departure from the ideal of integration. Their experience indicates, however, that the confidence and progress thus achieved facilitates subsequent success in Swedish. That practical experience, tested against experience elsewhere, should surely be the touchstone for deciding what is the best course of action to take in the circumstances of Britain.

To the extent that choice in education has been extended (choice which is independent of income), it seems inevitable that schools will become more diverse in their ethos and in their ethnic/class composition. In this respect, schools will more accurately mirror the plural nature of British society and move away from the homogenizing ideal which inspired wartime and postwar reform.

Britain's nations

The English, the Welsh, the Scots and the Irish all retain a strong sense of nationhood, deeply rooted in the history and geography of the British Isles (Hechter 1975). For centuries, the Irish refused to accept English domination, and although the creation of the Republic in 1921 solved many problems, difficulties in the six counties which comprise Ulster continue to the present (Ch. 8). Although the situation is peaceful in Wales and Scotland, and does not have the makings of the tragedy which afflicts Ulster, nevertheless we do have a nationalities question in mainland Britain which came to a head with the 1979 referenda on devolution for Scotland and Wales, an issue which may well again be on the political agenda.

Notwithstanding that a single Parliament legislates for the whole country, the actual administration of both Scotland and Wales differs from the arrangements for England. Both countries have a secretary of state who is of cabinet rank and therefore possesses considerable authority, and both have a devolved administration in support. The Welsh have been successful in maintaining their language and culture, and the Scots have a quite distinct legal system, as well as a distinct pattern of education at school and university. Both countries have rather generous representation in Parliament. If, when the 1983 apportionment was conducted, the average size of constituency had been set equal to that for England, Scotland would have only 58 Members of Parliament, compared with the present number of 72 who sit for that country. Similarly, Wales would have 31, 7 fewer than at present.

The differences noted in the previous paragraph are some of the more important but they do not exhaust the list. Manifestly, within Great Britain the territorial space is in fact divided at the two boundaries, even though individuals can pass freely and goods are traded without hindrance. The present arrangements, however, are not universally accepted, for two opposing reasons. Some Scots and Welsh consider that existing devolution does not go far enough. On the other hand, some of the regions of England consider that the two countries enjoy undue favours which work to the detriment of adjacent regions, from which some conclude that the English regions should have privileges similar to those accorded to Wales and Scotland.

One manifestation of the disquiet within Wales has been the arson committed against second houses purchased by the English in Wales, and even against the premises of estate agents who handle such transactions. This is not just a protest at the impact which second-home purchases may have upon property prices and the ability of local people to afford a dwelling; it is essentially a protest against the cultural dilution which is implicit in the intrusion of English people into areas which are perceived to be dominantly Welsh. Fortunately, these illegal acts are comparatively few in number.

Nationalist sentiment is embodied in Plaid Cymru and the Scottish National Party. Both political parties aspire to greater control of their respective nation's affairs at the regional level. Early in the 1970s, this sentiment became so strong that both the Labour Party and the Conservatives took fright and sought to placate the mood of resurgent nationalism. By Act of Parliament, provision was made for the devolution of certain powers to Welsh and Scottish assemblies, subject to the outcome of separate referenda in the two

41

countries. In the event, the 1979 affirmative vote fell just short of the requisite number in Scotland, while in Wales the voters decisively rejected devolution. For the time being, devolution ceased to be an urgent issue and the fortunes of both the nationalist parties waned. More recently, there has been a resurgence, especially in Scotland. The Labour Party was stunned when the 1988 by-election in Govan saw a massive general election majority turned into defeat by the SNP. The Conservatives could take little comfort from the discomfiture of Labour, having themselves been humiliated in Scotland in the 1987 general election.

Devolution is virtually certain to remain a major issue north of the Border. The Labour Party has promised that if it is returned to power it will legislate for Scottish devolution (and would do so for Wales also if the people of that country so wished), while the SNP advocates full independence for Scotland within the framework provided by the European Community. The Labour Party, trades unions and churches are all pressing for an assembly north of the Border. Given that the Conservatives obtained only 10 out of the 72 Scottish seats at the last general election, notwithstanding their handsome overall majority in Parliament, there are the ingredients for a divisive period in our history.

Conclusion

It is widely assumed that ours is a homogeneous culture, sub-divided by class, with only two rather special exceptions: the existence of legally distinct countries, in one of which (Ulster) there is a special problem of sectarian conflict; and the existence of a limited number of areas in which ethnic minorities comprise a large proportion of the population. Furthermore, it was certainly hoped that, if New Commonwealth immigration were kept under control, it would be possible for the postwar immigrants to 'integrate' with the host community, and that this would be evident in their wide dispersal. Or, as some would have had us believe, that the new immigrants were a temporary phenomenon, in that they would return whence they came. Consequently, the existence of actual or potential problems arising from ethnic differences has not been taken very seriously. In contrast, class differences have been given considerable prominence.

The material reviewed in this essay suggests that such a view of British society is limited or incomplete. Instead of assuming that the population is culturally homogeneous and admitting a few 'special cases', it seems more realistic to recognize that our society is in fact plural, with clear differences of class, ethnicity and sense of nationhood. Furthermore, this plurality has not appeared suddenly but is deeply embedded in our history – most notably, the differences between Scotland, Wales and Ireland, the Protestant/Catholic division, and the divisions by class. Postwar immigration has added a new dimension, with the advent of coloured minorities. Given the long-persisting differences between the English, Welsh, Scots and Irish, and given the religious distinctions which also have a long history, it seems improbable that the New Commonwealth immigrants would necessarily forsake their own culture. More important, should they be expected to do so?

If the host community is indeed homogeneous, and if the immigrant community is numerically small, then there may be a strong case for expecting the newcomers to adapt and integrate. If the host community is itself plural in character, and has so been for a long period, then the imperative for conformity is weakened, the more so if the immigrant group is quite large. Given that the host community itself is in fact plural, and given that immigrant groups have maintained their identity, it seems probable that diversity will in fact be maintained. The probability of this occurring must be increased by the stress which government presently lays upon the virtues of personal choice and responsibility.

If we assume that a goal of public policy must be the maintenance of peaceful and equitable conditions, we are next faced with the following fundamental question: is the ultimate aim to encourage the assimilation of the minority groups by the majority, host community? Or is it the lesser aim, that the minority groups should be integrated with the host community, however much the minorities maintain their own distinctiveness? The first possibility – assimilation – could only be a long-term goal, with a timespan measured in generations. It is not an immediate goal that could realistically be considered. Integration is clearly a much more practicable aim, but is integration necessary either for the maintenance of peace or for providing equity between citizens? In any case, what do we mean by integration? Is it possible that the best means for achieving integration is to recognize the reality of existing differences and to adopt policies which make it feasible for them to be maintained? If so, this will only be possible if individuals and groups are tolerant of each other's differences and if the distinctions are not translated into discrimination in jobs, housing, education and all facets of civilized life.

At one level, we can be thankful that we do not have the problems associated with legally enforced reservations, as for the Indians in the United States and in Canada, or the Aborigines in Australia. At another level, though, both Wales and Scotland represent territories within which a minority can lead some semblance of a separate existence, analogous perhaps with the French/English divide in Canada. And although we do not have legally enforced segregation of residence, schooling, etc., which is a striking feature of South Africa, it cannot be said that the spatial segregation of class and ethnic groups is entirely voluntary in character.

If segregation is voluntary in character, then it can only be regarded as a 'bad thing' if primacy is given to the imposition of an ideology which demands uniformity irrespective of individual wishes. Such a view is the very antithesis of the tolerance which I believe to be an essential ingredient of civilized life. If individuals are to be accorded maximum freedom to choose how to conduct their lives in a manner which is consistent with the exercise of that same freedom by others, then there is no *a priori* way by which we can determine whether the exercise of choice will lead to convergence on a common culture or to the maintenance of existing diversity. For the tolerance of diversity to be other than a rather hollow sham, however, expenditure out of public funds is often necessary to support or facilitate activities which minister to particular minorities. It is this lack of sensitivity to the needs of minority groups, including their need on occasion to be geographically separate, of which Rex complained in 1981.

Note

1 As defined in the *Shorter Oxford English Dictionary*, the term 'ethnic' conveys the idea of nations other than Christian or Jewish. For the purpose of this essay, the term will be used in a somewhat wider sense, to encompass race, nation and religion as differentiating characteristics for people.

References

Balchin, P. N. 1985. *Housing policy: an introduction*. London: Croom Helm.

Banton, M. 1967. *Race relations*. London: Tavistock.

Barnett, C. 1986. *The audit of war. The illusion and reality of Britain as a great nation*. London: Macmillan.

Boal, F. W. 1972. The urban residential sub-community – a conflict interpretation. *Area* **4**, 164–8.

Boal, F. W. 1976. Ethnic residential segregation. In D. T. Herbert and R. J. Johnston (eds), Vol. 1, 41–79.

Burtenshaw, D. & M. Bateman 1981. *The city in West Europe*. Chichester: Wiley.

Clarke, C., D. Ley & C. Peach (eds) 1984. *Geography and ethnic pluralism*. London: Allen & Unwin.

Collison, P. 1963. *The Cutteslowe walls. A study in social class*. London: Faber & Faber.

Hechter, M. 1975. *Internal colonialism. The Celtic fringe in British national development, 1536–1966*. London: Routledge & Kegan Paul.

Herbert, D. T. & R. J. Johnston (eds) 1976a. *Social areas in cities*. Vol. 1: *Spatial processes and form*. Vol. 2: *Spatial perspectives on problems and policies*. Chichester: Wiley.

Herbert, D. T. & R. J. Johnston 1976b. An introduction, in D. T. Herbert & R. J. Johnston (eds), Vol. 2, 1–16.

Hughes, G. & B. McCormick 1981. Do council housing policies reduce migration between regions? *Economic Journal* **91**, 919–37.

Jones, E. 1960. *A social geography of Belfast*. London: Oxford University Press.

Kerckhoff, A. C., R. T. Campbell & I. Winfield-Laird 1985. Social mobility in Great Britain and the United States. *American Journal of Sociology* **91**, 281–308.

Kleinman, M. & C. Whitehead 1987. Local variations in the sale of council houses in England, 1979–1984. *Regional Studies* **21**, 1–11.

Midgley, J. 1988. Flight from multiculturalism. *The Independent*, 15 December, 19.

References

Office of Population Censuses and Surveys 1984. *Census 1981. Key statistics for local authorities. Great Britain*. London: HMSO.

Peach, G. C. K. 1966. Factors affecting the distribution of West Indians in Great Britain. *Transactions, Institute of British Geographers*, **38**, 151–63.

Peach, G. C. K. 1968. *West Indian migration to Britain. A social geography*. London: Oxford University Press.

Peach, G. C. K. (ed.) 1975. *Urban social segregation*. London: Longman.

Peach, G. C. K. 1984. The force of West Indian island identity in Britain. In C. Clarke, D. Ley & C. Peach, 214–30.

Policy Unit, Bradford. Undated. *Bradford District Ward Profiles*. Bradford: City of Bradford Metropolitan Council

Ram, S. & D. Phillips 1985. *Indians in Bradford. Socio-economic profile and housing characteristics: 1971–1984*. Working Paper 433. Leeds: School of Geography, University of Leeds.

Ram, S. & P. Rees 1985. *A spatial demographic analysis of Indians in Bradford*. Working Paper 434. Leeds: School of Geography, University of Leeds.

Rex, J. 1981. Urban segregation and inner city policy in Great Britain. In *Ethnic segregation in cities*, C. Peach, V. Robinson & S. Smith (eds), 25–42. London: Croom Helm.

Rex, J. & R. Moore 1967. *Race, community and conflict. A study of Sparkbrook*. London: Oxford University Press.

Robertson, D. 1984. *Class and the British electorate*. Oxford: Basil Blackwell.

Robinson, V. 1979. *The segregation of Asians within a British city: theory and practice. Research Papers* 22. Oxford: School of Geography, University of Oxford.

Robinson, V. 1984. Asians in Britain: a study in encapsulation and marginality. In C. Clarke, D. Ley & C. Peach, 231–57.

Robinson, V. 1986. *Transients, settlers, and refugees*. Oxford: Clarendon Press.

Robson, B. T. 1969. *Urban analysis: a study of city structure with special reference to Sunderland*. Cambridge: Cambridge University Press.

Timms, D. W. G. 1971. *The urban mosaic. Towards a theory of residential differentiation*. Cambridge: Cambridge University Press.

3

Group identity and urban space: the North American experience

JOHN EYLES

Introduction: the meanings of race

More than ten years ago, in one of the most important summary papers written on divided space and ethnic residential segregation by a geographer, Boal (1976, 45) commented that:

> conflict situations in cities lead people to feel threatened. This will particularly apply to recent in-migrants, who may vary culturally from the 'host' population ... The perceived threat may materialize in the form of physical violence or remain as a psychological threat. At the same time, and indeed sometimes because of the threat, the ethnic group may have a strong urge to internal cohesion, so that the cultural 'heritage' of the group may be retained.

This realistic assessment is at odds with the integrationist ideal of the 'melting pot', which would see the absorption of in-migrants into the host society in terms of behaviour and social position. It is the purpose of this chapter to explore some of the differences between ideal and reality from a contemporary North American perspective through the examination of the maintenance of group identity and the significance of segregated living spaces in such maintenance.

This discussion will be preceded by a portrayal of the realities of segregated space in terms of measures of separation and followed by an exploration of the societal outcomes of divided spaces. While these examinations will note that at different times and in different cities ethnic groups have sometimes shared living space (altering the experience and effects of group interactions), we must, however, begin by considering the salience and meanings of race and ethnicity for social members. In the late 1980s and early 1990s, at least in the United States, there seems to be a silence over racial and ethnic issues, except where they pertain to crime. It may be that the increasing public perception of a close association between crime and race, with drug-related robberies and homicides being seen as black affairs, will lead to greater white intolerance. But the silence may be ominous for minority group individuals (and may therefore affect how they think, live and act), it allows the question of salience of race and/or ethnicity for society as a whole to be raised. While the reality of divided space cannot be denied, as will be documented below, the societal significance of such division can be addressed.

Indeed, Prager (1987) argues that there is a shifting meaning to race in American political culture and that today the 'racial problem' is the object of neither public discussion nor controversy. Prager suggests that race has only become an issue at four crucial phases in American history, these being, first, the slavery debate and the drafting of the US constitution; second, 19th-century abolitionism, the outbreak of the Civil War and the drafting of the 12th, 14th and 15th Amendments (which refer to the freedom of slaves, the legal basis of property ownership and voter rights respectively); third, the end of Reconstruction and the rise of Jim Crow legislation (which instituted black-only facilities); and, finally, the Brown v. Board of Education decision (which struck down separate facilities on the basis of their inherent inequality) and the rise of the Civil Rights movement in the 1950s and 1960s. In all these cases, race was an important focus for determining the meaning and values of the American community. Thus, Prager does not devalue the importance of race but places the category in a cultural and ideological context. At any given time, blacks themselves represent the success or, more usually, the failure of American principle and their status may be used to determine who should be included in society (appropriate social relations) as well as the aspirations for and desirability of political community (the inclusiveness of the definitions of public good).

The public good in the US is seen in a strong commitment to individualism. Bellah (1985) suggests that there are three competing individualisms, expressed respectively in terms of biblical language, that of civic morality and one of utilitarian and expressive individualism. It is argued that the last-named – the concern with self-improvement – has been dominant and that the visions of the others, which celebrate the individual in the context of a community recognizing its responsibilities to all, are unsustainable, although they burst through and shape and even redefine public consciousness and institutions. Prager (1987) suggests that the Civil Rights movement and its affirmative action programmes reshaped institutions and that the public commitment to racial equality remains strong. But, following Steele (1988), it may be seen as a peculiar commitment. Steele argues that blacks defined themselves as victims. Separating themselves by race guaranteed their continued isolation. And the reassertion of utilitarian individualism has worsened the situation because it means that problem solutions and conflict resolutions lie in the 'normal' processes of equal opportunity and individual attainment. Self-improving individualism sees the needy and disadvantaged as marginal to community; there is a public silence on social inequality, and private resentment concerning the resources directed at the disadvantaged. Community is now characterized by exclusionary sentiments, with the boundaries being firmly established between the in-group and the out-group. This boundary is marked by a powerful racial imagery in that for 'good' Americans the major problem is crime and the crime problem is largely a black problem. There is little desire to examine the social and economic causes of crime. The perceived association between crime and race seems to provide proof not only of the existence of a black underclass but also of its behavioural as well as material deficiencies (see Auletta 1982)). Value judgement becomes 'fact'. Prager (1987, 73) may, therefore, be optimistic to comment on the status of blacks that 'this time [is] one of rest; a period where there is occurring a solidification and crystallization of previous gains', but he is also correct to add that 'at the same time, the line is sharply drawn between the guarantee of civil rights and the extension of the meaning of social equality'.

From Prager's analysis, it is possible to see that race (and ethnicity – discussed in somewhat different terms below) has a shifting meaning. This shifting has implications for group interactions and identities and will affect the divisions and uses of space that different groups make. While affirmative action may lead to greater accessibility to scarce resources for certain ethnic groups, it may also heighten racial hostility and lead to a strengthened commitment to segregated living space. But the present climate of utilitarian individualism means that the reception of new migrants is, to say the least, unenthusiastic, as exemplified by the Haitians in Miami (see Stepick 1982). The meanings of race and ethnicity are medicated through political discourse, being functions of their negotiated and contingent public character. This may be well illustrated if we compare present-day meanings of and attitudes to race in Canada and the US. While recent surveys have documented that Canada is probably as racist as any other western nation (*Toronto Star*, 14 January 1989), its values are based on a sense of community (and consensus) rather than individualism (and competition). As Clift (1989) has recently noted, the Canadian character is quiet and compromising, respectful of authority, afraid of competition and tolerant of other people and their ideas. He suggests that ethnicity has been employed as a basis of consensus-building rather than competition. But the senses of consensus, community and egalitarianism mean that the race problem, manifested particularly in tensions and resource conflicts in Montreal, Toronto and Vancouver, is still very real and the subject of intense public debate and scrutiny.

The recognition of the negotiated and contingent nature and meaning of race enables us to see the inherent variability in group relations, identities and activities. These shifting meanings lead Prager (1987) to reject the concept of racism as a useful way of understanding the problem of race in the US, because it implies an unchanging and negative evaluation of a racial group. In this he errs. While racism implies a negative status, it is not unchanging. Hall (1978, 26) argues that it is not a permanent human or social deposit and that it does not always assume the same shape: 'there have been many significantly different racisms – each historically specific and articulated in a different way with the societies in which they appear'. To which Sivanandan (1983, 2) would add: 'racism does not stay still; it changes shape, size, contours, purpose, function – with changes in the economy, the social structure, the system, and above all, the challenges, the resistances to that system'. With 'racism' we have a term that enables consideration of the status of groups with respect to living space, occupation and so on, and the shifting experience of this status as well as its bases. Racism is structured and institutionalized, and while the boundaries of racial and ethnic disadvantage may shift, its consequences are real. The response to racism has also been institutionalized, with white America ceding to the victims of racism the definition of their problems (see Steele 1988). Solutions to problems – income, employment, etc. – have not been ceded. But before we examine the consequences of racism in terms of the social organization of American and Canadian society, we shall document the realities of racial and ethnic disadvantage.

The realities of shared and divided spaces: measuring disadvantage and segregation

While not all racial and ethnic groups experience disadvantage or segregated living spaces, for minority group members they are the dominant reality. This is especially the case for American blacks. But as Farley (1985) points out, there exist many indicators of the changing status of blacks, not all of which suggest that their social and economic position has worsened. For example, although social differences still exist in educational attainment, they are decreasing. In 1940 blacks averaged about three fewer years of schooling than whites. By the early 1980s the difference had lessened to one and a half years. There is, though, increasing questioning of educational attainment as a solution to black problems. Success in the school system may lead to the accusation of 'acting white' and a loss of black identity (Fordham & Ogbu 1986). But blacks also hold more prestigious and higher-paying jobs than they did. Black men and women have moved increasingly into white-collar occupations, although Farley (1985) calculates that there is still a 40-year gap separating the occupational attainments of black men and white men. Increases in occu-pational prestige have influenced earnings and the racial differences have gradually declined among men and are disappearing much more rapidly among women. We should note, however, that these reductions are closely linked to the gender biases in the labour market; while qualified black women earn as much as whites with similar attributes, they receives less than 60 per cent of the renumeration of white men. But Farley (1985, 14) is able to conclude that 'for almost all segments of the population, the actual earnings of blacks rose faster than those of whites and the apparent cost of labour market discrimination declined'.

The position of blacks in work shows improvement. But chief among the indicators showing no improved status for blacks is the unemployment rate. Black men are twice as likely to be unemployed as white men. And while black earnings are increasing, a decreasing proportion of black men are at work. There seems to be a growing reliance on the informal economy, especially during the late 1980s with the reduction in the number of programmes and real benefits for the poor. This is shown in the emergence of the so-called underclass, which is estimated to make up about one-third of the poverty population (see Auletta 1982). It is a differentiated grouping, including the passive poor (longterm welfare recipients), the hostile (street criminals and drug addicts), the hustlers (living on the informal economy) and the trauma-tized (drunks, drifters, the homeless), producing white intolerance, anxiety and concern. It is, as Auletta (1982, xviii) notes, 'both America's peril, and shame', but the dominant view of race today is likely to lead to an emphasis on control rather than emancipation.

Finally, there are indicators which show improvement in some places and at some times but not others. For example, in most of the rural South, in many small and medium-sized cities in all regions, and in southern metropolises where schools are organized on a county-wide basis (e.g. Tampa, Jacksonville, Nashville), there is by and large social integration in public schools. But little progress has been made in the largest cities and in Los Angeles, New York, Detroit, Chicago, Washington and elsewhere, public school districts are mainly colour-coded, with central cities having predominantly black or Hispanic enrolment and the suburbs being largely white. Indeed, it is important to remember that white flight to the suburbs concerned the perceived quality of education as well as of residential environments. The income of black husband-wife families has continued to improve, such that *per caput* income went from one-half to two-thirds that of whites between the early 1960s and the mid-1980s, although progress slowed throughout the 1970s and 1980s. The failure of the overall ratio of black-to-white median family income to improve after 1970 is explained by changes in living arrangements and family structure (see Norton 1983). Between 1960 and 1983 there was a doubling of the proportion of single parent black families, often headed by a woman. This impacts not only on family income but also on levels of poverty and helps to explain the increase and persistence of poverty among blacks in the 1970s and 1980s. The removal of many social and urban programmes has further exacerbated this problem (see Eyles 1989).

Residential segregation

The final indicator that will be examined is residential segregation, which has declined in some places but not in others. As we shall see, this segregation, whatever its level, is primarily the result of white prejudice (and preferences and discriminatory practices) rather than economic factors. But in large cities of all regions, racial residential segregation decreased little between 1940 and 1970 (see Taueber & Taueber 1965, van Valey *et. al.* 1977). Using the index of dissimilarity (which measures census tracts on a scale from zero – no segregation – to 100 – complete segregation), Taueber (1965) found the 1960 median index value to be 88. For 1970, van Valey *et al.* (1977) found that over half of the 237 cities that they examined had scores of 70 or more, with cities such as Chicago, Dallas and Las Vegas having scores of over 90. These studies indicate that the blacks are the most highly segregated group. Hispanics and Asians tend to be segregated but high scores are regarded as those which exceed 60 in these cases (Garcia 1985).

But it might be argued that the important indication of changing residential status is to be found in the decade 1970 to 1980 after the impact of Civil Rights legislation, increasing black incomes and the liberalization of white attitudes, i.e. after the redefinition of race (see Farley 1984). Initial analyses found a mixed pattern of change for both central cities (Taueber 1983) and suburbs (Logan & Schneider 1984); with Taueber's study showing significant decline in residential segregation in Houston, Dallas, Jacksonville, Richmond, Detroit and Los Angeles, increases in Cleveland and Philadelphia, and Chicago and St Louis close to the realistic maximum value of 90 or more. Since these analyses, however, there has been concern over the actual measurement of segregation, implying that the standard measure (the index of dissimilarity) masks other important dimensions. Thus Massey & Denton (1988a, 283) argue that 'residential segregation is a global construct that subsumes five underlying dimensions of measurement, each corresponding to a different aspect of spatial variation: evenness, exposure, concentration, centralization and clustering'. They go on to define evenness as the differential distribution of two social groups among areal units of the city; exposure as the degree of potential contact between minority and majority group members within urban areas; concentration as the relative amount of physical space occupied by a minority group in the urban environment; centralization as the degree to which a group is spatiality located near the centre of an urban area; and clustering as the extent to which overall units inhabited by minority members adjoin one another in space. Their multivariate analyses show the significance of the five dimensions, with evenness and exposure being the dominant factors; the remaining three are correlated more with the former than the latter.

This investigation by Massey & Denton (1988a) is important. It clearly demonstrates that the picture we obtain of segregation and divided space is dependent on the tools of measurement. Further, it points to a complex picture of residential segregation; or that there are important variations in the spatiality of segregation, in that its spatial outcome varies in terms of causation and also with respect to the patterns themselves, depending on how segregation is defined. A detailed investigation of pattern may enable a significant increase in the understanding of process. This will be illustrated with typologies of divided space but first the portrayal of segregation trends will be completed.

Massey & Denton (1988a) comment on the difficulties of finding good measures of the different dimensions of segregation. In their own empirical work, Massey & Denton (1987) concentrate on evenness (measured by the index of dissimilarity) and on exposure (measured by the potential interaction index). The context of the exposure (or, put differently, isolation) is that, throughout the 1970s, minorities became increasingly predominant in most large urban areas. The proportion of blacks increased greatly in Chicago, New York, Memphis and New Orleans and that of Hispanics in Los Angeles, Miami, El Paso and San Antonio. Asians formed significant minorities in San Francisco and San Jose. Massey & Denton (1987) show that the black isolation decreased in 50 of the 60 SMSAs and the likelihood of white contact increased in 47. But blacks remain the most spatially isolated minority. Exposure remains low where the vast majority of blacks live in the slow growing cities of the north-east and north-central states (e.g. Baltimore, Chicago, Cleveland and St Louis). In fact the likelihood of contact decreased in Detroit, Newark, New York and Philadelphia. The increases in exposure were found mainly in the rapidly growing cities of the south and west (e.g. Anaheim, Austin, Denver, Fresno and Oklahoma City). These cities have few blacks. With respect to Hispanics, there is increasing spatial isolation brought about mainly by a shifting population composition with rapidly growing Hispanic populations and declining Anglo ones. The number of Asians is too small for meaningful conclusions.

Turning to evenness, most metropolitan areas experienced a clear lowering of black segregation between 1970 and 1980, suggesting progress towards desegregation in US cities. There are again significant regional differences. Northern cities housing the majority of the blacks remain highly segregated, with Cleveland, New York, Detroit and St Louis (and Los Angeles) having scores of over 80. The largest declines are found in the low black populated cities of the south and west (e.g. Anaheim declined from 84 to 46, Phoenix 82 to 59 and Tucson 71 to 47). Other work indicates that blacks are less segregated in the suburbs than in central cities – although segregation remains quite high – and they are the least suburbanized of all the minorities (Massey & Denton, 1988b). Residential dissimilarity for Hispanics is highly variable. Slow-growing Hispanic communities with little immigration showed declines in spatial unevenness (e.g. Dayton, Columbus), while the largest or fastest growing groupings demonstrated stable (New York, Phoenix) or increasing (Los Angeles, Anaheim) dissimilarity.

These measures of ethnic residential segregation in the US show that blacks, Hispanics and Asians occupy very different positions in urban society. This is well illustrated by the example of San Francisco, where the groups each form roughly 11 per cent of total population. 'In 1980, the probability of black contact with Anglos was 0.299, compared with 0.582 for Hispanics and 0.564 for Asians; and black-Anglo dissimilarity stood at 0.717, with respective figures of 0.444 and 0.402 for Asians and Hispanics. In other words, given the same relative numbers, blacks are nearly twice as segregated as Hispanics or Asians' (Massey & Denton 1988a, 823).

Race thus has a particular meaning in American society. Racial situations, we may argue, have been worsened in the 1980s by the public silence on racial equality issues and growing white intolerance of perceived black crime rates. Indeed, race and language can conspire against the more optimistic picture for Hispanics. Guest & Weed (1976) indicate that Puerto Ricans are nearly as segregated from Anglos or blacks, while Hwang & Murdock (1983) and Farley (1987) show that Hispanic–black segregation exceeds Hispanic–Anglo segregation in most cities and many southern rural areas. Mohl (1985) shows how Haitians have received scant welcome in Miami; they remain concentrated in the Edison–Little River section of the city which provides cheap housing in overcrowded conditions and access to job opportunities if not social services.

The Hispanics and Asians are important elements in the ethnic mosaic of the US. Indeed, as Woolbright and Hartmann (1987) point out, Asia and Latin America replaced Europe as the major source of immigration to the US in the post-1945 period, with significant numbers from Cuba, Mexico, the Philippines, Indochina and Korea. Many of these migrant streams have different adjustment profiles, with Puerto Ricans who arrived mainly when job opportunities were few in the 1950s being less well integrated than Mexicans (despite their general low economic status) and Cubans (despite their recent arrival). Cubans were aided by government assimilation programmes. As Mohl (1985) points out for Miami, Cubans are residentially concentrated in Little Havana, a large area south and west of the CBD. But despite their large numbers, they have adjusted well to American life. Adjustment is not the same as assimilation and Cuban Miami is an active ethnic community, the landscape of which is shaped by language, religion, family, food, culture and politics. Indeed, parts of Miami can be said to be Latinized just like the ghetto in Los Angeles (see Rogers & Uto 1987). But with these processes of change, adjustment and assimilation, we move from describing trends to understanding and explaining the socio-spatial outcomes.

But before examining these processes, it remains for us to comment on these new patterns of segregation because they concern not only new groups but new places. For example, the Southeast Asian refugees were initially scattered throughout the US; now they are beginning to congregate according to clan and kinship groups, especially in California, where, for instance, 34 per cent of all Vietnamese live (11 per cent in Los Angeles County: Woolbright & Hartmann (1987)). Further, new places are seeing the emerging patterns of segregation and divided space, graphically described as the ghettoization of paradise by Ford & Griffin (1979) in their analysis of segregation in San Diego. In this city, the 'ghetto' is in part a positive and distinctive place, suburban both in age and character. Ford & Griffin suggest, therefore, a new typology of segregated places. From their typology, we may place the San Diego-style ghetto, characterized by black sectors reaching the urban and rural fringes of the city and reflecting changes in the socio-economic characteristics of blacks in

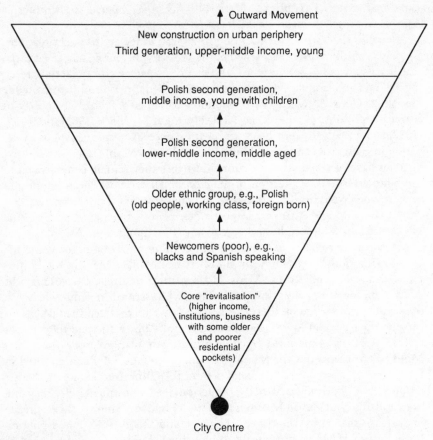

↑ Outward Movement

New construction on urban periphery
Third generation, upper-middle income, young

↑

Polish second generation,
middle income, young with children

↑

Polish second generation,
lower-middle income, middle aged

↑

Older ethnic group, e.g., Polish
(old people, working class, foreign born)

↑

Newcomers (poor), e.g.,
blacks and Spanish speaking

↑

Core "revitalisation"
(higher income,
institutions, business
with some older
and poorer
residential
pockets)

City Centre

Figure 3.1 Ethnic sector in Detroit.
Source: Thompson 1983, 352.

contrast to the classic 'northern' ghetto which is inner-city in location and characterized by high levels of segregation and much housing decay and abandonment. An obvious conclusion must be drawn. Not all segregated places in the US are alike, a point made as tellingly by Thompson (1983) in his ethnic sector model of Detroit which emphasizes ethnic mixing (blacks, Poles, Hispanics) as well as social and spatial change (Figure 3.1). This complexity of urban space is also well illustrated in Canadian cities (Balakrishnan 1976 and 1982, Matwijiw 1979, Massey 1985) with extensive acculturation and pro-gressive dispersal away from ethnic enclaves over time. To understand assimilation and dispersal and the retention of group identities and social areas we need to examine the social chemistry of ethnic interactions. To begin this process, we can explore two typologies of divided spaces (Hernandez 1985, Agocs 1981) which point, explicitly and implicitly, to those factors that enhance or impede community-building.

Typologies of ethnic relations in space

Hernandez (1985) is concerned to develop a typology of urban immigrant community-building which respects the local ecologies of places where new migrants and their descendants settle. He draws extensively on the Chicago and New York cases, being critically aware of data shortages and problems. The first of the five community types is the ghetto or barrio, in which today more than one racial or ethnic group may live but one is dominant. There is a limited capacity for such areas to absorb new immigrants, who must compete with other groups for scarce housing, jobs and other services. In this, they may be aided by their own social networks. Such competitions lead to the second type – the heterogeneous new immigrant districts in which no single group predominates. For example, the core of Haitian settlement in New York lies in the Crown Heights–East Flatbush area, but elsewhere in Brooklyn they share their neighbourhoods with other groups.

The third community type is distinguished by its instability and eventual colonization by white middle-class gentrifiers. New immigrants are renters who can be more easily displaced by real estate developers and speculators. These in turn encourage the more profitable refurbishment and back-to-the-city movements, as in the Old Town in Chicago. Fourthly, new immigrant communities appear in the older neighbourhoods of satellite cities. As part of the acculturation process, migrants and their descendants move spatially (and socially), becoming in part the middle and upper-middle strata of the local social order. They may arrest local economic decline and although ethnic attachment may limit mobility, the settlers become significant local actors, e.g. Cubans in Union City, NJ, and Italians in Hamilton, Ontario. Finally, affluent migrants live interspersed with native whites and blacks in communities such as Skokie, Illinois, or Nassau County, Long Island. They are indistinguishable residentially from native Americans, so Hernandez's fifth type is scattered suburban settlements varying from lower-to-upper-middle class, according to American majority standards.

Hernandez presents a model of assimilation which is, in the main, integrationist and central-city focused. A more complex model of ethnic relations in space is presented by Agocs (1981). Her study of Detroit between 1940 and 1970 examined ten ethnic groups on the basis of three key measures: segregation, clustering and suburbanization. She shows how blacks and Hispanics are characterized by centralization, clustering and segregation; Jews, Italians and Hungarians by segregation, clustering and suburbanization; Britons and Germans by suburbanization, dispersal and integration; and Poles, the Irish and Russians by centralization of the immigrant generation and suburbanization of their descendants. This rich study already demonstrates the complexity of ethnic community-building. It is further enriched by her typology of ethnic communities (Table 3.1). Thus the ghetto is a clearly bounded concentration of blacks in the older decaying parts of the city. Recent

Table 3.1 Typology of ethnic communities.

Ethnic population distribution	Clustered and segregated	Dispersed and integrated
Centralized	1 Ghetto 2 Immigrant reception centre 3 Urban village	4 Residual community
Suburbanized	5 Transplanted community 6 New suburban settlement	7 Community without neighbourhood

Source: Agocs 1981, 132.

immigration reception centres can be found in inner areas (e.g. for Mexicans) or in industrial suburbs which are generationally mixed, while urban villages are stable concentrations dominated by second-generation migrants, supported by ethnic institutions such as schools, churches, business and political organizations. Residual communities are ethnic concentrations in inner-city and working-class neighbourhoods and transplanted communities are clustered, segregated groupings in areas distant from initial reception areas, rather like Jewish settlements in Detroit and Chicago (see Rosenthal 1961). New suburban settlements are less dense and bounded than transplanted communities and are often the product of sectoral segregation, as Thompson (1983) documents for the Poles in Detroit. Finally, communities without neighbourhood are displaced groupings held together not by residential closeness but interactions and shared activities. This typology seems again to imply an assimilationist progression and a movement from constraints on ethnic behaviour to the choices that ethnic groups may make. If it is recognized that some racial and ethnic groups may not progress through all stages and indeed may not regard the community without neighbourhood, or Hernandez's scattered settlement, as desirable, then the schemes of Agocs & Hernandez contain within them mention of the processes that shape ethnic identity and organization as well as the creation and maintenance of divided space. In this regard, we come full circle to Boal's (1976) words that opened this chapter, focusing on ethnic group cohesiveness and majority group actions and beliefs. These parameters set the tone for our discussion of the social bases of ethnic organization and segregation.

The social bases of segregation and ethnic organization

In general terms, ethnic separation and division are generated through the interplay of two opposing spatial forces, concentration and dispersal:

the concentration of ethnic groups is rooted in the spatial differentiation of the urban economy, and reinforced by the nature of immigrants and immigration. Dispersion is driven by socio–economic mobility and acculturation, and is based on the fact that a differentiated urban economy distributes resources and opportunities unevenly in space, encouraging immigrants to move in order to improve their position in society. (Massey 1985, 317).

But chain migration and the institutionalization of ethnic neighbourhoods emphasize concentration, as does the structure of the housing stock and high degree of land–use specialization found in large cities. But the same structural differentiation of society that makes segregation possible also leads to spatial assimilation. In industrialized societies, social and family status produce a fragmented urban space and the need for movement for advancement for ethnic members. Indeed, it may be argued that the decentralized spatial structure of Canadian cities at the time of immigration in the 1950s and 1960s resulted in low levels of segregation and more rapid dispersal. But dispersal is dependent on migrant willingness to acquire the language, values and mores of the host society, to acculturate (see Gordon 1964). Thus 'acculturation provides the desire, and social mobility the means, for immigrants to achieve spatial assimilation' (Massey 1985, 320). From the evidence above, we may note that the spatial assimilation of Hispanics in the US, by and large, follows this underlying process of acculturation.

These ideas present a generalized picture of ethnic relations in North America. They enable a societal contextualizing of these relations in terms of urban development, economic structure and social and group mores. The significance of ethnicity (and race) is found in these structural conditions of society. Ethnicity is more than the result of a labelling process but its meaning can only come from the context of its containing society. While this view accords with our earlier discussions, support may also be found in Ward's (1982) examination of the ethnic ghetto in the US. He shows how the meaning of 'ghetto' developed in the late 19th century in the US to describe common disabilities suffered by immigrants rather than the variable conditions of their residential districts. He outlines the assumptions on which this view was based, e.g. behavioural consequences of overcrowding, the composition of foreign immigration and the temporary and sequential nature of ghetto residence. But Ward (1982) goes on to show how these assumptions might be challenged by pointing to the stability of family and institutional life amongst the immigrants; the influence of ethnic heritage on living and health conditions such that the mortality rates of Russian Jews in many American cities were lower than those of the more established Irish and Italians (see Ward 1969); the role of ethnic institutions in allaying fears, threats and the transition itself, documented for the Italians (Williams 1938) and Poles (Thomas & Znaniecki 1958); the elaborate and dispersed kinship networks (see Guttman 1974, Modell &

Hareven 1977); and the establishment of ethnic politics to counter economic and political deprivation, as with the Cubans in Miami. Further Ward (1982) points out that most migrants and their descendants lived in shared districts and also in suburban locations. Most newcomers experienced, therefore, neither disorganization nor assimilation. Ward proposes then a useful elaboration of the notion of assimilation. 'The migrant generation and their descendants experienced rapid cultural assimilation but relatively limited structural assimilation, since their primary group relationships remained concentrated in the ethnic community. The migrant community did not transplant its ancestral culture but organized institutions and social networks based upon family, friends and acquaintances of a common ethnic origin' (Ward 1982, 265). Thus early cultural assimilation led to the emergence and persistence of structural pluralism. This may be seen to persist despite rapid rates of structural assimilation which have occurred with increased ethnic consciousness, the importance of this being seen in part in the continuing significance of religious affiliation and sensitivity of intermarriage (see Greeley 1970). In such circumstances, ethnicity becomes one form of associational behaviour. Residential proximity is no longer of great significance but ethnic identity remains important.

An ethnic division of labour?

We shall return to ethnic identity but as yet we have not really addressed the persistence of highly segregated deprived minorities. The exclusion of these highly visible groups from good housing, jobs and access to other resources may be explained by what Ward (1982) calls the ethnic division of labour. Many ethnic migrants came to the US and Canada as labour migrants and a buoyant, developing economic structure created (albeit unequal) employment opportunities in which, for example, the Irish, European Jews and Slavs found their niches. The transition from labour migrant to immigrant was slow and variable. The arrival of European migrants in fact reduced the range of occupations available to blacks in many northern cities such that black Americans encountered a diminished range of job options and have predominated only in the least secure sections of the labour market (Bonacich 1976, Ward 1982). Thus black Americans may be seen as labour migrants, a status held for several generations and one which enables their residential districts to become ghettoized and deteriorate.

In this reasoning, we have an economic argument for the social position and segregated existence of blacks: an existence escaped by most white ethnics because of favourable labour market conditions. Such a view is supported by Wilson (1978) who suggests that while racial status determined black life chances in the antebellum South, and both race and economic position shaped opportunity during early-20th-century industrialization, class position is now of overriding significance. Black life chances in general and the black underclass in particular exist not as a function of racism but because of the incapacity of the economic system to absorb the population. Further support is provided by Rogers & Uto (1987) in their examination of residential segregation in Los Angeles. They argue that social and ethnic categories are the result, in part, of ideological processes which are mainly but not exclusively significant in relation to production and its particular sectors. They suggest that 'residential segregation both expresses and impacts upon social and spatial division of labour, which in turn have their origins in the labour processes associated with commodity production, circulation and consumption. The co-ordinates of this process are provided by the social formation, which also defines the terrain of class relations' (Rogers & Uto 1987, 54–5). To understand the status of visible minorities, they employ the ideas of Sassen-Koob (1985). In her study of New York, she argued that there is a 'peripheralization at the core', with areas of declining American cities being re-employed with foreign capital and Third World labour (and we should add indigenous labour migrants). In Los Angeles, there is a polarization of the inner-city occupation structure, with high-status jobs being complemented by low-wage producer services. There also exist labour-intensive, low-wage, vertically disintegrated, highly clustered industries such as garment-making in the downtown (Scott 1984). This industry employs predominantly Latino and Asian women. Finally, there is a creation of immigrant areas in the built environment which face competition from gentrification and condominium development. Although Rogers & Uto stress the economic, they also recognize the political and cultural parameters of race and ethnicity, with the ghetto forming an important political power base. But these cultural parameters are seen by others as being more important in understanding ethnic relations and divisions.

Blacks as a distinct microcosm of society?

The basis of such work stems from the fact that in the main blacks remain segregated despite economic advancement. Rose (1981) shows that, residentially, black professionals remain largely segregated. Indeed Gordon (1964) introduced the idea of 'ethclasses' to demonstrate that blacks form a distinct and separate microcosm of society as a whole, in that ghettos are socially differentiated along class lines, as for example in Chicago's Black Belt. While it may be argued that such work underemphasizes economic context, it stresses isolationist tendencies in both majority and minority communities. With respect to the majority community, the arguments in relation to white prejudice and individual and institutional discriminatory practices are well-known. But such phenomena ensure that living spaces are not shared and that structural assimilation (i.e. equality of opportunity in labour, housing and educational markets) will not occur. Thus Ford & Griffin (1979), for example, point to housing market discrimination and racial steering in creating San Diego's ghetto, while Dingemans (1978) documents the redlining of poor and black areas in Sacramento by banks and mortgage companies. Further, in San Diego, it was found that white residential settlement increased in density, so that areas close to the black ghetto did not have to be developed. Many of these institutional and developmental constraints on black actions have been documented by Forman (1971) who provides a less than rosy picture of the actions of realtors, lawyers, developers and government. It should be further noted that the development process itself, particularly in the refurbishment of downtown, has removed much cheap black and ethnic housing. Even when development is delayed, as occurred in San Francisco in the late 1970s, the land is often assembled and cleared so that the effect is the same.

Prejudice and hostility are important dimensions in ensuring separate and segregated ethnic existences and spaces. Indeed, Park (1927) saw racial prejudice as helping to define a sense of group position, with conflict between classes or ethnic groups helping to fix their social positions (see Park 1921). But in such situations, colour or any other ethnic characteristic must be given a cultural meaning which accords with the structural conditions of the society in question. The psychological and societal significance of race and prejudice have been well established for US society by Baran & Sweezy (1966) when they argue that the white working class will often see blacks or migrants as competitors for scarce jobs and housing. Racist or ethnic discrimination becomes not just a matter of objective reality but also involves a belief system. This system is a device to protect psychological well-being in a status-conscious world. Groups in a competitive system need to compensate for feelings of inferiority and envy towards those above them by feelings of superiority and contempt for those below. A pariah group at the bottom helps distil the frustration and hostilities for all others, especially those nearer the bottom. The pariah group acts as a stabilizer of the social structure, and in time such a society may become saturated with racial prejudice which becomes part of 'human nature' and which is legitimized by a belief in individualistic competitiveness and achievement. The visibilities of race as documented by Prager (1987) help redefine institutions, but they may be inadequate to shake 'human nature'.

Prejudice and segregation

Prejudice is, therefore, seen by many to be a major reason for the lack of progress towards racial equality and shared space. Galster (1982) points to three possible causes of segregation, namely class (unequal distributions of income, education and occupation), discrimination (unequal access to housing and other resources) and preference (blacks and whites prefer segregated neighbourhoods). But it has been shown that blacks prefer mixed and suburban neighbourhoods (Darden 1987). In fact after reviewing the evidence Darden (1987, 37) suggests that 'black residential segregation is best explained by exclusion and discrimination motivated by racial prejudice. Economic factors are of minor importance.' Further as Wolfe (1981) points out, voluntary segregation is unlikely except as a response to threat. Racial concentration is largely compelled and it will remain widespread and unresponsive to both economic progress and the assimilative processes that dispersed ethnic groups. Discrimination and prejudice mean, therefore, that the relationships between identity and urban space will differ for race and ethnicity. It also means that the bases of identity will differ. While racial and ethnic groups will both emphasize their own similarities and differences from the majority, the former often takes the form of the community of the oppressed when the latter have been communities of hope and assimilation. In other words, blacks have little choice in whether or not they assimilate or remain isolated. An isolatist strategy is all that they are given.

We must not, however, underestimate the importance of marginality or oppression in developing ethnic strength and identity and racial pride. Herbstein (1983) shows how Puerto Ricans on the US mainland developed organizations to deal with their shared circumstances despite their class, racial and religious differences. But majority group practices prevent the possibility of these organizations working for assimilationist ends. Yet common interests, affective ties and marginality are the three main sources of ethnic strength (see Yinger 1986). This ethnic strength is employed when 'ethnicity emerges as the basis of collective action when there are clear advantages attached to ethnic (versus religious, kinship, class, or some other) identity' (Olzak 1982, 254) as evidenced by the Irish and Italians in many cities, the Cubans in Miami and the Asians in California. But as the differences between racial and ethnic groups aver, the internal sources of strength or weakness of ethnic attachments cannot be separated from the interactions with influences of the surrounding society, as the devaluing of schooling for racial group attachments indicates (see Fordham & Ogbu 1986). These influences then affect ethnic relations and contacts, and Table 3.2 lists the factors which may affect the salience of racial or ethnic group membership.

We may regard the table as a summarizing device for many of the group encounters and situations discussed in this chapter. It must be remembered that ethnic identity may not diminish with improved group status: it may, as with the Irish and Italians, for example, become an important dimension of self-definition in the undifferentiated and fragmented space of American and Canadian cities. As Yinger (1981) notes, ethnicity helps to preserve some sense of community, to know who one is, and to overcome the feeling of being a cipher in an anonymous world.

Table 3.2 Variables that affect the salience of group membership.

	Tend to increase salience	Tend to decrease salience
1	Large group (relative to total population)	Small group
2	Residentially concentrated by region and community	Residentially scattered
3	Short-term residents (high proportion of newcomers)	Long-term residents (low proportion of newcomers)
4	Return to homeland easy and frequent	Difficult and infrequent
5	Speak a different language	Speak the dominant language
6	Different religion from majority	Share majority religion
7	Different race	Same race
8	Entered the society by forced migration or conquest	Entered voluntarily
9	Come from culturally different society	Come from culturally similar society
10	Attracted to political and economic developments in land of origin	Repelled by those developments
11	Homogeneous in class and occupation	Diverse in class and occupation
12	Low average level of education	High average level of education
13	Experience a great deal of discrimination	Experience little discrimination
14	Resident in a society with little social mobility	Resident in open-class society

Source: Yinger 1986, 31.

Conclusion

This chapter began with an examination of the significance of the meaning of race and ethnicity. It has also shown how the effects of race and ethnicity vary in the North American context. For blacks, race and place remain closely intertwined because of majority group prejudice and discrimination as well as the operation of the urban economy. For the members of groups based on religion and ethnic origin, ethnicity and place have become more or less dissociated, with associations being determined largely by ethnic desires rather than majority group pressures. It is perhaps unfortunate that most theories of ethnicity emphasize assimilation rather than pluralism, separation and conflict. Thus Glaser (1958) sees groups moving from segregating, through marginalized and desegregating to assimilation stages. A more complex model is put forward by Greeley (1971) who sees migrants entering the US experiencing 'culture shock' before beginning to organize their emerging consciousness in institutions and organizations. There follows the assimilation of the ethnic elite and a phase of militancy in which the ethnic group organizes with zeal and often comes into conflict with other groups vying for similar resources. Then comes a phase of 'self-hatred and antimilitancy' in which the ideals, values and institutions of the wider North American society are used as models. Finally, there is a phase of 'emerging adjustment' with a renewed commitment to an ethnic heritage while remaining embedded in mainstream society. Integration, assimilation and a degree of pluralism are suggested. It is largely the experience of European migrants to North America.

Such theories and phases perhaps underemphasize the struggles and conflicts of the European migrants themselves. Banton (1983) is right when he stresses intergroup competition and bargaining as is Rex (1983) when he comments that the oppression of the market is heightened in race relations situations by group conflicts mediated by deterministic belief systems. But these emphases again point up the importance of class, discrimination and preference as the bases of ethnic interaction and conflict. We must also continue to stress that the operation of these forces (as with the sources of ethnic strength) is contingent under specific cultural, political and economic configurations. Culture, polity and economy have a shifting and variable influence on group relations and boundaries. Indeed, Parkin (1979) argues that social closure may be used to restrict access to resources and opportunities to a limited number of eligibles. Blacks remain largely excluded while ethnic minorities may more successfully alter the boundary relations between themselves and the majority. Minorities may create their own bounded spaces, as with ethnic identity maintenance and the informal economy of many ghettos. The boundaries themselves are not fixed, however. They shift by activity, group and space. Such contingency makes firm conclusions difficult, especially with respect to the likelihood of assimilation, pluralism or ethnogenesis. We may perhaps conclude with Yancey *et al.* (1985). From their analyses of Philadelphia, they comment that ethnicity is a multidimensional phenomenon. Thus its meaning depends on the structural location of individuals and groups. These structural (and ideological) parameters generate groups and define their positions and possibilities. Emphasizing the parameters enables us to get behind the rhetoric of 'integration', 'melting pot' or 'multiculturalism' to understand the changing status of different racial and ethnic groups. Group identity and urban space are interrelated but the nature of the relationship is difficult to generalize. Unpacking the relationship in concrete settings allows an 'advance beyond the debate over whether ethnicity matters, to learn how and why ethnicity matters' (Hirschman 1983, 416). It (as well as race) matters because of its individual and societal implications and significance. They matter because they help configure American and Canadian societies.

References

Agocs, C. 1981. Ethnic settlement in a metropolitan area. *Ethnicity* **8**, 127–48.

Auletta, K. 1982. *The underclass*. New York: Random House.

Balakrishnan, T. R. 1976. Ethnic residential segregation in the metropolitan areas of Canada. *Canadian Journal of Sociology* **1**, 481–98.

Balakrishnan, T. R. 1982. Changing patterns of ethnic residential segregation in the metropolitan areas of Canada. *Canadian Review of Sociology and Anthropology* **19**, 92–110.

Banton, M. 1983. *Racial and ethnic competition*. Cambridge: Cambridge University Press.

Baran, P. & P. Sweezy 1966. *Monopoly capital*. New York: Penguin.

Bellah, R. 1985. *Habits of the heart*. Berkeley, Calif.: University of California Press.

Boal, F. W. 1976. Ethnic residential segregation. In *Social areas in cities*, Vol. 1, D. T. Herbert & R. J. Johnston (eds). Chichester: Wiley.

Bonacich, E. 1976. Advanced capitalism and black–white race relations in the US. *American Sociological Review* **41**, 34–51.

Clift, D. 1989. *The secret kingdom*. Toronto: McClelland & Stewart.

Darden, J. T. 1987. Choosing neighbours and neighbourhoods. In *Divided neighbour-hoods*, G. A. Tobin (ed.). Beverly Hills: Sage.

Dingemans, D. 1978. Redlining and mortgage lending in Sacramento. *Annals Association of American Geographers* **69**, 225–39.

Eyles, J. 1989. Urban policy? what urban policy? In *Social problems and the city*, D. T. Herbert & D. M. Smith (eds). Oxford: Oxford University Press.

Farley, R. 1984. *Blacks and whites: narrowing the gap?* Cambridge, Mass.: Harvard University Press.

Farley, R. 1985. Three steps forward and two back? Recent changes in the social and economic status of blacks. *Ethnic and Racial Studies* **8**, 4–28.

Farley, R. 1987. Segregation in 1980. In *Divided neighbourhoods*, G. A. Tobin (ed.). Beverly Hills: Sage.

Ford, L. & E. Griffin 1979. The ghettoization of paradise. *Geographical Review* **69**, 140–58.

Fordham, S. & J. U. Ogbu 1986. Black students' school success. *Urban Review* **18**, 176–206.

Forman, R. *Black ghettos, white ghettos and slums*. Englewood Cliffs, NJ: Prentice-Hall.

Galster, G. C. 1982. Black and white preferences for neighbourhood racial com-position. *American Real Estate and Urban Economics Association Journal* **10**, 39–67.

Garcia, P. 1985. Immigration issues in urban ecology: the case of Los Angeles. In *Urban ethnicity in the US*, L. Maldonado & J. Moore (eds). Beverly Hills: Sage.

Glaser, D. 1958. Dynamics of ethnic identification. *American Sociological Review* **23**, 31–40.

Gordon, M. M. 1964. *Assimilation in American life*. New York: Oxford University Press.

Greerley, A. M. 1970. Religious intermarriage in a denominational society. *American Journal of Sociology* **75**, 949–52.

Greerley, A. M. 1971. *Why can't they be like us?* New York: Dutton.

Guest, A. M. & J. A. Weed 1976. Ethnic residential segregation: patterns of change. *American Journal of Sociology* **81**, 1088–1111.

Gutman, H. G. 1974. *The invisible fact: the black family in American history*. New York: Free Press.

References

Hall, S. 1978. Race and reaction. In *Five views of multi-racial Britain*, CRE (ed.). London: CRE.

Herbstein, J. 1983. The politicization of Puerto Rican ethnicity in New York. *Ethnic Groups* **5** (7), 31–54.

Hernandez, J. 1985. Improving the data: a research strategy for new immigrants. In *Urban ethnicity in the US*, L. Maldonado and J. Moor (eds). Beverly Hills: Sage.

Hirschman, C. 1983. America's melting pot reconsidered. In *Annual Review of Sociology* **9**, R. H. Turner & J. F. Short (eds). Palo Alto: Annual Reviews.

Hwang, S. S. & S. H. Murdock 1983. Segregation in metropolitan and nonmetropolitan Texas in 1980. *Rural Sociology* **48**, 607–23.

Logan, J. R. & M. Schneider 1984. Racial segregation and racial change in American suburbs, 1970–80. *American Journal of Sociology* **89**, 874–89.

Massey, D. S. 1985. Ethnic residential segregation: a theoretical synthesis and empirical review. *Sociology and Social Research* **69**, 315–50.

Massey, D. S. & N. A. Denton 1987. Trends in the residential segregation of blacks, Hispanics and Asians. *American Sociological Review* **52**, 802–25.

Massey, D. S. and N. A. Denton 1988a. The dimensions of residential segregation. *Social Forces* **67**, 281–315.

Massey, D. S. and N. A. Denton 1988b. Suburbanization and segregation in US metropolitan areas. *American Journal of Sociology* **94**, 592–626.

Matwijiw, P. 1979. Ethnicity and residence. *Canadian Geographer* **23**, 45–61.

Modell, J. & T. K. Hareven 1977. Urbanization and the malleable household. In *Family and kin in urban communities*, T. K. Hareven (ed.). New York: Oxford University Press.

Mohl, R. A. 1985. An ethnic 'boiling pot': Cubans and Haitians in Miami. *Journal of Ethnic Studies* **13**, 51–74.

Norton, A. J. 1983. Keeping up with households. *American Demographics* **5**(2), 17–21.

Olzak, S. 1982. Ethnic mobilization in Quebec. *Ethnic and Racial Studies* **5**, 253–75.

Park, R. E. 1921. Sociology and the social sciences. *American Journal of Sociology* **26**, 401–4 and **27**, 1–21, 169–83.

Park, R. E. 1927. Human nature and collective behavior. *American Journal of Sociology* **32**, 733–41.

Parkin, F. 1979. *Marxism and class theory*. London: Tavistock.

Prager, J. 1987. American political culture and the shifting meaning of race. *Ethnic and Racial Studies* **10**, 62–81.

Rex, J. 1983. Review of 'The ethnic phenomenon'. *Ethnic and Racial Studies* **6**, 368–71.

Rogers, A. & R. Uto 1987. Residential segregation retheorized: a view from southern California. In *Race and racism*, P. Jackson (ed.). London: Allen & Unwin.

Rose, H. M. 1981. The black professional and residential segregation in the American city. In *Ethnic segregation in cities*, C. Peach (ed.). London: Croom Helm.

Rosenthal, E. 1961. Acculturation without assimilation? The Jewish community of Chicago. *American Journal of Sociology* **66**, 275–88.

Sassen-Koob, S. 1985. The new labour demand in global cities. In *Cities in transformation*, M. P. Smith (ed.). Beverly Hills: Sage.

Scott, A. J. 1984. Industrial organization and the logic of intra-metropolitan location: a case study of the women's dress industry in the Greater Los Angeles region. *Economic Geography* **60**, 3–27.

Sivanandan, A. 1982. *A different hunger*. London: Pluto Press.

Steele, S. 1988. I'm black, you're white, who's innocent? *Harper's* **267** (1657), 45–53.

Stepick, A. 1982. Haitian boat people: a study of the conflicting forces shaping US immigration policy. *Law and Contemporary Problems* **45**, 165–96.

Taueber, K. E. 1965. Residential segregation. *Scientific American* **213**, 12–19.

Taueber, K. E. 1983. *Racial residential segregation, 28 cities, 1970–80.* Working paper 83–12. Wisconsin: Center for Demography and Ecology, University of Wisconsin.

Taueber, K. E. & A. F. Taueber 1965. *Negroes in cities.* Chicago: Aldine.

Thomas, W. I. & F. Znaniecki 1958. *The Polish peasant in Europe and America.* New York: Free Press.

Thompson, B. 1983. Social ties and ethnic settlement patterns. In *Culture, ethnicity and identity*, W. C. McCready (ed.). New York: Academic Press.

Van Valey, T. L. 1977. Trends in residential segregation. *American Journal of Sociology* **82**, 826–44.

Ward, D. 1969. The internal spatial structure of immigrant residential districts in the late nineteenth century. *Geographical Analysis* **1**, 337–53.

Ward D. 1982. The ethnic ghetto in the US. *Transactions, Institute of British Geographers* **7**, 257–75.

Williams, P. H. 1938. *Southern Italian folkways in Europe and America.* New Haven, Conn.: Yale University Press.

Wilson, W. J. 1978. *The declining significance of race.* Chicago: Chicago University Press.

Wolfe, E. P. 1981. *Trial and error: the Detroit school segregation case.* Detroit: Wayne State University Press.

Woolbright, L. A. & D. J. Hartmann 1987. The new segregation. In *Divided neighborhoods*, G. A. Tobin (ed.). Beverly Hills: Sage.

Yancey, W. L. *et al.* 1985. The structure of pluralism. *Ethnic and Racial Studies* **8**, 94–116.

Yinger, J. M. 1981. Toward a theory of assimilation and dissimilation. *Ethnic and Racial Studies* **4**, 249–64.

Yinger, J. M. 1986. Intersecting strands in the theorization of race and ethnic relations. In *Theories of race and ethnic relations*, J. Rex and D. Mason (eds). Cambridge: Cambridge University Press.

4

Nationhood and statehood in Canada

PETER SLOWE

Introduction

Ethnicity and nationhood are concepts which are open to a variety of interpretations. Here they are used quite specifically. 'Nationhood' is taken to be the same as 'ethnicity' except that it occurs within state boundaries and is thus created or reinforced by the power of the state (Slowe 1988). The Canadian state, therefore, has two main ethnic groups, the English Canadians and the French Canadians, but it has also created a new ethnicity, including the whole of Canada, Canadian 'nationhood'.

Ethnicity is the consequence of affinities and transactions outside the framework of the state among a group of people coherent enough to be called an ethnic group. Similar affinities and transactions to those which characterize an ethnic group are also actually generated by the state itself, for the state is extremely powerful, deriving its power from its sovereignty over clearly defined territory, its complete and compulsory jurisdiction within definite boundaries. The state can easily generate the affinities and transactions which occur naturally within an ethnic group, and when it does so, the consequence is nationhood.

Not every state generates nationhood; but every state aspires to do so because nationhood provides the state with a consensus and thus with the power to mobilize and motivate its citizens and to obtain their loyalty. In the case of Canada it will be shown that two main ethnic groups developed before independence from Britain, but that the independent Canadian state has been able to generate the affinities and transactions of one Canadian nationhood.

So Canada has become a nation-state. The ethnic groups have not of course disappeared, but nationhood has become a more important source of power than ethnicity. The nation-state is the most consistently powerful organization in the political geography of the world today, combining consensus, legality and international recognition. Therefore it is of great importance to Canada that it has achieved the status of 'nation-state'.

Ethnicity and territory

Traditionally, ethnic groups are described mainly in terms of affinities. Anthony Smith (1986, 283–4), for example, said that any social group may be called an ethnic group if its members claim a common origin, share a common history and culture, and possess feelings of mutual solidarity which mark them off from other groups. A shared feeling of identity is important, but transactions between people who share characteristics are also essential if a group is to be cohesive. Indeed, this cohesion or 'integration', measured by the quality and quantity of transactions between individuals and groups, has been the focus of study by geographers and political scientists, such as Soja (1968) in geography and Deutsch (1969) in political science during the last few decades without being applied specifically to ethnicity. Transactions can be political – such as participation in political decision-making, chains of command and the exercise of political power; they can be cultural – such as schooling, the diffusion of literature and broadcast or performed entertainment; they can be social – such as intermarriage and social class relations; and they can be economic – such as trade and transport. These transactions benefit from shared territory, although this need not necessarily be bounded or controlled in the style of the modern state.

Before European settlement, the land of Canada was inhabited by North American Indian tribes. Oswalt (1966), Snow (1976) and others have differing opinions on the number of tribes in Canada. There were probably about thirty groups which were sufficiently similar and integrated to be described as ethnic groups, sharing language and myth, and combining into single collective economies and societies. Oswalt's study of the Chipewyan, for example, illustrates a degree of integration and sharing of tradition which would never be matched by either English Canadians or French Canadians, both of whom can certainly be described as ethnic groups (Oswalt 1966, 36–76). The Chipewyan had an unambiguous sense of their own identity with their own mythology. Although they had no concept of state or bounded territory, they saw themselves as part of the land. They shared a creation myth, which they related in their Na–dene language, that their ancestors were a woman and a dog who loved each other in an ancient cave in the mountains. Their mother was the earth and their father the animals who provided sustenance. North American Indians, such as the Chipewyan, could scarcely understand the European view of territory. The ideas of ownership and boundaries and the European view of the land as an object contrasted with the Indian view of the land as sacred.

Both the European and Indian views of the land were shared by a people large enough to retain some measure of cultural, economic and therefore political independence and continuity at the time. Both were therefore distinct views of viable ethnic groups. The vital difference was that the European view of land ownership was exclusionary. Canada, divided into English and French

Canada with occasional bounded reserves for Indians, was the result of the inability of Indians who knew no boundaries to resist European encroachment politically, economically or militarily. Now Indians account for only just over 0.5 per cent of Canada's population. Nearly half of the rest are anglophone ('English Canadians'), about a quarter are francophone ('French Canadians') and the remainder are originally from other parts of Asia and Europe.

English Canadian ethnicity

The creation myth of anglophone or English Canada is just as elaborate as that of a Chipewyan and equally contentious:

> In days of yore
> From Britain's shore
> Wolfe the dauntless hero came
> And planted firm Britannia's flag
> On Canada's fair domain.
> Here may it wave, our boast, our pride
> And joined in love together
> The Thistle, Shamrock, Rose entwine the Maple Leaf for ever.
>
> (Muir 1891).

The British conquest of New France and the consequent enrolment of Canada into the British Empire constitutes the first part of the mythological history of English Canada. The unequal struggle between the representatives of two European empires became a heroic history of the origin of a people whose ascendancy was proven by their ability to control most of North America.

The significance of Canadian territory only really became apparent after the United States had won independence. 40 000 loyalists to the British Empire moved north. Their allegiance to the British Crown was reified by the 1783 Treaty of Versailles which drew most of the modern boundary between the colony of Canada and the independent United States. A tract of land for Empire loyalists was clearly defined. The loyalist immigration tipped the population scales firmly in favour of loyalty to the British Crown and, under vigorous Lieutenant-Governors, British political power was asserted throughout the British North American provinces defined by the Canada Act of 1791. At the same time the society and economy of British North America retained a distinctly American flavour:

> The loyalists who came to Canada were British Americans who, although they might have rejected the American Revolution politically, neverthe-less reflected the aggressive, acquisitive, Protestant, individualist society of the American colonies. Like the Americans, they were interested in new

techniques in agriculture and in developing new markets for their products. (Verney 1986, 177)

18th- and 19th-century treaties ensured Britain's political ascendancy in Canada. Canadians were linked to the Crown through legislative councils and the Lieutenant-Governor, but a distinctly American flavour to loyalism characterized the English Canadian economy and society. English Canada started to acquire its own identity with political allegiance to Britain but the economic and social characteristics of North America.

This crucial early history provided English Canadians with the shared origin and the shared culture essential for an ethnic group, and loyalty to the British Crown in the face of challenges from French Canadians and the new United States provided stable political foundations for the mutual solidarity of an ethnic group. English Canadians remained, however, very diffuse both in geography and character, and the cohesion of the English Canadian ethnic group, which now accounts for some 10 million Canadians, has been developed over nearly two centuries by political, cultural and social transactions.

Following American independence, the British territories in North America were politically divided into Upper Canada (west of the Ottawa River), Lower Canada (which included French-speaking Canada), the four Atlantic provinces and the vast areas controlled by the Hudson's Bay Company extending to the Arctic and the Pacific. It was not until 1867 that Canada became a united dominion with four provinces, Ontario, Quebec, New Brunswick and Nova Scotia; it was recognized by the United States in 1871 in the same year as British Columbia was included in the confederation. Prince Edward Island came into the confederation in 1873, so the Canadian national motto 'From Sea to Sea' was realized. The French-speaking minority was swamped, but supported confederation on the grounds that the cultural threat from incorporation within the United States, a real possibility at a time of uneasy relations, was more serious: the Canadian confederation appeared to offer a chance for them to retain some ethnic identity.

At that time, before the major immigration of the 1890s and 1900s, the English Canadians accounted for some 75 per cent of the population. With an inbuilt English Canadian majority, Canada's political transactions were either with Britain or in the British political tradition, in which a Westminster style of government was taken for granted. Indeed, the transactions directly with Britain through the Governor-General, the Judicial Committee of the Privy Council and the British Parliament itself at Westminster, were seen as guarantees against domination by the Ontario elite within the English Canadian majority.

The importance of the transatlantic connections with Britain as a factor in the ethnic identity of English Canadians was illustrated first by the response to the threat from the United States in the 1860s, but it was through participation

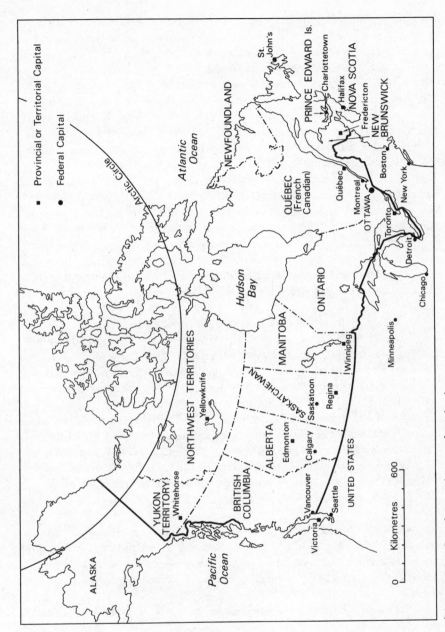

Figure 4.1 Canada: provinces and territories.

in the wider British imperial destiny that English Canadians were able to express their identity through loyalty to the Crown. They were, for most practical purposes, politically independent but saw themselves also as 'the eldest daughter of the empire' and later as the 'Senior Dominion' (Verney 1986, 113). They were Canadian citizens and British subjects.

It was first the Boer War and then, most important, the First World War which enabled English Canadians to express their English ethnicity but political independence; these wars helped to clarify English Canadian ethnicity. The English Canadian connection with Britain forced Prime Minister Laurier's hand into sending eventually over 7000 Canadians to fight in the Boer War, despite widespread sympathy with the Boers among French Canadians. 'Fighting Britain's wars' from the Boer War to the Second World War and beyond was a way for English Canadians to express a sense of belonging which held them together as one ethnic group. It was in the First World War that the youthful loyalty of independent Canadians was contrasted with British decay, German woodenness and French barbarity. There was little recognition of French Canadian interest in the role of France and nearly all Canadian troops supported the British Western Front.

> The Canadians crossed the Atlantic to fight for King and Country. They did so with enthusiasm and gusto ... their feelings of patriotism were uncomplicated. Like most soldiers, they relished the excitement of war and loathed its horrors, but their simple belief in the rightness of the Empire's cause made them brave – more effective than the reluctant British drafts and more fervent than the 'blood and steel' Germans.
> At St. Eloi on Vimy Ridge, the Canadians looked forward eagerly to their formidable task: 'The boys were in high spirits and glad of the opportunity to demonstrate again the quality of the New World troops ... We would uphold all the traditions of the Canadian Army and our Battalion would prove to be one of the best in France!' (Becton & Odell 1918, 55–6, quoted in Slowe & Woods 1986, 120.)

Becton & Odell in the same passage go on to explain the role of the French Canadians in the First World War in disparaging terms, and the same tension can be found in other English Canadian war memoirs, such as those of Lieutenant Pedley (1927), a founder-member of the first ever Canadian Corps.

By the time of the outbreak of the Second World War, there was less doubt than ever about Canadian participation. Again, the French Canadian interest in neutrality or supporting first the French republic and then the Free French was scarcely recognized, but there was increasing frustration at the lack of political influence over British decisions leading up to the war, eventually bringing about a belated direct intervention with Hitler by Canadian Prime Minister MacKenzie King (Neatby 1976, 315–16).

Cultural affinities and transactions also play an important part in defining English Canadian ethnicity. Their shared English language gave rise to a substantial literature. Most popular literature among English Canadians tended to reflect the same values as they felt and expressed in the First World War: young, brave and undecayed, not unlike the pioneering America to the south but with the British connection as well. For example, in the first decades of dominion status, Canadians recited Wild-West-style ballads:

> A bunch of the boys were whopping it up in the Malamute
> saloon;
> The kid that handles the music-box was hitting a jag-time
> tune;
> Back of the bar, in a solo game, sat Dangerous Dan McGrew,
> And watching his luck was his light-o'-love, the lady that's
> known as Lou.   (Sutherland, 1982, 425).

At the same time Helen Johnson's 'Our Native Land' reflected other sentiments, like those of 'The Maple Leaf For Ever' (above):

> How many loving memories throng
> Round Britain's stormy coast!
> Renowned in story and in song,
> Her glory is our boast!
> With loyal hearts we still abide
> Beneath her sheltering wing;
> While with true patriot love and pride
> To Canada we cling.   (Sutherland 1982, 409).

The popularity of later Canadian novels set in the prairie and the west, some in a stilted literary style, is also accounted for by their reflection of the English Canadian ethnic self-image. A prime example would be Grove's 1928 novel, *Our daily bread* set in a youthful land with great open spaces offering unlimited opportunity.

Just as English Canadian literature reflects the English Canadian self-image, so do certain landscape characteristics. The allegiance of English Canadians to Britain is commemorated by war memorials in nearly every town. At the same time the rugged independence of English Canadians is illustrated by symbols of the Canadian north, singling out English Canadians both from French Canadians and from the Americans to the south, for example in the work of the artist, F. H. Varley (Nasgaard 1984). Konrad in 'Recurrent symbols of nationalism in Canada' claims that

> the work of Varley and his colleagues etches the severity of [Canadian] Shield existence and suggests the strength of body and character necessary to survive in this formidable land.

He goes on to illustrate how northern symbols, such as the moose and caribou, provide an incongruous decor for government buildings in Ottawa (Konrad 1986, 176–8).

Finally, English Canadian ethnicity has been held together by elite cohesion in economic, political and social affairs. Presthus (1973) described this 'elite accommodation'; he showed that public policy for the whole of Canada was in the hands of certain economic interest groups and senior politicians, almost all English Canadians, and suggested that the involvement in federal decision-making by French Canadians and other groups amounted to mere tokenism. The lack of political sophistication amongst most Canadians made it impossible for them to penetrate the 'bureaucratic ethos' which characterized the governance of Canada.

Through their numerical domination and elite cohesion, English Canadians took – and hold on to – power in federal Canada. They have retained a clear ethnic identity through their shared history, mythology and language and through their political, cultural and social integration.

French Canadian ethnicity

The 6 million francophone or French Canadians who make up about a quarter of the population share the common myths necessary for ethnic identity.

> We are nourished by myths, by ideals, whose relationship to reality are at the very best highly vague; this is a most irritating characteristic of our culture ... We envisage a highly patriotic national project without ensuring that an exciting and imperious reality provide the essential elements of the dynamic policy that is capable of being fulfilled. Our national mystique therefore remains necessarily sentimental and idealistic. It ... is based on an antiquated reality, fixed in tradition, which reached its zenith perhaps in the middle of the last century. This reality was for us the plausibility of becoming a small nation in the 19th-century conception of that. (Vadeboncoeur 1952, quoted in Behiels 1985, 87).

The mythical origins in the mind of French Canadians referred to by Vadeboncoeur had to do with a common idea of an Arcadian past dominated by the church and by rural patriarchal family life. French Canadians shared a myth of allegiance to an ancient French way of life. They felt themselves Frenchmen who had been abandoned on a hostile English continent.

Only French civil law and the Roman Catholic church actually remained of the French imperial state institutions. Ouellet (1980, 10–13) described French Canada in the days of French imperial rule as untouched by American enterprise and acquisitiveness and virtually unaware of industrialization. It was dominated by seigneury and church, and the peasantry was mainly apathetic.

74

The seigneury was weakened fatally by the war with the British. The church was the sole remaining powerful French Canadian institution; it found no appeal in post-revolutionary France nor in the secular United States. On the contrary it felt more able to fight tenaciously for its own spiritual autonomy and consequently for the cultural autonomy of its adherents, the French Canadians, within a loose Canadian confederation.

Even the significance of the church at the time the French were defeated in 1760 was itself a 19th-century myth, since there were in fact only 138 priests for 70 000 people, but by the 1840s the church dominated French Canada. The church dominated French Canadian ethnicity, with a stranglehold on education, including the two French Canadian universities at Montreal and Quebec, on welfare institutions, on early trade unions and on everyday life:

Life in St. Denis is a flow of traditional behavior. Upon rising there are family prayers: then the animals must be fed and the cows milked; the workers returned to cross themselves and sit down to breakfast ... Incidents in this stream of events can be singled out as sacred and secular, but such distinction is not part of the native's own conceptualization of life. (Falardeau 1971, quoted in Woolfson 1982, 352).

The church became the focus of not just social but also political and economic transactions. The church was enormously wealthy and directly involved with politics. Church officials used their moral and political authority to censor critical debate and used their economic and social power to silence critics if they thought it necessary (Behiels 1985, 17–20).

It was during the 1950s and 1960s that a group of intellectuals successfully challenged these traditional features of French Canadian ethnicity. This group was dominated by contributors to radical journals, especially *Le Devoir*, *L'Action Nationale* and *Cité Libre*, and included future Prime Minister Pierre Trudeau, and their method was political education and campaigning, taking advantage of postwar economic and social change. The crude conservative nationalism of the church-dominated politics of French Canada, with its racial certainties and antisemitism, was rejected in favour of a new French Canadian ethnicity based on a modern industrial society and not a rural idyll of seigneurs and priests. The new ethnicity was no longer to be centred around the integration of a theocracy but instead to be based on the realities of cultural affinity within French Canada and of economic integration with the rest of Canada and the wider world. It was to be based on fact not myth. It was to be French Canadians' 'quiet revolution', a cultural and economic transformation.

Education was the first target of the new ethnicity; it was to be secularized and democratized with state financing loosening church control at primary, secondary and university levels. The social and economic inferiority of French Canadians to English Canadians, even within French Canadian Quebec, let alone within Canada as a whole, was attributed in large part to outmoded educational institutions. The reform of education would enable French Canadians to participate in the reality of economically advanced, industrialized North America. Each individual would have a wider choice of role in society. The clerical classical college system would be replaced by a universally accessible public secondary system which would prepare students for the entire range of secular career opportunities. The reduction of the power of the church changed French Canada's ethnic self-image. In particular a new cultural self-confidence emerged in the 1970s. Only Quebec in the whole of Canada was to have a Ministry of Culture and a National Library. A good deal of money was spent on a French Canadian art centre, a French Canadian theatre and a French Canadian museum. There was a French Canadian renaissance; publishers and film companies flourished in response to the new creativity.

The new cultural self-confidence of Quebec found a metaphor in Langevin's 1976 novel *Une chaine dans le parc*. A child, Pierrot, is brought up in an orphanage and a traditional school in French Canada. But he is independent and refuses to accept religious and other traditional ways. There is a beautiful girl who is distant from him; she is hard to reach and all the authorities discourage him; but through force of intellect he wins through. It is an intellectual revolution that has destroyed the Old French Canadian national ethnicity based on the cohesion of church control and replaced it with an ethnicity based on cultural affinity.

Cultural self-confidence has enabled French Canadians to escape the territory of the francophone province of Quebec. While French Canadian ethnicity had been preoccupied with crude nationalist aspirations, national territory was needed as a focus and Quebec was the only realistic choice. Once the constraint of an aspiration to national territorial independence was dropped, French Canadian ethnic culture could assert itself beyond territorial boundaries. French Canadians recognized their unique North American francophone culture and actively encouraged cultural activity among francophone minorities in Ontario and even Louisiana. Indeed, one of the main North American francophone literary figures, Antoine Maillet, winner of the Prix Goncourt, came from New Brunswick. No longer confined by a clear contiguous territory, French Canadian ethnicity was free to set its own cultural boundaries.

The new French Canadian culture also recognized the internationalization of economic transactions. Officials from Quebec, for example, started to participate fully in the work of the annual meetings of the Eastern Canadian Premiers and New England Governors, dealing with such issues as energy transfers, acid rain, fisheries and trade in agricultural products. Hero and Daneau (1984) discuss the burgeoning field of Quebec–United States relations, particularly the relations between Quebec and New York State covering several cross-border agreements on energy, water supply and the environment. Duchacek (1986, 270–7) discusses the wider cultural and economic activities of Quebec in Tokyo, Dusseldorf, London and Caracas, and quotes the journalist Elliot Feldman of the *Toronto Globe and Mail*:

Has any one noticed that the United States is no longer anxious about Quebec? Quebec has enlarged and polished its international profile. This remarkable accomplishment is attributable largely to three developments: the redirection of Quebec nationalism, the cultivation of policies sympathetic to US interests and the responsible conduct of international affairs. (Duchacek 1986, 276–7).

French Canadian ethnicity has undergone an extraordinary rehabilitation. The method used to get from conventional nationalist aspiration to cultural and economic power was essentially a process of political education by astute intellectuals, described fully by Behiels (1985) and Quinn (1979). Senior positions in the financial, commercial and industrial world had been closed to French Canadians narrowly tutored in the church schools. Only in the public sector did French Canadians have any power in Quebec, and this small elite was rigidly committed to the *status quo* which they could only preserve through English Canadians in the private sector and the Catholic Church. The political education campaigns aimed to publish scandals in the operation of the old regime, the Union Nationale, to discredit it, and to encourage western democratic ideas at a time when modern levels of literacy and modern communications meant that more and more people would hear the message. The pattern of economic activity was also changing, as French Canadians abandoned the poverty of overmanned farmsteads for the labour-hungry cities and the beginnings of a more liberal church. The new ideas coincided with the new realities. They were pushing at an open door. The 'quiet revolution' produced a new ethnicity.

Canadian nation-statehood

In addition to English and French Canadian ethnicity, the Canadian state has created its own special ethnicity – or 'nationhood' – to embrace all Canadians. The Canadian state, like many other states, is the creator of a nation.

The state can create a nation, because its sovereign authority ensures that intense transactions and affinities, just as intense as those within any ethnic group, take place within its clear territorial boundaries. This sovereign authority derives in part from the universal jurisdiction of the state, which means that legal citizenship applies everywhere within its territorial boundaries, making no distinction, for example, between Quebecois and British Columbians, German-speaking Canadians and indigenous Indians. Sovereign authority also derives in part from the state's compulsory jurisdiction, which means, for example, that people living in Canada have no choice about Canadian state jurisdiction; it may be possible to have nothing to do with family, religion or ethnic group, but there is no escape from the jurisdiction of the state. So much of human life is carried on within the sovereign state, through the state and by the state, that almost inevitably it generates its own affinities and transactions which eventually make up a nation, incorporating even those who might have been excluded by ethnic groups before the state came into being. Thus, in effect the state creates its own ethnicity on its own territory, a special type of ethnicity called 'nationhood'. The Canadian state has created a new nationhood to coincide with sovereign territory and has, therefore, become more than just a state and more than just a nation; Canada has become a sovereign nation-state.

The Canadian state was confronted with two strong ethnic groups in British and French Canadians. To fulfil its function of creating and maintaining internal order through the consensus of nationhood, it has had to adopt a dualist stance, incorporating and preserving two equal and competing ethnicities into one Canadian nationhood.

The Canadian state emerged after the Second World War with few links with an impoverished Britain and barely half its population able to trace any British origin. It was increasingly powerful and independent economically and politically and in a good position and a clearly defined state, well able to defend undisputed boundaries and to develop the affinities and transactions which would make up Canadian nationhood. These would have to incorporate both English and French Canadian ethnic groups through a forthright policy of dualism encouraged by the growing self-confidence of French Canadian ethnicity and a desire for a clear identity to contrast with the United States.

It would, however, be no simple triumphal march to nation-statehood. The French Canadian 'quiet revolution' had rejected political independence for French Canada in favour of the cultural, economic and political assertion of French Canada within the Canadian state. This was a difficult concept. It was perhaps inevitable that greater assertiveness and greater prosperity would lead to a revival of aspirations to the cruder and simpler concept of independent statehood. Daniel Johnson, Premier of Quebec from 1966 to 1968, sought electoral popularity through his appeal for 'separatism' and tried to establish close ties with France; President de Gaulle returned the compliment with his famous call for 'Québec Libre' from a balcony of Montreal's City Hall in 1967. Separatism was finally politically defeated by one of the leaders of the 'quiet revolution' who, in 1968, became Prime Minister of Canada, Pierre Trudeau. The determined pursuit of dualism took the wind out of the political sails of separatism; then much of what remained of its political appeal evaporated with an outburst of violence and terrorism culminating in the kidnap and murder of Quebec Minister of Labour and Immigration, Pierre Laporte. Nevertheless, there would be no relapse in the insistence of dualism at federal level and the absolute primacy of French culture in Quebec itself. These were the issues, not separatism (which was played down), which swept the Parti Québecois into power in Quebec in 1976 under René Levesque, and they are also the issues that Prime Minister Brian Mulroney will confront in the 1990s.

French is encouraged and learned as an official federal language and there is a

Table 4.1 Canada: population by province or territory.

Alberta	2 340 265
British Columbia	2 849 585
Manitoba	1 049 320
New Brunswick	701 860
Newfoundland	564 000
Northwest Territory	52 020
Nova Scotia	864 150
Ontario	9 001 170
Prince Edward Island	125 090
Quebec	6 454 490
Saskatchewan	996 695
Yukon Territory	23 360
Total	25 022 005

Source: 1986 Census.

Table 4.2 Canada: population by origin.

British	8 406 555
Mixed British and other	2 262 525
French	6 099 090
Mixed French and other	325 655
Mixed British and French	1 139 345
Other European	4 467 840
Asian	931 555
Indigenous Indian	373 265
Other or uncertain	1 016 175
Total	25 022 005

Source: 1986 Census

vigorous national programme of biculturalism intended to permeate education from primary through to university level. The April 1987 Meech Lake agreement between Prime Minister Mulroney and all the provincial premiers produced an agreement to include in Canada's new constitution the recognition of francophone Quebec as a 'distinct society' within Canada, the strongest statement of dualism yet by the official Canadian state.

In recognition not just of the special nature of Quebec but of the growing sophistication of all Canadian provinces, the Meech Lake proposals also include the right of provinces to veto constitutional changes, their rights over immigration, financial and welfare policy and gives them more say in appointments to the Supreme Court. This represents a strong swing away from centralization; some talk of the Balkanization of Canada, but the agreement is likely to be ratified. There is less need for central control. A state with two major competing ethnic groups does not need power concentrated at the centre. It is good order and not central government power that is the aim of the Canadian state, and in this case diversity is clearly associated with good order; uniformity would be unenforceable and would not create a stable order. Because there is now no perceived threat from a fast-growing French Canada with evangelical Catholic priests or from a British Empire seeking conscripts to fight in foreign wars, no province is threatened by the relative independence of another. Diversity is encouraged and Canadian nationhood may eventually develop from dualism to pluralism with each province representing one dimension of that pluralism.

A threat to Canadian nationhood has always come from the south. The cultural and economic power of the United States has at times threatened to swamp Canada. By the 1960s, television and light entertainment were dominated by American themes and products. To visitors Canada also started to look like the United States. The Canadian philosopher George Grant put it this way:

> The United States is the most progressive society on earth and therefore the most radical force for homogenizing the world. By its very nature the capitalist system makes of national boundaries only matters of political formality. (Grant, 1965, 43).

It was not just technology that flooded across the state boundary. The intellectual influence of the United States led to the ascendancy in Canada of American social science over European humanities, of American political science based on the study of interest groups and public opinion over the British study of parliamentary government, and of American political sociology and comparative politics over European political philosophy. But Grant's gloomy analysis was not accepted:

> Just as there was no threat to Canada's identity if a Canadian satellite were launched from American rockets, so there seemed no threat to Canadian scholarship if political scientists used the research methods, the computer technology, and the data archives of American survey research. (Verney 1986, 100).

The Canadian nation-state would prove strong enough to absorb American high culture without losing its national identity and the unique characteristics of Canadian national culture. A dualist nation does not need a unified approach to knowledge. Indeed, disagreement on fundamental issues has become part of the Canadian intellectual tradition; a mixture of philosophical ideas, whether imported from Europe or the United States, is adapted to local conditions. In Canadian national philosophy, as in Canadian national politics, there is dualism or pluralism, not victors and vanquished. Canadian philosophy and epistemology aim to take from and to transcend British, French and American traditions.

Different interpretations of pluralism in academic philosophy, while important, are unlikely to provoke a terrorist incident or a battle for secession. Different English and French Canadian interpretations of political dualism are far more significant from this practical point of view. To English Canadians, dualism means collaboration between the national majority and a provincial minority, whereas to the French Canadians it means a joining together on equal terms of the two founding peoples of Canada and their cultures.

Whether of not this can be resolved successfully is a constant problem. The particular difficulty, arising from these contrary interpretations, in 1988 and 1989, has been a law passed in Quebec making it illegal to display a public sign in any language except French. Both the Quebec Court of Appeal and the Canadian Supreme Court decided that it was a violation of the right to freedom of expression in the charter of rights of both Canada and Quebec. A compromise may be reached allowing small English language signs inside buildings but still not outside; if no agreement is reached New Brunswick and Manitoba may refuse to ratify the Meech Lake agreement. If the Meech Lake agreement is not ratified, Quebec could consider itself outside the jurisdiction of the Canadian constitution in 1990. Such are the tensions created by conflicting interpretations of dualism. Different views and opinions are invited, making uniformity and agreement unlikely and, as in this case, whole perspectives may differ.

This illustrates the most important point about Canadian nationhood. It provides a framework for peaceful association under dualism and a sense of belonging and identity for both major ethnic groups, but it is not a rigid statism. Although the state creates nationhood and nationhood has the same boundaries as the state, dualist nationhood or pluralist nationhood can actually reduce the power of the state. Canadian dualist nationhood recognizes that there are many cases where state sovereignty gives way to superpower strength or to ethnic groups within the state. An example of the former is the economic agreement between Canada and the United States to promote free trade reached in principle in 1987. An example of the latter would be the Quebec language laws, however they are finally drawn up. For most purposes, the sovereign state still provides territorial focus of activity and thought, but Canada has shown how nationhood can preserve the order of the state by reducing its power; the bounds of nationhood remain the territory of the state, but by no means all human activity need be incorporated. The sovereign territorial nation-state is weakening in Canada.

The weakening of the state would be disastrous if people needed sovereign authorities to solve disputes without chaos. But Canadian nationhood shows that there are many ways of solving disputes such as by debate, mutual consideration, even through respect and friendship. Occasionally fighting political disagreement will also play a part in solving a dispute, but strong unitary states also often use violence both externally and internally. Sometimes it is useful for individuals or groups within the state to apply to the state to act as final arbiter but earlier simpler arbitration might solve many disputes more quickly in a pluralist state. Open disagreement is often healthy anyway and there is always a risk in a strong unitary state of state-imposed uniformity which may well be worse than having disagreements.

Canada is full of open disagreements but it is likely to remain a nation-state. English Canadians and French Canadians will still be Canadian nationals. They will share a dualist state with power distributed internationally, to the provinces and, above all, to Canada's two main ethnic groups. Only dualism or pluralism could possibly work in Canada.

Summary

Canada is shared between two major ethnic groups, English-speaking Canadians and French-speaking Canadians which together account for three-quarters of its population. The English Canadians share a self-image promoted originally by comparisons with the Americans, British and French in the two world wars and elsewhere; they were pioneers but sought to retain many of the traditions of the British Empire. They are held together and controlled by an economic and social elite accommodation. The French Canadians have shifted from nationalism which was the aspiration to have their own independent territorial state, to a self-confident identity based on cultural affinity and economic realism.

Since the Second World War, in a statist age, Canada has emerged as an economically and militarily powerful sovereign state (although the constitution was only formally patriated in 1982). It was in a position to develop a Canadian nationhood. The economy is being internationalized; low culture and academic culture have long been internationalized but traditional high culture is increasingly under the control of the two main ethnic groups within the state. In some ways, then, the dualism of Canadian nationhood makes it weak, yet its flexibility may be its strength. The days of state centralism in societies with more than one important ethnic group may now be numbered. Many Canadians are culturally ethnic, politically national and economically international. The state still provides a clear symbolic territory and an important sense of belonging and, as yet, there is no real questioning the powerful world system of nation-states. There is certainly no clear indication of what will succeed it, although Canada suggests one possible future.

References

Becton, J. & E. L. Odell 1918. *Hunting the Hun*. Toronto: Appleton.
Behiels, M. D. 1985. *Prelude to Quebec's quiet revolution: liberalism versus neo-nationalism (1945–60)*. Montreal: McGill-Queen's University Press.
Deutsch, K. 1979. National integration: a summary of some concepts and research

References

approaches. In *Tides among nations*, K. Deutsch, (ed). New York: Free Press.

Duchacek, I. 1986. *The territorial dimension of politics: within, among and across nations.* Boulder, Col.: Westview.

Grant, C. 1965. *Lament for a nation: the defeat of Canadian nationalism.* Toronto: McClelland & Stewart.

Grove, F. P. 1928. *Our daily bread.* Toronto: Macmillan.

Hero, A. O. & M. Daneau (eds) 1984. *Problems and opportunities in US–Quebec relations.* Boulder, Col.: Westview.

Konrad, V. 1986. Recurrent symbols of nationalism in Canada. *Canadian Geographer* **30**, 175–80.

Langevin, A. 1976. *Une chaine dans le parc.* Toronto: McClelland & Stewart.

Muir, A. 1891. The maple leaf for ever. In *The Scottish student's songbook*, The Scottish Student's Songbook Committee (ed.). Glasgow: Bayley & Ferguson.

Nasgaard, R. 1984. *The mystic north: symbolist landscape painting in northern Europe and North America, 1890–1940.* Toronto: University of Toronto Press.

Neatby, H. B. 1976. *Willian Lyon Mackenzie King 1932–39: the prism of unity.* Toronto: University of Toronto Press.

Oswalt, W. H. 1966. *This land was theirs: a study of the North American Indian.* New York: Wiley.

Ouellet, F. 1980. *Lower Canada 1791–1840: social change and nationalism.* Toronto: McClelland & Stewart.

Pedley, J. H. 1927. *Only this.* Toronto: Graphic.

Presthus, R. 1973. *Elite accommodation in Canadian politics.* Toronto: Macmillan.

Quinn, H. F. 1979. *The Union Nationale: Quebec nationalism from Duplessis to Levesque.* Toronto: University of Toronto Press.

Slowe, P. M. 1988. *Geography and political power: the geography of nations and states.* London: Routledge.

Slowe, P. M. & R. H. Woods 1986. *Fields of death: battle scenes of the First World War.* London: Hale.

Smith, A. D. 1986. *The ethnic origins of nations.* Oxford: Basil Blackwell.

Snow, D. 1976. *The American Indians: their archaeology and prehistory.* London: Thames & Hudson.

Soja, E. J. 1968. Communication and territorial integration in East Africa: an introduction to transaction flow analysis. *East Lakes Geographer* **4**, 39–57.

Sutherland, R. 1982. A literary perspective: the development of a national consciousness. In *Understanding Canada: a multidisciplinary introduction to Canadian studies*, W. Metcalfe (ed.). New York: New York University Press.

Verney, D. V. 1986. *Three civilisations, two cultures, one state: Canada's political traditions.* Durham N.C.: Duke University Press.

Woolfson, R. F. 1982. An anthropological perspective: the ingredients of a multicultural society. In *Understanding Canada: a multidisciplinary introduction to Canadian studies*, W. Metcalfe (ed.). New York: New York University Press.

5

The Soviet federation: from corporatist to crisis politics

GRAHAM SMITH

One of the most striking features of Gorbachev's USSR is the way in which the nationality-based republics have moved from the periphery of Soviet domestic politics to occupy centre stage. This ascendancy is inextricably bound up with the so called 'national question'. As the programme of *perestroika* (restructuring) has unfolded across the country, and having purposely encouraged the liberalization or 'opening up' (*glasnost'*) of society, the new regime has inadvertently invited the nationalities to re-evaluate their status within the world's largest multi-ethnic polity. As a consequence, an ethnic revival on a scale and magnitude hitherto unknown in Soviet history has occurred. It has embraced not only those regions, like the Baltic republics and Georgia, where nationalist tensions have periodically spilt over into the arena of federal politics, but also those republics like Belorussia, Moldavia and Armenia, hitherto considered as the most loyal. Such is the intensity of demands for greater self-determination, and since the scope of ethnic tensions is so widespread, it is the national question which poses probably the greatest threat to Gorbachev's 'revolution from above' (Motyl 1989, Smith 1989a).

This chapter examines the changing nature of state–nationality relations from the Brezhnev period of corporatist politics to the crisis years of Gorbachev's *perestroika*. It will be argued that while particular centrally managed political practices succeeded in maintaining stability during the 1970s and early 1980s, nonetheless important developments were also occurring within the regions which help shed light on the nature of the nationalities problem now facing the Gorbachev administration. Next we explore how the impact of the rolling agenda of *perestroika*, and its handmaiden, *glasnost'*, have recast state–nationality relations. The Baltic republics are then singled out for special attention, for it is suggested that not only is this region pivotal to the success of *perestroika* but that developments there threaten the future of the Soviet federation.

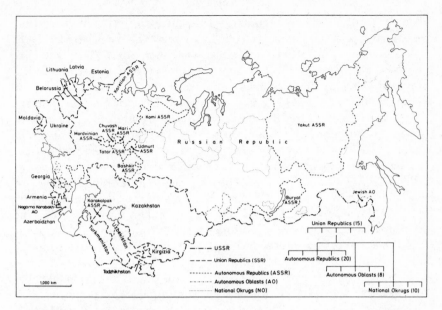

Figure 5.1 The Soviet federation.

Brezhnevism, corporatism and the non–Russian republics

The Soviet federation of hierarchically organized national republics (Fig. 5.1) is a product of a socio-territorial formation grounded in a compromise between a Russian dominated Communist Party and its urban-based non-Russian allies, in which, in return for territorial re-annexation following the Bolshevik Revolution, the major nationalities were promised a degree of cultural and administrative autonomy. In using federalism as a means of managing the national question, it would however be inappropriate to consider Moscow as practising a form of rule analogous to either 'internal colonialism' or, at the other extreme, one based on what is officially claimed as 'a federation of sovereign states'. Rather, relations between Moscow and its 14 non-Russian union republics can be considered as one of federal colonialism (Smith 1989b and 1990). It contains four essential features.

1 The Soviet federation denies the nationalities the right to national self-determination, with only a minimal degree of political manoeuvrability being granted to the local party-state machine in running the union republic. The notion, as embodied in article 76 of the Soviet constitution, that the USSR is 'a federation of sovereign states' is unverifiable. Moreover, despite the claim of article 72 that 'each republic shall retain the right freely to secede from the USSR', this is emasculated by article 73, notably clauses 2 and 4, which affirm that the highest bodies of USSR state authority have the right both to 'determination of the state boundaries of the USSR' and 'settlement of

85

other matters of All-Union importance'. In essence, article 72 'is merely a front to create an appearance that union republics are sovereign states' (Bruchis 1988, 123). Through its control over the *nomenklatura system* (that is, the right to hire, promote and sack party and state officials), the centre is able to ensure the loyalty of the local political leadership, while the established practice of appointing 'outsiders' (usually Russians) to certain key local positions, notably to the post of Second Party Secretary, whose primary function, analogous to that of a proconsul, further reinforces native elite loyalty and the successful expedition of central policies. However, provided that federal politics are confined to 'safe issues' (e.g. questions of resource allocation and distribution), and do not spill over into the arena of state security, the union republics do have some autonomy in the running of local affairs. For the union republic leadership this means that 'their role is far more complex than one of obedient lieutenants carrying out directives from Moscow: confronted with demands from above and below, they are activists out to protect local interests in the face of a limited budget' (Bahry 1987, 2).

2   As a product of central policy, each of the non-Russian republics has developed a specialized, core-dependent economy (ranging from the export-based agrarian economies of Central Asia and Moldavia to the fully industrialized European republics of the Ukraine, Belorussia and the Baltic), and concomitant specialized territorial divisions of labour. In some republics, notably the Baltic, Georgia and the Ukraine, native standards of living are comparable to if not higher than that of the Russian republic; but despite Russian capital undoubtedly having played a part in improving the material wellbeing of Central Asia, this region continues to lag well behind most other republics (Table 5.1).

3   The upward mobility of natives within their union republic homelands has been aided by affirmative action policies which have contributed to the nativization of the local political leadership and to the growth of an indigenous middle class through preferential access to higher education and to party membership (Zaslavsky 1988).

4   Each of the non-Russian republics possesses a flourishing native culture and language aided by a variety of institutional supports provided as a consequence of their territorial status. Yet local cultures, while supported by the Soviet federation, have also been subject to standardizing linguistic and cultural pressures from a Russian-dominated state.

The Soviet federation can therefore be considered as a form of socio-territorial control: its centralized character limits the political and economic autonomy of the non-Russian union republics but as a result of union republic status provides its indigenous peoples with certain privileges of place. It is a form of political rule based on the need to contain ethnic tensions but which provides for the possibility of national group articulation within the formal arena of federal politics. This situation contrasts for those nationalities which have been granted more limited territorial recognition (ASSRs and below) or those

Table 5.1 The union republics: indices of socio-economic development.

	Population (millions) 1987	Urbanization % of total population		Rate of economic growth (1970 = 100)		Income distribution (% monthly earnings in rubles), 1988			Students in higher education per 10 000 population	
		1940	1987	1980	1986	less than 75r.	75–200r.	over 200r.	1940/1	1986/7
USSR	281.7	33	66	163	202	12.6	70.2	17.2	41	181
Russian republic	144.3	34	74	164	204	6.3	71.7	22.0	43	200
Ukraine	51.2	34	67	148	182	8.1	77.7	14.2	47	166
Belorussia	10.0	21	64	191	266	5.0	75.5	19.5	24	179
Moldavia	4.2	13	47	160	204	13.0	76.0	11.0	10	126
Estonia	1.6	34	72	161	197	3.9	62.5	33.6	45	151
Latvia	2.7	35	71	158	201	3.2	68.5	28.3	52	164
Lithuania	3.6	23	67	147	201	3.6	72.4	24.0	20	178
Armenia	3.4	28	68	210	286	18.1	72.4	9.5	82	160
Azerbaidzhan	6.8	37	54	204	265	33.3	60.4	6.3	44	155
Georgia	5.3	31	55	188	233	16.3	67.1	16.6	77	163
Kazakhstan	16.2	30	58	151	169	15.9	71.1	13.0	16	169
Turkmenistan	3.4	35	48	141	168	36.6	58.2	5.2	22	117
Tadzhikhstan	4.8	19	33	169	203	58.6	40.0	1.4	15	115
Kirgizia	4.1	22	40	154	195	37.1	58.3	4.6	19	141
Uzbekistan	19.0	25	42	183	217	44.7	52.5	2.8	28	153

Sources: Gosudarstvenniyi komitet SSSR po statistike (1987) *Narodnoe Khozyaistvo SSSR za 70 let*, Moscow, Financy i Statistika, 20, 132, 374, 378–9, 550; Kovalev, A(1989) Kto i pochemu za chertoi bednosti, *Ekonomicheskaya gazeta* **25**, 11.

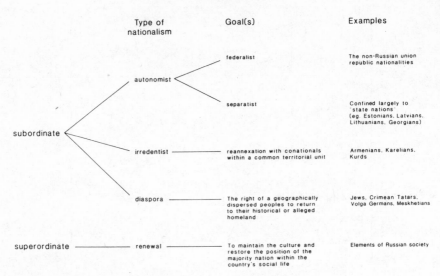

Figure 5.2   A typology of nationalism in the USSR.

whom the federal map excludes altogether. (This includes those nationalities, like the Crimean Tatars, Volga Germans and Meskhetian Turks, who, for supposed geostrategic reasons, were forcibly moved by Stalin during the Second World War from their native homelands to other parts of the Soviet Union, but it also in effect includes the Jews because of their token territorial status.) Consequently, for many, the struggle for political power is confined to informal and generally less effectual channels of protest demonstration. Given, then, their particular territorial status and native homeland-based concentration, it is only in the non-Russian union republics that an autonomist nationalism, based on some form of home rule, can arise. Other forms of sub-state nationalism, of the irredenta or diaspora types (Fig. 5.2), do not, therefore, provide the same challenge to state stability.

During the years of the Brezhnev leadership (1964–82) there was little evidence to suggest that autonomist nationalism presented a problem to the Soviet state. Confined largely to dissident politics in the Ukraine and in the Baltic region, it was relatively easily contained by a state willing and able when necessary to use coercion. But there were also other reasons why it remained on the fringes of political life. The Brezhnev regime preferred the pragmatic preservation of the status quo to any more radical quest for social and economic transformation. Sacrificing reform for stability was inextricably bound up with an administration which refrained from repeating the promises of an imminent communist society. Within the arena of nationalities policy, the notion of *sliyanie* (the eventual merger and ending of differences between the nationalities) disappeared from Politburo member speeches. Instead, in the new Brezhnev-designated era of 'developed socialism', emphasis was placed on taking cognizance of the interests and peculiarities of different peoples, and to raising all Soviet people in the spirit of proletarian internationalism. The socialist federation, despite its critics, was to remain the backbone of institutional and cultural support for the nationalities but any prospect for further experimentation with regional decentralization – as experienced during the Khrushchev administration – was abandoned. Within the political arena more generally, a number of western commentators began to see in the conservatism of Brezhnev's rule, and in its ability to ensure social stability, the emergence of a new set of state-managed political practices, essentially corporatist in character (e.g. Bunce & Echols 1980).

As Bunce (1983, 134) has argued, 'developed socialism' represented 'a corporate vision of a consensual society, in which conflict could be managed by deals struck between the state and functionally based interests'. Corporatism in effect involves a system of interest representation in which a limited number of hierarchically organized and functionally differentiated constituent units at the upper echelons of the political system are granted a representational monopoly within their respective categories, in exchange for observing certain controls on their selection of leaders and articulation of demands and supports (Schmitter 1974). As in western-style corporatism, identification of common aims and purposes is the hallmark based on ensuring economic growth, social stability and national unity. Western analysts, however, have tended to confine their studies of corporatist politics to institutional interests being acted out within Moscow, whereas an important territorial dimension can also be identified, in which a political compromise existed between the centre and the non-Russian union republic leadership. This compromise, however, was not restricted to interests within the centre-union republic party-state apparatus. A number of centrally declared social commitments were extended to the population in general, including, most notably, the affirmation of a regional policy based on improving the material wellbeing of the more backward nationality republics. And yet, as I shall argue below, the stresses and strains of this territorial compromise could be detected before the Brezhnev regime had ended.

Corporatist territorial politics and the native leadership

In contrast to Khrushchev, who alienated the regional political leadership, Brezhnev engaged in extensive fence-mending. There was, in effect, a willingness on behalf of the centre and republic leaders to administer their particular territorial and political spheres of influence. Republic *apparatchiks* wanted security of status and autonomy, while from the regions Moscow required political stability and only moderate overall commitment to realistic economic growth targets. The Brezhnev regime was also prepared to allow greater flexibility in native appointments to local positions, a process which was complemented by the less frequent appointment of 'outsiders' to key republic party posts. Even in the area of state security, traditionally earmarked for Russians, the appointment of natives increased (Jones & Grupp 1984). The type of Russian official appointed also changed. In most cases they were either descendants of Russian settlers from the republic or had climbed to the top of the republic bureaucracy after serving time at its lower levels. Analysis of key posts in republic party-state organizations also shows far lower rates of personnel turnover, particularly among natives, than in the previous era. In short, Brezhnev's policy of putting greater trust in native and local cadres made party and state life in the republics less volatile and more comfortable (Moses 1985). In return, the native political leadership could be relied upon to ensure social stability within their fiefdoms. Events which threatened to undermine regional stability, as for instance when the echoes of unrest resulting from the activities of Solidarity in Poland in 1980–1 reverberated around the western borderlands of the Soviet Union, were quickly and effectively dealt with by the local political leadership (Vardys 1983). But although republic leaders closely identified themselves with the centre's conservatism, they also enjoyed a degree of influence. The centre was prepared to examine initiatives and proposals from the regions but disagreements were generally moderated. The issues which arose were to do with tinkering with current policies rather than pushing for systemic changes.

Within the arena of resource allocation in particular, native elites were willing to champion local interests. Lithuania's leadership continued to lobby for the republic's industrial development, while at the same time ensuring that it did not occur at a pace which would facilitate the need for extra Russian labour, as had happened in the neighbouring republics of Estonia and Latvia (Smith 1982). Central Asia's leadership also continued to argue for more developmental resources, while in the Ukraine, the new First Party Secretary, Volodymyr Shcherbytskyi, while distancing himself from his predecessor's concern with Ukrainian cultural autonomy, argued for more capital in order to regenerate the republic's ailing heavy manufacturing base. In short, the native political leadership was prepared to engage in politicizing republic needs but only in so far as they did not undermine the Brezhnevite compromise.

The centre's policy of 'trust in cadres', combined with its increasing benign neglect of republic administration, had furnished the native leadership with a degree of power and patronage over their territories probably far greater than at any time in Soviet history. Local empire-building also made those in positions of authority susceptible to wide-scale corruption. By the late 1970s, racketeering, report padding, nepotism and organized crime were rife in a number of republics. This was notably so in Central Asia; in Uzbekistan, the First Party Secretary, Sharaf Rashidov, and several ministers, maintained an organized crime syndicate, having stolen about 4 billion rubles from the state over a number of years, which included charging the state for extra cotton that was never produced (Medvedev 1988).

Regional policy and social welfare

Corporatist territorial politics, however, were not just confined to striking an accord between native elites and the centre. It pervaded all aspects of economic and social life within the national republics. Certainly a degree of continuity from the Khrushchev years could be detected within the material sphere of social life; of giving society a stake in the system through implementing populist policies designed to improve social welfare, standards of living and to guarantee full employment. For the non-Russian republics, attempts to tie them into the system were bound up with a purposeful regional policy, which was also to remain a backbone to nationalities policy. Although Brezhnev had declared in 1972 that ethno-regional equalization had largely been carried out, he was careful to temper his remarks by restating Moscow's commitment to protecting the interests of all the republics, which was again reaffirmed at his last Party Congress speech in 1981. Important signals were therefore sent out to the republics that their socio-economic interests would be safeguarded. During the 1970s, the union republics were able to retain a higher proportion of their turnover tax than previously and, in the case of the Central Asian republics, this meant retaining the full amount (*Pravda*, 19 December 1969 and 1 December 1979). Employment continued to be created for natives within their own regions, even where there was an overabundance and overconcentration of particular skills or types of labour. Greater tolerance for the activities of the second economy and private initiative in the republics as compared to Russia proper has also been noted which, in the case of the Central Asian and Transcaucasian countryside, meant that the standard of living enjoyed by the peasantry was probably higher than that of their counterparts in Russia proper (Bialer 1986).

It was, however, becoming increasingly apparent as the 1970s progressed that with economic stagnation and the state's unwillingness to take on board structural economic reform, the country could no longer afford to meet the growing material and employment expectations of the republics. In Central Asia, with the continuing growth of the Muslim population, the state was finding it increasingly difficult to meet the welfare needs of its population (Zwick 1979) and to generate employment in the countryside. This inability to meet the region's growing material expectations must have been of concern to a Brezhnev leadership witnessing the resurgence of Islamic fundamentalism in neighbouring Muslim states and the region's potential for religious unrest following the USSR's occupation of Afghanistan in December 1979. Indeed, there is evidence to suggest that, although considerable strides had been made during the Brezhnev years to improve the material lot of the less developed republics, in terms of real *per caput* consumption, republic differences were increasing throughout the 1970s, with the Russian and Baltic republics gaining ground (Schroeder 1986). Moreover, by the late 1970s, a number of republics (Kirgizia, Belorussia, Moldavia, Lithuania and the Ukraine) saw their levels of total investment decline (Bahry 1987, 104). There were, therefore, signs that the unprecedently high standards of living enjoyed throughout the regions could no longer be sustained.

Federation, social privileges and the intelligentsia

Despite growing pressures leading up to the formulation of the 1977 Soviet constitution to abolish the federal structure, the Brezhnev leadership was astute enough to realize that it would have been 'premature and dangerous' (*Pravda*, 5 October 1977) to eradicate formal nationality boundaries, even though, as federalism's adversaries argued, such administrative divisions made little economic sense (Ebzeeva 1982). Reaffirmation of the federal structure, therefore, continued to ensure an important support for native institutions, while preservation of affirmative action policies, again not without its critics, continued to facilitate local native upward mobility.

For the native intelligentsia – that official but disparate class of specialists made up of those drawn from the cultural professions, administration, scientific and technical personnel, and economic management – reaffirmation of support for the Soviet federation had particular benefits. Besides affirmative-based action policies favouring indigenous social mobility within their namesake union republic, native language-based educational systems have also furnished the conditions under which an ethnic intelligentsia has flourished, which helps us to understand why, at the republic level, this broad social group has not needed to assimilate into the dominant (Russian) culture in order to gain position and status. The development of educational facilities in the native language, which includes the opportunity to attend native-based schools, for which the majority opt, has also resulted in the demand for a large native intelligentsia equipped to read and speak the native tongue. This community of native speakers has continued to grow and shows no signs of linguistic assimilation, in spite of social pressures to adopt the Russian language. In the 1959–79 inter-censal period, for example, the proportion of each nationality declaring their namesake nationality language as their native tongue remained relatively static at over 98 per cent; only the two Slavic nationalities, the Ukrainians and Belorussians, partly because of their closer historical and linguistic ties to the Russians, have a lower proportion of native speakers (89.1 and 83.5 per cent respectively) (Ts 1962 and 1980, *Nar.Khoz* 1987). The creation and continuation, then, of native-based republic institutions continued to establish niches for incumbents who adhere to the native culture.

The native intelligentsia, however, is not spread uniformly throughout specialist employment (Kulichenko *et al.* 1977, 97; Arutyunyan *et al.* 1986, 66); it tends to be particularly well represented in the culturally related professions like teaching, and in the arts. That such clustering should occur is certainly linked to the monopoly the native intelligentsia enjoys over access to the language and culture of their indigenous communities (Russian migrants are notorious for their unwillingness to learn the native language), and of the employment opportunities which are made available as a result of their union republic status. It is, however, also important not to underestimate the linguistic difficulties, particularly apparent in less developed Central Asia, faced by non-Russians in entering a higher educational system which demands of its would-be scientific and technical intelligentsia a high degree of fluency in the Russian language. Overall, then, the humanistic intelligentsia in particular, and specialists in general, have been guaranteed employment within their own homelands to the point that, certainly in the more developed republics, there is an over-concentration and over-supply, often contrary to the economic interests of the state. Indeed, the reluctance of specialists in republics like Georgia and Estonia to move to regions where their specialisms are in short supply but where they would be stripped of privileges from remaining within their namesake republic, has become an issue of growing concern within the Soviet Union (Ostapenko & Susokolov 1984).

It was this native stratum which represented one of the fastest growing social groups during the Brezhnev years (e.g. Jones & Grupp 1984). They contrasted with previous generations of specialist personnel who had gained position more by their political credentials than by educational qualifications. It is this more articulate and assertive native urban intelligentsia, having largely replaced the *praktiki* (that is, those in top level positions whose training was inadequate or practically non-existent), who have come to dominate the local economic, political and administrative machine.

While their growth and interests cannot be analytically divorced from the privileges which have accrued as a consequence of federation, neither centralism nor the erosion of cultural freedoms are likely to endear the native intelligentsia to a social compromise which undermines professionalism or inhibits both their symbolic and material interests in the creation of a more culturally pluralistic society. It is a stratum conscious of and frustrated by the discordances of the Brezhnev years: by an overly centralized production system inhibiting technical and professional initiative; of a migration policy which brings Russians into competition with natives for jobs, based on Moscow's inadequate knowledge of local labour markets; of a culturally standardizing centre (increasingly by the late 1970s) insisting on fluency in Russian as a precondition for professional employment and to expanding opportunities for the teaching of Russian in republic schools and universities; and of centrally managed industrial ministerial interests running roughshod over the local environment. Not surprisingly, then, it is this new social stratum which came to form Gorbachev's natural constituency of support but which also contains within its ranks, particularly within the culturally related professions, those most supportive of home rule, if not national separatism (Smith 1988).

Perestroika, glasnost' and the national question

Gorbachev's 'revolution from above' has changed the nature of relations between the centre and the national republics. From the outset, however, the national question was treated by the new administration as incidental to reform. The Gorbachev leadership preferred to reiterate Brezhnev's faith in the concept of 'the Soviet people' (*Sovetskii narod*), although it was conceded at the 27th Party Congress in March 1986 that success with the socio-economic convergence of the nationalities was not in itself sufficient to erase nationality-based identities (Gorbachev 1986, 101–3). Yet at this historic Party Congress, when *perestroika* was outlined, little time was wasted on the national question (Bilinsky 1986). By February 1988, however, less than two years later, having endured a series of ethnic crises, the Gorbachev leadership had promoted the national question to being a vital political issue on the Kremlin's agenda (*Pravda*, 18 February 1988).

The nature and scale of the problem which the Gorbachev leadership now faces is a product of two essential paradoxes. First, in order to ensure the socio-economic acceleration (*uskorenie*) and modernization of the economy, later widened to include economic decentralization, Gorbachev had first to reassert central control over the regions, control which had been weakened during the Brezhnev years. Secondly, having acknowledged that socio-economic reform could not be effectively implemented without wider socio-political reforms (*glasnost'* and democratization), the centre purposely invited a multi-ethnic society actively to engage in the making of *perestroika*, without having considered the likely repercussions of its actions.

Reasserting control over the republics

While successive Soviet leaders since the mid-1950s acknowledged the importance of linking material improvement among the citizenry to political stability, the Gorbachev leadership went further in recognizing that stability was not only to do with improving living standards but was also bound up with social justice. As Shlapentoch (1988) notes, social justice became 'almost the fulcrum of a new party ideology'. A new word found its way into the vocabulary of reform, *razlozhenie*, meaning the abuse of power; amongst that stratum of the population singled out as guilty of *razlozhenie* were corrupt republic and provincial *apparatchiks*, who were also recognized as a source of much animosity amongst their constituents. Moreover, if Moscow were successfully to implement a programme of reform, then it first needed to reaffirm control over the republics, and that required a reform-minded and loyal local party machine. As Gorbachev noted in his speech to the 27th Party Congress in 1986: 'At some stage some republics, territories, regions and cities were placed outside the bounds of criticism'. Furthermore, 'in the party there neither are nor should be organizations outside the pale of control and closed to criticism, there neither are nor should be leaders fenced off from party responsibility' (Gorbachev 1986, 157). Identified with the era of Brezhnevism and deemed guilty of corruption and economic mismanagement, a purge of cadres on a scale unknown since Stalin's time began, focusing on Central Asia and Kazakhstan. As a *Pravda* editorial noted with regard to Uzbekistan, which experienced the first major shake-up of personnel: 'The actual situation [in Uzbekistan] during these years [the late 1970s and early 1980s] was such that . . . one can refer to the departure from socialism of province and republic "great leaders", those present day emirs, and about the ignoring of all legal and moral norms' which led the republic 'into a state of slow and agonising decay' (*Pravda*, 23 January 1988).

Up until 1987, therefore, the removal of leading party officials, largely Brezhnev-era appointees, suggested 'a continuing high priority attached by Moscow to fighting corruption and reasserting central control' (Gustafson & Mann 1988). Of the six First Party Secretaries who were dismissed by Gorbachev, four were from Central Asia (including Kazakhstan). But while non-Central Asian First Party Secretaries remained in office there was a more or less universal purging of their seconds in command, with 11 of the 14 non-Russian union republic Second Party Secretaries losing their positions. The strategy of cross-regional transfers of cadres, as a means of ensuring centre accountability, was employed by the Gorbachev administration, which in effect meant sending Russians from Moscow.

Such reaffirmation of central control also illustrated the insensitivity of the Gorbachev leadership to nationality sensibilities. Nowhere was this more apparent than in Kazakhstan, a republic where Russians outnumber Kazakhs by 41 to 36 per cent. In July 1986, following the plenary session of the Kazakh Party Central Committee, Moscow strongly criticized the plenum's failure to do something about the republic's poor economic performance, with accusations being made of mismanagement, corruption and bureaucratism amongst those in positions of responsibility (*Pravda*, 7 July 1986). Further accusations of 'report padding' and the falsification of republic statistics followed (*Kazakhstanskaya Pravda*, 9 December 1986). On 16 December the native First Party Secretary, Dinmukhamed Kunaev, was replaced by a Russian from outside the republic, which triggered off the first major ethnic riots of recent times, in Alma Ata. Such a method of reaffirming central control broke with the hitherto universal practice of reserving the symbolic post of First Party Secretary for a member of the titular nationality.

The Gorbachev leadership also began to link the purge of local leaders as a necessary prerequisite for the successful implementation of *perestroika*, with the conservatism and inaction by the local leadership in many republics also being officially interpreted as causally related to the upsurge of nationalism. It was noted in a recent plenary session of the Kazakh Central Committee, for example, that as a result of the change of leadership *perestroika* was now proceeding, and that the republic's ethnic riots in December 1986 were a consequence of the previous republic leadership's poor economic management and widespread corruption (*Pravda*, 4 February 1988). For Moscow, then, the problem was that the party and bureaucratic machine in many republics was not sympathetic to economic restructuring. Such conservative misgivings within the republics was, however, symptomatic of Soviet public life more generally. As Battle writes: 'It is no accident that the process of restructuring was widened to include the concept of democratisation. Gorbachev made it clear that the further democratisation of society was necessary to overcome inertia and conservatism' (1988, 379).

Glasnost', democratization and decentralization

The idea was that pressure 'from below' would facilitate the successful implementation of 'reform from above'. In the process, *glasnost'* provided the opportunity not only for ethnic issues to be discussed more openly but it also enabled the proliferation throughout the Soviet republics of informal movements and clubs with varying agendas, espousing linguistic, cultural, environmental and other concerns. A new political vacuum had been created which, in the national republics, was quickly filled by locally based organizations willing and able to champion concerns bound up in one way or another with national self-determination. New opportunities were also opened up for the nationalities to rediscover their sense of nation-ness and to reassess their position within Soviet society. Issues previously the domain of containable dissident politics now became part of the public arena. Once out in the open, they have become more difficult to suppress.

The emergence of such centrifugal tendencies should not, however, be viewed as necessarily working against *perestroika*, for the national republics see in Gorbachev's reforms the means to achieve greater cultural and territorial autonomy. Rather, the issue at stake is to do with the scope and tempo of the reforms, as most clearly demonstrated and misjudged by the political leadership of the ethnically Armenian enclave of Nagorno-Karabakh. On 20 February 1988, a resolution was passed by its regional soviet demanding the region's transfer from Azerbaidzhan to Armenia. Moscow rejected the request as *ultra vires*, stipulating that constitutionally any border changes between republics must be approved by both parties (Herzig 1990). In the non-Russian republics more generally, what has been implemented so far, and what is proposed in the short term, falls short of local expectations, although the union republics have been offered economic decentralization, including moving towards greater republic economic accountability or self-financing (*khozras-chet*). This, the republics argue, should involve more priority being given to territorial planning and to the regional management of local resources, which they feel would remedy many of the problems associated with over-bureaucratization and sectoral planning. Support for greater regional self-financing, however, as proposed by Estonian economists and specialists in September

1987, has received a mixed reception. While the wealthier non-Russian European republics, along with Georgia, favour such proposals, which a leading article in *Kommunist* (1988) put down to 'a reaction to the compulsory giving of indeterminate amounts of aid' to the less developed, the poorer Central Asian republics have remained silent but without doubt are concerned about future prospects of having to rely more on generating their own capital investment. This is acknowledged to be increasingly problematic given the region's burgeoning rural population, decreasing employment opportunities, and growing demands for more and improved social services.

The Gorbachev leadership must have mixed feelings over regional economic decentralization, and in part this is reflected in the cautious way in which it has been enacted. Besides requiring a loyal and committed local leadership, decentralization also means possessing power and authority over those conservative-minded centralist interests which have most to lose from decentralization, notably the industrial ministries and the state bureaucracies. In addition, Gorbachev is only too well aware of the pitfalls of going too far with regional devolution, as Khrushchev's shortlived experiment in the late 1950s with the setting up of regional economic councils (*sovnarkhozy*) showed only too clearly. Rather than leading to more effective regional management and inter-republic co-ordination, that scheme became dogged by the promotion of regional self-interests, and in some republics, notably in the Baltic, by localism (*mestnichestvo*) and nationalism (Smith 1979 and 1982). As Bialer (1986, 137) puts it:

> The multi-ethnic and nominally federal character of the Soviet system . . . exerts a conservative influence on reformist tendencies. Undoubtedly, a decentralising reform would diffuse economic authority. If the rewards were high enough, the leadership might tolerate such a diffusion among the Russian provinces, but it would be much more reluctant to introduce similar changes among non-Russians.

And he continues:

> A fundamental economic reform could – and probably would – upset the balance. Indeed, the leaders may well believe that radical economic reform would necessarily entail a thorough restructuring of the relationships among the nationalities. This is a price they are probably unwilling to pay.

Meaningful devolution is therefore likely to reinforce locally based interests as union republic-based elites are increasingly armed with the resources of decentralization. The idea of promoting inter-republic liaison through the setting up of new regionally based political bodies may be one way of reducing inter-ethnic tensions (*Pravda*, 24 February 1989), particularly in Transcaucasia (e.g. Armenians and Azerbaidzhanis) and in Central Asia (e.g. Tadzhikhs and Uzbeks) but it is hardly likely to be welcomed by the centre, who would have to contend with formidably powerful regional alliances able more effectively to challenge Moscow's power and authority. There is also one further dimension to going too far down the path of accommodating the economic and political interests of the non-Russian republics. Demands for greater decentralization sit uneasily with the emergence of a particular brand of neo-conservative Russian nationalism which has also flourished under *glasnost'*. Hidden beneath what otherwise would appear as laudable aims – namely the promotion of the Russian language and culture and protection of the Russian countryside – is a cult of Stalinism which views Mother Russia as being weakened by a state which has given priority to the material welfare and development of the national cultures of the non-Russian regions. Such a nationalism, most clearly represented in the activities of a number of literary and environmental movements, represents a synthesis of the traditions of totalitarianism with what Anthony Smith (1976, 5) calls 'renewal nationalism', namely, a nationalism born out of a dominant ethnic group desirous of the rejuvenation and renewal of their nation in the country's social and political life. It is a nationalism from which the Gorbachev administration distances itself but which is condoned, if not supported, by more conservative elements within the party-state apparatus, notably, the KGB, the military-industrial complex, and *Komsomol* (the Young Communist League) (Duncan 1988).

It would seem that despite having to manage a series of ethnic crises of growing intensity, frequency and variety (Fig. 5.2), 'restructuring the national question appears to be far less pressing an issue for Gorbachev than containing it' (Motyl 1989, 160–1). Where ethnic crises have arisen, essentially non-territorial solutions have been offered to territorial problems of reorganization, decentralization and accommodation. Thus the response to the Kazakh riots has been to provide more resources for Kazakhstan, particularly better educational facilities for the teaching of the native language (*Kazakhstanskaya Pravda*, 18 February 1987), but as *perestroika* has failed to deliver any material improvement, or more fully to accommodate political demands for greater autonomy, ethnic problems remain very much to the fore in Kazakh politics (*Pravda*, 25 June 1989; *Izvestiya*, 24 June 1989). In response to demands by the Crimean Tatar diaspora to re-establish their homeland's status as an autonomous republic, a State Commission was set up which came to the conclusion 'that there were no grounds for establishing a Crimean autonomy' (*Pravda*, 9 June 1988). Although the Commission did accept the right of the Crimean Tatars to settle in the Crimea, migration has been limited, no doubt linked to the official view that the Crimea does not require additional labour and to concern in some circles that resettlement in this now predominantly ethnic Russian area of the Ukraine could fuel social discontent. And having failed to appease the Armenian irredenta with a seven-year regional development package for Nagorno-Karabakh, Moscow took the unprecedented step in

January 1989 of transferring the enclave's administration to Moscow. Clearly, Gorbachev is only too well aware that meeting the demands of the Armenian irredenta would fuel further ethnic unrest in Azerbaidzhan (with the possibility of it spreading to other Muslim republics), as well as opening the floodgates for further diaspora and irredentist demands elsewhere. His speech at the special 19th Party Conference in June 1988, in which he stated that he had no intention of redrawing the federal map, is hardly likely to appease those nationalities seeking accommodation within the Soviet federation (*Pravda*, 29 June 1988).

The autonomist challenge: the Baltic republics

The idea of the inevitable Balkanization of 'the world's last empire' has been a dominant theme in western Sovietology (e.g. Conquest 1986; Rakowska-Harmstone 1980). Under certain circumstances, there is no doubt, as evidence of nationalist movements elsewhere shows (Orridge 1982), that demands for greater national self-determination within a reconstituted polity can become separatist, a development which would clearly present the reform programme with its ultimate challenge. Yet, as has been argued elsewhere, the differing socio-political constitution of regions means that the facility for mobilization around the separatist cause is going to be easier for some nationalists than for others (Smith 1985 and 1989c). The nation must imagine itself as a community, based on a territorial relationship which subsumes other cross-cutting divisions (e.g. language, possibly religion, occupation/class, party/non-party membership) if nationalism is to proceed to being a movement for mass mobilization. Moreover, contained within the image of the nation must be the ideal of being sovereign (Anderson 1983). And an instrumental precondition to facilitating such a sense of nation-ness must be some form of political organization willing and able to champion the separatist cause. Not only do we find a sense of nation-ness potentially more easily mobilized around the separatist cause in the Baltic republics, but as a result of recent political developments, organizations now exist in the region which have the capability of promoting national separatism.

Popular Movements in support of *perestroika* were set up in each of the three Baltic republics, first in Estonia (the Popular Front or *Rahvarinne*) in April 1988, and during that summer in Latvia (the Latvian People's Front or *Latvijas Tautas Fronte*) and in Lithuania (the Movement in Support of *Perestroika* or *Sajudis*). They have emerged to become truly mass movements, with their membership drawn from both party and non-party members. Paradoxically, Moscow gave its blessing to their formation precisely because it saw the Baltic as being central to the success of the *perestroika* experiment. In his February 1987 'revolution of expectations speech', Gorbachev drew upon the experience of his preceding visit to Estonia and Latvia to make the point that there were those who were growing impatient with the speed of restructuring and who wanted tangible and speedy social and material return (*Pravda*, 20 and 22 February 1988). There were good reasons why expectations were high in the Baltic republics and why, during his trip there, his task of convincing the population of the necessity of *perestroika* was not difficult. In contrast to Russia proper and to many other regions, democracy is no stranger to the Balts. A civic culture of democracy, embedded in the experience of the interwar years of independent statehood, 'has provided better standards for judging Soviet reality and thus served as a more inspiring means of protest demonstration' (Vardys 1982, 123) than is the case elsewhere. Those elements of the enterprise culture contained within the economic programme of *perestroika* are also no strangers to the Balts. Both private enterprise and the co-operative idea formed an integral part of their national economies during the interwar years. Under successive post-Stalin regimes, Estonia has also proven itself to be a receptive laboratory to market-oriented experimentation, while throughout the region the second economy has continued to flourish. It is therefore not surprising that the prospect of *perestroika* has been received with greater enthusiasm in the Baltic region than in most other parts of the federation. The socio-economic restructuring of the national economy, with its emphasis on investing in industrial high technology, is also likely to favour the region's highly skilled and more technologically based economies, and also accords with the generally held view in the republics that the modernization of industrial plants, together with increased labour productivity, would halt the need for the continuing in-migration of Russian labour, an issue which has done much to fuel ethnic discontent in Estonia and Latvia. The opening up of the region to foreign trade through joint venture schemes is also acknowledged as being particularly conducive to their more 'outwardly-oriented' economies.

The Popular Movements were set up in order to facilitate the restructuring process, with the local political leadership coming in for particular criticism. Having been deemed guilty of acting 'indecisively' and 'without initiative', and having 'failed to take public opinion into account' (see, for example, *Pravda*, 29 September 1988), both the Estonian and Lithuanian leaderships were dismissed. In Latvia, following promotions at the top, the installation of a new Baltic political leadership sympathetic to a more radical reform programme was complete. At its Inaugural Congress in autumn 1988, Estonia's Popular Front, like its counterparts in Latvia and Lithuania, affirmed its support for 'the course of socialist renewal and its implementation in all fields of government and public life', which was also to include (clause 2.4) 'a fight for the union republics to be recognised as sovereign states' within a socialist federation (*Molodezh Estoniya*, 6 September 1988, 2). In all three republics, the new local party leadership were in attendance while Gorbachev sent greetings of support. What Moscow underestimated, however, was not only the increasingly radical stance that the Popular Movements have taken but that, at least in the case of Estonia, the new local party leadership was unwilling to act in the interests of the central party machine. This became clear during the constitutional crisis in November 1988. Fearing that the proposed new constitutional powers of the Congress of People's Deputies – which included the right to repeal laws of individual republics which it deemed unconstitutional – undermined the very basis of federal democratization, the Estonian Parliament, with the support of the local party leadership, declared that Moscow had no such authority. The rapidity with which the Gorbachev leadership amended its proposals clearly showed its concern that, in pursuing a policy of non-accommodation, not only was it likely that Latvia and Lithuania would follow a similar path but that the Popular Movements would be pushed into taking an even more radical stance on the issue of territorial sovereignty.

What has also become evident is that while Estonia's party leadership has continued to identify closely with its Popular Movement, an increasing divergence has occurred within in Latvia and Lithuania. Analysis of the election results to the new Congress of People's Deputies showed that support for Popular Movement candidates or candidates endorsed by the Popular Movements was considerable; in Lithuania *Sajūdis* and its supporters won 36 of the 42 seats, while in both Estonia and Latvia over half of the seats were won by the Popular Movements and those sympathetic to their aims (*Izvestiya*, 5 and 15 April 1989). In Estonia, leading party officials fared better than in the other two republics precisely because of their more radical stance.

While the Popular Movements have consistently argued that their appeal is not confined to the indigenous nationality but rather to those 'living and working' within the national territory, it is increasingly the case that their attraction is primarily to a titular constituency. Simple ethno-demographics make support for the Latvian People's Front a particularly problematic affair, for Latvians now constitute a bare majority (53.7 per cent) within their own republic, compared with their titular counterparts in Estonia (64.7 per cent) and Lithuania (80 per cent). So the Popular Movements need to retain a nationalistic flavour in order to mobilize support and to prevent more extreme (separatist) demands gaining ground. The more nationalistic they become, however, the more they are deprived of a territorial constituency. For the large Russian community in particular, both the promotion of the titular languages and proposals to halt the continuing influx of Russian labour raise the question of what sort of citizenship rights they could expect within a reconstituted federal polity. Anxious to maintain control over events in their republics, the local political leadership has consistently stressed that the restructuring of social life means accommodating all ethnic groups within their territory but at the same time should ensure the protection of the titular nationality. As Estonia's First Party Secretary, Vaino Valjas, put it:

Under conditions in which further migration threatens to transform the Estonian nation into a minority on its ancient land, the Estonian

Communist Party and all party members must struggle against unjusti-
fied migration. Like all other nations, Estonians have their right to
territory, which they have always inhabited. (*Sovetskaya Estoniya*, 10
September 1988).

In the same speech it was also made clear that 'any national discrimination
should be excluded' and that everyone should have the opportunity to conduct
their affairs in Estonian and Russian.

The continuing support given by the native political leadership to the Popular
Movements, especially evident in Estonia, and the extent to which it is willing
and able to champion the autonomist cause, is going to be crucial. Elsewhere,
local political leaderships have tended to distance themselves from attempts
within their republics to challenge Moscow's authority. Where the leadership
has been seen to be sympathetic to the nationalist cause or unable to control
events in the region, as in Armenia, dismissals have followed. The establishment
of mass-based Popular Movements of the Baltic variety in other republics,
notably in Belorussia, Georgia and the Ukraine, have been actively discouraged
by the local leadership. The new Central Asian political leadership has been
especially critical of the more radical stance taken by their counterparts in the
Baltic, in which they have condemned what they label as the region's 'rally-type
democracy' and the unacceptable behaviour of 'certain republics' (a reference to
Estonia) in attempting to suspend the application of all-union laws (*Izvestiya*, 30
November 1988, 4). Indeed, Kazakhstan's new First Party Secretary even went
so far as to suggest that 'it would seem we have made mistakes in our choice of
the teachers of *perestroika*' (*Izvestiya*, 30 November 1988, 5). All this must
contain mixed blessings for a Gorbachev leadership which requires its republic
leaders to maintain social stability but not at the cost of abandoning *perestroika*.
Nowhere is this more of a dilemma for Moscow than in the Ukraine, pivotal to
the maintenance of the internal empire, due to its size (Europe's largest stateless
nation) and its contribution to the USSR's economic and military might. Gorbachev has, in effect, put the republic's stability before reform by keeping in
power the only Brezhnevite First Party Secretary, Volodymyr Shcherbytski,
until his dismissal in September 1989, for it has been the Ukrainian conservative
leadership, widely criticized for its indifferent attitude towards *perestroika*,
which has succeeded in keeping the lid on Ukrainian nationalism.

The prospects for *perestroika* now look less hopeful. In the non-Russian
regions, the Gorbachev leadership is finding it increasingly difficult to contain
ethnic demands. In some instances, notably in the Baltic, it can no longer rely
on the local political leadership to ensure restructuring within acceptable
parameters, whereas in other republics local political leaderships are increasingly at odds with the aspirations of their constituents. How far the Gorbachev
administration can continue to 'muddle through' without succesfully incorporating the nationalities into the restructuring process will determine the future
prospects for *perestroika*.

Acknowledgements
.

This is a revised version of a paper given to the Soviet History and Politics Study Group, King's College, Cambridge, on 28 February 1989. I am grateful for the valuable comments from those who attended this seminar. I am also grateful to the British Academy for its financial support.

References

Anderson, B. 1983. *Imagined communities*. London: Verso.

Arutunyan, Yu V. *et al.* (1986) *Sotsial' no-kul' turnyi oblik Sovetskikh natsii (po materialam etnosotsiologicheskogo issledovaniya)*. Moscow: Nauka.

Bahry, D. 1987. *Outside Moscow. Power, politics and budgetary policy in the Soviet republics*. New York: Columbia University Press.

Battle, J. 1988. Uskorenie, glasnost' and perestroika. The pattern of reform under Gorbachev. *Soviet Studies* **40**(3), 367–84.

Bialer, S. 1986. *The Soviet paradox. External expansion, internal decline*. London: Tauris.

Bilinsky, Y. 1986. Nationality policy in Gorbachev's first year. *Orbis* **30**, 331–42.

Bunce, V. 1983. The political economy of the Brezhnev era. *British Journal of Political Science* **13**, 129–58.

Bunce, V. & J. Echols 1980. Soviet politics in the Brezhnev era: 'pluralism' or 'corporatism'? In *Soviet politics in the Brezhnev era*, D. Kelly (ed.), 1–26. New York: Praeger.

Bruchis, M. 1988. The nationality policy of the CPSU and its reflection in Soviet socio-political terminology. In *The Soviet Union, party and society*, P. Potichnyi (ed.), 121–41. Cambridge: Cambridge University Press.

Conquest, R. (ed.) 1986. *The last empire: nationality and the Soviet future*, Stanford: Hoover Institution.

Duncan, P. 1988. The party and Russian nationalism in the USSR: from Brezhnev to Gorbachev. In *The Soviet Union, party and society*, P. Potichnyi (ed.), 229–44. Cambridge: Cambridge University Press.

Ebzeeva, S. 1982. Sovetskaya federatsiya na etape zrelogo sotsializma. *Sovetskoe Gosudarstvo i Pravo* **7**, 10–14.

Gorbachev, M. 1986. *Politischii doklad tsentralnogo komitera· KPSS XXV11 s'ezdy Kommunicheskoi Partii Sovetskogo soyoza*. Moscow: Politizdat.

Gustafson, T. & D. Mann 1988. Gorbachev and the 'circular flow of power'. In *Elites and political power in the USSR*, D. Lane (ed.), 21–48. Aldershot: Edward Elgar.

Herzig, E. 1990. The Armenians. In *The nationalities in Gorbachev's USSR*, G. E. Smith (ed.). London: Longman.

Izvestiya, 30 November 1988.
Izvestiya, 5 April 1989.
Izvestiya, 15 April 1989.
Izvestiya, 24 June 1989.

Jones, E. & F. Grupp 1984. Modernisation and ethnic equalisation in the USSR. *Soviet Studies* **36**, 159–84.

Kazakhstanskaya Pravda, 9 December 1986.
Kazakhstanskaya Pravda, 8 June 1988.

Kommunist **15** (1988), 22–3.

Kovalev, A. 1989. Kto i pochemu za chertoi bednosti. *Ekonomicheskaya gazeta* **25**, 11.

Kulichenko, M. I. *et al.* 1977. *Natsional'nye otnosheniya v razvitom sotsialesticheskom obshchestve.* Moscow: Mysl'.

Medvedev, Z. 1988. *Gorbachev.* Oxford: Basil Blackwell.

Molodezh Estoniya, 6 September 1988.

Moses, J. 1985. Regionalism in Soviet politics: continuity as a source of change, 1953–82. *Soviet Studies* **37**, 184–211.

Motyl, A. 1989. The sobering of Gorbachev: nationality, restructuring, and the West. In *Inside Gorbachev's Russia*, S. Bialer (ed.), 149–73. New York: Westview.

Nar. Khoz. 1987. Gosudarstvennyi Komitet SSSR po statistike. *Narodnoe Khozyaistvo SSSR za 70 let.* Moscow: Financy i Statistika.

Orridge, A. 1982. Separatist and autonomist nationalisms: the structure of regional loyalties in the modern state. In *National separatism*, C. H. Williams (ed.), 43–74. Cardiff: University of Wales Press.

Ostapenko L. & A. Susokolov 1983. Etnostial'nye osobennosti i vospriozvodstva intelligentsii. *Sotsiologicheskii Issledovaniya* **1**, 10–16.

Pravda, 19 December 1969.

Pravda, 5 October 1977.

Pravda, 1 December 1979.

Pravda, 7 July 1986.

Pravda, 20 February 1987.

Pravda, 22 February 1987.

Pravda, 23 January 1988.

Pravda, 4 February 1988.

Pravda, 18 February 1988.

Pravda, 9 June 1988.

Pravda, 29 June 1988.

Pravda, 24 February 1989.

Pravda, 25 June 1989.

Rakowska-Harmstone, T. 1980. The nationalities question. In *The Soviet Union. Looking to the 1980s*, R. Wesson (ed.), 129–53. New York: Hoover Institution.

Schmitter, P. 1974. Still the century of corporatism. *Review of Politics* **36**, 85–91.

Schroeder, G. 1986. Social and economic aspects of the nationality problem. In *The last empire. Nationality and the Soviet future*, R. Conquest (ed.), 290–313. Stanford: Hoover Institution.

Shlapentoch, V. 1988. The XXVIIth Congress – A case study of the shaping of a new Party ideology. *Soviet Studies* **40**(1), 1–20.

Smith, A. 1976. *Nationalism in the twentieth century.* Oxford: Martin Robertson.

Smith, G. E. 1979. The impact of modernisation on the Latvian Soviet republic. *Co-Existence* **16**, 45–64.

Smith, G. E. 1982. Die probleme des Nationalismus in den drei Baltischen Sowietrepubliken Estland, Lettland und Litauen. *Acta Baltica* **21**, 43–177.

Smith, G. E. 1985. Ethnic nationalism in the Soviet Union: territory, cleavage and control. *Environment and Planning C. Government and Policy* **3**(1), 49–73.

Smith, G. E. 1988. Ethnoregional societies, 'developed socialism' and the Soviet ethnic intelligentsia. In *Nationalism, self-determination, and political geography*, R. J. Johnston, D. Knight and E. Kofman (eds), 166–88. London: Croom Helm.

Smith, G. E. 1989a. Gorbachev's greatest challenge: perestroika and the national question. *Political Geography Quarterly* **8**(1), 7–20.

Smith, G. E. 1989c. Administering ethnoregional stability: the Soviet state and the nationalities problem. In *Community conflict, partition and nationalism*, C. Williams and E. Kofman (eds), 224–50. London: Routledge.

Smith, G. E. 1989b. Development, federal colonialism and the non-Russian regions. In G. E. Smith, *Planned development in the socialist world*, 68–81. Cambridge: Cambridge University Press.

Smith, G. E. 1990. Federal colonialism and the nationalities question. In D. Shaw, J. Pallot, G. Smith, A. Helegson and R. North, *The Soviet Union. Geography of an administered society*. London: Longman.

Sovetskaya Estoniya, 10 September 1988.

Ts 1962. *Itogi vsesoyuznoi perepisi naseleniya 1959 goda*. Moscow: Tsentral'noe statisticheskoe upravlenie pri Sovete Ministrov SSR.

Ts 1980. *Naselenie SSSR. Po dannym vsesoyuznoi perepisi naseleniya 1979 goda*. Moscow: Tsentral'noe statistcheskoe upravlenie SSSR.

Vardys, V. S. 1982. The nature and philosophy of Baltic dissent: a comparative perspective. *Nationalities Papers* **10**, 121–36.

Vardys, V. S. 1983. Polish echoes in the Baltic. *Problems of Communism* **32**(4), 21–34.

Zaslavsky, V. 1988. Ethnic group divided: social stratification and nationality policy in the Soviet Union. In *The Soviet Union, party and society*, P. Potichnyi (ed.), 218–28. Cambridge: Cambridge University Press.

Zwick, P. 1979. Ethnoregional socio-economic fragmentation and Soviet budgetary policy. *Soviet Studies* **31**(3), 380–400.

6

Religious vs. regional determinism: India, Pakistan and Bangladesh as inheritors of empire

GRAHAM CHAPMAN

Introduction

In the last 40 years, the two largest nations of South Asia, India and Pakistan, have been at war with each other three times. They are currently engaged in a covert nuclear arms race. For much of the 40 years trade and other contacts between them have been almost completely severed. The region has been dogged by other conflicts, such as tribal problems on the Bangladesh–Indian border and the communal dispute in Sri Lanka. Yet in 1985 the states of South Asia, that is to say Pakistan, India, Bangladesh, Nepal, Bhutan, Sri Lanka, and the Maldives, founded the South Asian Association for Regional Co-operation (SAARC). It is significant that these countries have found it in their interests to promote a new forum for the exchange of ideas and the development of new economic and cultural links, because the last decades have shown the extent to which their destinies are intertwined in this one region, and the extent to which opportunity costs have been incurred by confront-ation rather than co-operation. The theme of this essay is the extent to which communal divisions have been countered by regional forces of integration. It considers in particular the nature of the space shared by the big three – India, Pakistan and Bangladesh – and makes only passing reference to the mountain kingdoms of Nepal and Bhutan, and the island states of Sri Lanka and the Maldives.

The space that the big three occupy as separate and independent sovereign states has quite often in history been divided in different ways. There is little that is inherently 'natural' about the current arrangement: indeed, there are many questions which are raised by the current political map which command immediate attention. Why is it that the Punjab is divided between the Indian and the Pakistani Punjab – though both sides use the same language? Why is it that Bengal, throughout which there is a continuity of Bengali language and culture, is similarly divided? Why, if India can include Assam and Kerala within a federation, is Bangladesh a sovereign state and not part of the federation?

106

There are other questions which the map does not pose directly, but which seem curious given the proximities of the countries. Why do India and Pakistan trade so little with each other? Why do India's neighbours seem to fear that she meddles in their affairs, when India protests that she never does unless invited in or unless trouble spills over her borders? Why has India, such a large polyglot federation, survived as a democracy, when Pakistan and Bangladesh have not?

Behind all of these questions is the assumption that South Asia is in some sense a well-defined geographical region of the world, and that there are few obvious natural subdivisions within it. This is the starting point.

South Asia as a geopolitical region

Cohen (1963) divides the world deductively into, first, geostrategic regions, and then geopolitical regions. His geostrategic regions are multi-featured in cultural and economic terms, but are single-featured in trade orientation and are also distinct arenas within which power can be projected. His division of the world broadly follows Mackinder's views: there is the Maritime Dependent Trading world and the Eurasian Continental power. Between these two are the 'shatterbelts' of Southeast Asia and the Middle East. The geopolitical region is defined as a sub-division of the geostrategic:

It expresses the unity of geographic features. Because it is derived directly from geographic regions, this unit can provide a framework for common political and economic actions. Contiguity of location and complementarity of resources are particularly distinguishing marks of the geopolitical region. (Cohen 1963, 62).

So the Maritime Dependent Trading world is divided into Europe and the Mahgreb; Africa minus Egypt, Sudan and Ethiopia (part of the Middle East shatterbelt); North America; South America; and Australia with New Zealand and Oceania. The Eurasian Continental region is divided into the USSR and China. South Asia is distinctive: Cohen classifies it as an independent geopolitical region, not within a geostrategic region. It is big enough to be a sub-continent in its own right, it has been and is guarded from the Eurasian power(s) by the massive wall of the Himalayas, from the Middle East by the Hindu Kush and other mountains of the Northwest frontier, and from Burma and Indo-China by lower but heavily forested jagged mountain ranges.

Like Gaul, this sub-continent can be divided into three parts: the high montane regions of the north, the depositional lowlands of the Indus and Ganges, and the ancient Deccan block of peninsular India. These three regions are of course sub-divided: principally by moisture availability, either directly from rainfall or from littoral extraction from rivers. In the Ganges valley, it is

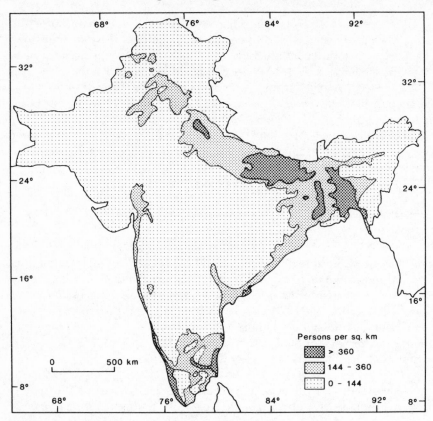

Figure 6.1 Rural population density in South Asia.
Source: Spate and Learmonth 1967, 121

the lower or eastern parts which are wetter: the western parts and the Indus valley are much drier. In the Deccan, the extreme southwest coast (Kerala) is wet, and so are some of the coastal regions on the eastern side. But much of the interior is substantially drier, although not as dry as the Thar desert.

The map of the distribution of rural population (Fig. 6.1, using 1961 data) shows little more differentiation from region to region than it would have shown centuries if not millennia ago. Perhaps the greatest change would be the higher relative densities now in the Punjab (between latitudes 26 and 30, and longitudes 71 and 76 on the map). It is a map which displays the agricultural potential of South Asia, defined principally by a combination of fertile riverine plains and higher and more reliable rainfall. There is one other factor. Movement in the plains has historically been much easier, whether using ox carts, or deploying armies, or using the river system. In the Deccan, navigation is more restricted seasonally, with shorter and smaller navigable reaches in the rivers; between the river basins where settlement may be possible are barren marchlands, or jagged ghat ranges, and forest areas.

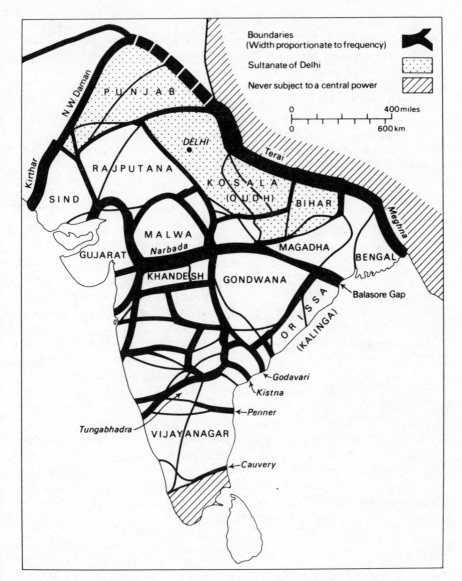

Figure 6.2 Relative frequency of boundaries in South Asia from *c.* 300 BC to *c.* AD 1750. The map is suggestive: no absolute value is given to line widths.
  Source: Spate & Learmonth 1967, 176.

Figure 6.2 shows the frequency with which boundaries between states have occurred in South Asia, and the fact that the northwestern, northern, and eastern mountains are the sub-continental frontier. (The northeastern frontier is historically more complicated – Assam has historically not often been incorporated by the powers of the Gangetic plains.) It also portrays quite clearly the threefold division of mountains, plains and Deccan.

The major variables to be considered in understanding the way in which this vast region has been divided and integrated over the centuries are linguistic, religious, cultural and economic. The arenas within which these variables have expressed differing kinds of forces and within which they have been manipulated are obviously political and military.

Language

As a result of its settlement history, South Asian linguistic geography is extremely complex. There are two major language groups: the Indo-Aryan group (derived from Sanskrit) of the North dominates the Indus and Ganges valleys, and includes Hindi (and the vernacular Hindustani), Punjabi, Sindhi, Bihari, and Bengali. This group also permeates the Thar desert and the northern parts of the Deccan – Rajasthani, Gujerati, Marathi, Oriya. All of these languages are within the Indo-European group, of which French and English are also a part. The northern languages are indeed closer to European languages than they are to the southern Dravidian group, comprising Malayalam, Kannada, Telugu and Tamil. In addition to these languages there are others, many associated with small tribal groups. There are also many scripts. In the contemporary Republic of India there are 14 recognized languages for constitutional purposes (plus Sanskrit, which is not in common use), and nearly as many scripts, and in addition, depending on the distinction between dialect and language, somewhere between 400 and 1000 others (*A Social and Economic Atlas of India* 1987). In Pakistan there are four major languages, and a fifth of significance. Even in uniform Bangladesh there are distinct tribal languages in the Chittagong Hill Tracts.

Religion

South Asia is pre-eminently the land of the Hindus – a word derived originally from the Indus. Outside India the country is often known as Hindustan. But South Asia is also home to 250 million Muslims – a number which dwarfs the numbers associated with the Muslim heartlands of· the Middle East. The history of the relations of these two religious groups has had a significant impact on the varying patterns of state formation in South Asia. There are also many other major religions in South Asia: Jainism and Buddhism both have adherents (both are reformist offshoots from Hinduism), Sikhism commands the loyalty of a people small in number but significant in so many fields and

Table 6.1 Percentage distribution of communities in the Indian Empire 1941.

	Caste Hindu	Untouchable	Muslim	Sikh	Other	Total
British provinces						
Madras	70.4	16.4	7.9	0.0	5.3	100.0
Bombay	70.5	8.9	9.2	0.0	11.4	100.0
Bengal	29.3	12.2	54.7	0.0	3.8	100.0
United Provinces	62.0	21.3	15.3	0.4	1.0	100.0
Punjab	22.2	4.4	57.1	13.2	3.1	100.0
Bihar	61.0	11.9	13.0	0.0	14.1	100.0
Central Provinces	58.8	18.1	4.7	0.1	18.3	100.0
Assam	34.7	6.6	33.7	0.0	25.0	100.0
NW Frontier Province	5.9	0.0	91.8	1.9	0.4	100.0
Orissa	64.1	14.2	1.7	0.0	20.0	100.0
Sind	22.9	4.2	70.7	0.7	1.5	100.0
Princely states						
Hyderabad	63.5	17.9	12.8	0.0	5.8	100.0
Mysore	72.1	19.2	6.6	0.0	2.1	100.0
Travancore	51.8	6.5	7.1	0.0	34.6	100.0
Kashmir	17.3	2.8	76.4	1.6	1.9	100.0
Gwalior	86.4	0.0	6.0	0.0	7.6	100.0
Baroda	68.8	8.1	7.8	0.0	15.3	100.0
Total these and other states	59.3	9.5	13.6	1.6	16.0	100.0
Total	53.0	12.5	23.7	1.5	9.3	100.0

Source: Coupland 1943, Pt 2, 339.

locally so important in problems in the Punjab. Zoroastrians, Christians and animists are also found.

To understand the relations between the two major religions, Hinduism and Islam, we need to understand the origins and theology of each. We can then see how they could relate at the popular everyday cultural level, and the grander political level.

HINDUISM

Around the second millennium BC there started a series of periodic invasions by a pastoral and nomadic people from Central Asia, the Aryans, who were light-skinned, fair-haired, blue-eyed. They also penetrated northern Europe, and are presumed to be the ancestors of the Nordic people. They are in one sense the founders of Hinduism, though such a phrase will be heavily qualified below. They are the 'master race' that Hitler tried to refound, and from Hinduism Hitler took the everyday symbol of the swastika, a symbol of the sun and good fortune. Their language, in its most refined form, is known as Sanskrit, and when first encountered by European scholars was thought to be the original stem of all Indo-European languages, though now it is known that it, like they, is an offshoot of the lost stem.

There clearly was considerable mixing between the various invading groups in India, and today there is some kind of colour gradient from the lighter and sometimes blue-eyed peoples of the Northwest, to the darker skinned and always dark-eyed peoples of the South. But there was also a limit to the mixing in an important sense. Imagine that in Britain there had been an apartheid that prevented the Roman-British from marrying the Celts (and language barriers and social stigma would certainly have made such a barrier for quite some time), that the Saxons never married the Celts, that in their turn the Danes and the Normans stayed aloof from the society which they had conquered (and to a large extent they did). Imagine society as frozen layers of serfs, and serfs of serfs. In Britain some would say we still have such a society, hidebound by class distinctions. But we have had since Roman times a dogmatic and egalitarian religious philosophy, which does not limit permissible marriages. The important qualification about India is this: the Aryans evolved their own religious philosophy before much homogenization had taken place, and this philosophy in practice embraced a doctrine of the inequality of man, of the ritual hierarchy of caste. There is no space here to go into any detail about the immensely complex subject of Hinduism and caste (Cohn 1971, Bougle 1971, Dumont 1971), so the following resumé is only a guide. Doctrinally, there are four grades of caste, the Brahmins (priests and pundits – guardians of knowledge), the Kshatriyas, or warriors, the Vaisyas, or merchants, the Sudras, or menials. Below them come groups of untouchables (now known as Harijans), and tribals, not normally embraced by Hinduism. The major groups are divided into 3000 sub-castes, and then into 90 000 endogamous marriage groups. Such groups have traditionally each had their own occupation, which in any one area are complementary. The untouchables carry out the most polluting jobs, such as cesspit cleaning, and labourers have always been Sudras of some type or other low caste groups. The Brahmins traditionally eschew any manual work, but are the keepers of the *Vedas* the sacred hymns of the Aryans, often recited by the Brahmins in their role as priests at important life ceremonies. Though such texts exist, Hinduism is not dogmatic. It does not claim a revealed truth, and does not prescribe one God. There is only one force in the universe, and it is in everything, but it has many faces and hence there are many gods. Different groups worship different deities, many will worship different deities for different purposes. One of the few common threads is that all groups traditionally believe in reincarnation, and that one's obligation in this life is to carry out one's duty according to one's rank at birth. Reward comes in the next incarnation. Other common features of Hinduism are a preference for vegetarianism, though lower classes may eat chicken or goat, and the untouchables frequently keep and eat pigs. The cow, the central pivot of agricultual life, is sacred to all, and in theory always allowed to die a natural death.

This complex society evolved with distinctive regional variations, and has bequeathed contemporary South Asia with the regional languages noted above. Hinduism, however, crossed the north/south lingustic divide, and Brahminism is in many ways stronger in the South today than in the North. But within this umbrella of life philosophies, there are always, by caste and by region, a myriad of societies. Economically and culturally, until the advent of cities with populations of a million-plus, India can best be described as divided into numerous *pays*, as defined by Vidal de la Blache.

But there was a major difference. The *pays* of de la Blache existed within a well-defined and centrist state, whose laws were made centrally and recognized universally. In India there was no such centrist tradition – partly for reasons of scale. Given the early technologies, there was plenty of cost but little economic advantage in the integration of large areas of India. More significantly, it was because such functions as maintaining the social order were organized within caste, each having a tribunal (*panchayat*) for its own members. Inter-caste matters would be settled by the dominant caste of any one area, but by involving the *panchayat* of lesser castes to take action against its members where necessary. In such a society the concept of king or monarch had a very different connotation. The Rajah, usually a Kshatriya and ritually inferior to the Brahmins, might be rich, but his wealth had, beside his own gratification, two major functions (Bayly 1983). One was for pomp and ceremony which was for public consumption, the other was that of a general, or minister of defence. In other words, the interpretation of customary law was the preserve of the Brahmins, the Rajah's was the defence of the principality.

ISLAM

The establishment of Islam as a major political and military force occurred remarkably quickly after its foundation by the Prophet Mohammed. The Quran, or Koran, which he wrote is, according to Muslims, not his words but the direct dictation to Mohammed by God. This therefore is a revealed religion, with a dogmatic source, much as fundamentalist Christians believe the Bible to be The Word. But, unlike Christianity, Islam does not recognize the distinction of the secular and the religious in human affairs: it prescribes rules for nearly all contingencies in life, and sets the aim of introducing the comprehensive Islamic state on earth.

Muslim influences reached India through Arab traders in Sind and in Bengal, and through the teachings of wandering Muslim saints or mystics, known as Sufis, not unlike the wandering Christian monks who took Christianity to Ireland and Scotland. But when Islam came in force, literally, when the first of the successful Muslim invasions burst into India through the northwest in the 12th century, it brought something radically different from anything India had encountered before. The Guhrids established in North India an empire (or more correctly a confederacy) acknowledged by the Khalif of Baghdad as the Sultanate of Delhi, and very rapidly after its establishment in India Islam was known to be precisely that – Islam-in-India, and not simply an extension of Islam in general. This was the beginning of 600 years of Muslim domination.

This Islam was iconoclastic, and brought destruction to many Hindu temples, and the forcible conversion of some subjects. Other subjects voluntarily chose the new religion, and this was particularly true of the untouchables and low-caste people, perhaps attracted by the doctrine of the equality of man. But one of the central tenets of Hinduism is that one cannot renounce one's birth, hence many, especially the higher castes, resisted conversion. Mass conversion of lower castes seems to have been greatest in East Bengal, for reasons which are not clear but may have been connected with Arab seafarers. Muslims are concentrated in the Indus valley, contiguous with the Middle East, and in East Bengal. These are roughly the areas of contemporary Pakistan and Bangladesh. In addition there were important Muslim populations in the imperial urban centres of the Ganges plain and in many imperial cities in the central Deccan.

Culture

Religion and culture may overlap, but cannot be seen as the same thing. In India, we have already noted the complexity of social groups that Hinduism spawned. When some of these groups were converted to Islam, they did not abandon their origins overnight, no more than someone today could expect to change his job tomorrow by proclaiming himself a Christian. Islam may prescribe the equality of man, but it does not command that people marry at random. Within Islam-in-India, therefore, caste persists in significant ways defined not so much by pollution rules as family marriage rules. It even persists to the extent that persons who were once distillers, who by being Muslim are not allowed to drink, nevertheless continue to make and market alcohol. In Pakistan, the network of families, each known as a *Bradri*, is fundamental to all social and political life. Further, the acceptance of Islam and the recitation of the Quran in Arabic does not deprive a man of his native tongue – so that a Bengali Muslim is first and foremost a Bengali, yet also a Muslim.

In other words, within Islam as within Hinduism local regional cultures persisted. Usually the same regional culture pervaded both religions in one place. The major religious difference was that for Muslims the common and exact reference point of a dogmatic revealed and egalitarian religion *could* be established with Muslims from different areas, whereas for Hindus such common references were much harder to establish and were always confounded by caste.

Economy

Economic variables enter into the question of integration from two viewpoints. One concerns the benefits that accrue from complementarities exploited, and the other the costs of integration.

The benefits argument is simply that of comparative advantage, that two regions linked together can each specialize to the ultimate advantage and increase in welfare of both. For this to happen, though, there have to be complementarities and there has to be a transport system whose operating costs are below the increased gains that trade engenders. Economic advantage must also obviously not be nullified by one-sided political power. In the case of South Asia, before the railways there were few complementarities that could be exploited. Those regions which could be connected by transport, primarily the northern plains, were fairly homogenous. Indeed, if any complementarities could be established, they would be with regions outside India, not within – hence the interest of European traders once ocean transport became sufficiently advanced. The exploitation of internal complementarity, particularly linking regions in or across the Deccan, could only occur after the coming of the railways, and even then could only occur fully with a change in the political regime.

Integration and empire

We need to think of three forces of integration, and to consider their interplay at two social levels. The forces are identitive, utilitarian, and coercive. The two levels are those of the elites and the masses.

The identitive bonds are those mutually recognized by a people as the symbols of their community, and are usually associated with language and religion, but they may also be associated with territory. Where these are strong, utilitarian integration can also follow if the technology permits. Utilitarian bonds are those of economic self-interest. The British now know that they are bound economically to Europe and that to break away would be injurious, no matter if they do not 'feel' European. The only comment one needs to make about coercion is that it is expensive, and fundamentally its premise is the threat of destruction. So after the costs of an invasion, which may instantaneously be met by plunder, a period of accommodation and reconstruction has to occur.

The elite–mass distinction is useful in elaborating all three of these forces. An elite may have identitive bonds in common, although the subject peoples do not. These bonds can then form the cement of integration, and while the masses are divided they will not combine to eject the elite. In the case of utilitarian bonds, these may be perceived more easily by the elite than by the masses. In the case of the use of coercive force to achieve integration, this almost by definition has to be controlled by an elite. The use of force by the masses against other masses is more likely to lead (as we shall see) to anarchy, genocide and disintegration.

There were four major imperial periods in South Asia before the advent of the British (see Fig. 6.3). They all had the following features in common. They were based on the agricultural and population heartland of the Gangetic plains, they projected power from this northern resource base into the Deccan, but none ever included the whole of peninsular India, and each decayed internally as much as collapsed because of external pressure. A major distinction between them was that the first two were Buddhist-Hindu or Hindu, whereas the third and fourth were formed by Muslim aristocracies which ruled over Hindu India. The exact heartland of these empires did vary a little: the first two, the Mauryan and Gupta empires, were centred on East Uttar Pradesh and Bihar (modern names), whereas the Muslim empires of the Sultanate and the Moghuls were based on Western Uttar Pradesh and the Punjab.

The Mauryan and Gupta empires

The Mauryan empire (Thapar 1966) at its zenith was synonymous with one man – Karla Asoka. At the time that he forged the empire, by force, there were many differentiated local communities – the *pays* referred to above. There was therefore no mass identitive integration, and the empire relied on integration through fealty by subsidiary chiefs to the emperor. There was no, or very little, utilitarian integration – the transport technology did not allow it. Although a well-ordered empire, and order and stability were no doubt constructive, it was expensive to maintain. It went into decline after Asoka's death, many of its troubles blamed on inflation. Asoka in his lifetime tried to promulgate his own version of Buddhism as a state religion. Clearly, he

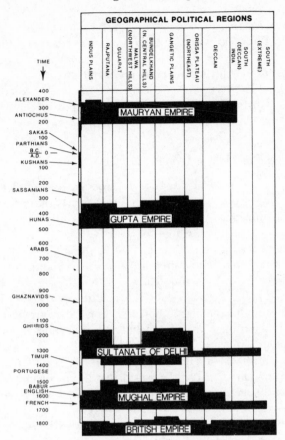

Figure 6.3 The empires of South Asia in time and space.
Source: Malik 1989.

perceived the need for a common identitive bond – but it did not take root. The next empire, that of the Guptas, echoed in many ways the emergence and decline of the Mauryan. It, too, never penetrated far into the Deccan. It was, however, remarkable for its development of applied science, mathematics and astronomy, and much that Europe was thought to have learnt from the Arab world was in fact knowledge that had diffused to it from this Indian empire.

There is, however, a problem here in that it seems easy to put a line round an area on a map and say of a historical past 'here was an empire'. What does this mean? The exact tributary status of many of the component parts is often unknown to us: and the tributary status may be near to fiction, paid more in protocol than hard cash or armed levies. It may also involve more of a treaty alliance than acknowledgement of overlordship. Where documentary evidence is weak, we are left to surmise.

There is also a possibility that we may have introduced a North Indian bias.

There were great empires in the South, which have left temples and ruins for us to marvel at. But there is one significant difference between them and the northern empires: their resource bases were neither as great nor as dense spatially as those of the North, and no southern empire ever threatened to take over the North. (This is true even of the Marattas, who could only have dominated the North by becoming an imperial power in, and the new aristocracy of, the North.)

The Sultanate and the Mughal empire

The Sultanate and the Mughal empire were, amongst many other differences they had compared with the earlier empires, particularly different in that they were led and dominated by Muslims. The added complication of Hindu–Muslim relations could be used both to work for and against empire. These relations posed questions hitherto unknown in the Indian context. India is renowned for its syncretic civilization, capable of absorbing and moulding a great many imported and invading cultures. Even the Huns were absorbed within Hinduism as the Rajputs of Rajasthan. But in the case of Islam, India and Hinduism, though having profound effects on the nature of Indian Islam, failed to absorb or dominate it. We may think of the relations between the two religions at theological, daily, and political levels.

Islam is the antithesis of Hinduism in nearly all ways. It is dogmatic, evengelical, egalitarian. The latter is inegalitarian, but tolerant of divergent views and practices, and is by definition not evangelical: you have to be born into a caste to be a Hindu. Where Hindus believe in reincarnation, Muslims believe in one life and heaven or hell afterwards. Where the Hindus believe all life is unitary, the Muslims, like the Christians, have their version of the Garden of Eden, in which Adam was placed last so that mankind could use the garden (the environment) as his birthright.

There are clear differences observable in daily life. Where Hindus worship idols, Islam prohibits all graven images – all ornamentation in a mosque is abstract. Muslim males go publicly to prayer as a congregation on a fixed day. Hindus usually go individually to a temple when they feel the need, and women, though not overtly the equal of men, are not debarred, and appear bare-faced in public where Muslim women appear veiled, if at all. Hindus are largely vegetarian. Muslims eat mutton and beef. No Muslim would eat pork, deemed, as the Jews deem it, to be unclean. There are no pigs in Pakistan: there are many troughing in the rubbish dumps of India. Muslims bury their dead, the Hindus cremate theirs. Where differences are as great as these, though communities living alongside each other may normally be tolerant, small accidents or even contrived events can set off a riot, that may degenerate into long-lasting communal strife. In this there is the further problem that Indian culture stresses the family and the community more, and the individual less than in the West. The result is that a slight against one member of a community is more likely to be felt equally by his brethren. Thus riots may start when music is heard near a mosque at prayer time, when a cow is killed by a Muslim, when a pig is let loose in a mosque, when a roadside idol is vandalized.

At the grand political level Muslims could secure the political support of their Hindu subjects by minimizing the discrimination against Hindus in public service, by reducing or eliminating the taxes levied on non-believers, by marrying into Hindu dynasties. But they could also close ranks by stressing their Muslim identity and persecuting Hindu idolaters.

The problem of maintaining the integration of these Muslim empires was essentially still the same as with previous ones: that though large areas could become incorporated by force, given that there were few utilitarian bonds that could develop because of inadequate transport, what was to prevent regional aristocracies breaking away, once established? So long as the empires were expanding and could therefore call on unification for the armed struggles, with the anticipation of reward after victory, mutual support provided the integrating impetus. In the case of the Sultanate, it became clear after the failure to dominate the Deccan that there were fissiparous tendencies, which were suppressed by some sultans only at great cost (Thapar 1966). An aristocracy, once seated and landed, rapidly becomes more and more rooted in its own locale, seeing less and less interest in distant centres of taxation.

The Mughal empire (Spear 1965) faced the same problems. But the manipulation of religious factors in seeking a solution is more in evidence. Different leaders pursued different policies towards their solution. Akbar, the greatest of the Mughals, who delineated the state most clearly, chose not to use Islam as the identitive bond of the ruling class, to keep it integrated by virtue of its opposition to the subservient masses. He indulged in patronage of Hindu nobles, took a Rajput princess as a wife, and went so far as to found a new religious cult centred around himself, in effect becoming an apostate. He also devised a system of appointments to the vice-royalties of the empire, which gave an incumbent wealth and tenure in his lifetime, but by which the state resumed all property and wealth at his death. The positions were not hereditary, and he thus avoided the development of powerful local rooted aristocracies, and maintained the dependency of the aristocracy as a class on the emperor.

By the time of Aurangzeb, the fragility of the empire had been displayed. His solution was to unite the aristocracy by reasserting Islamic purity and domination; he became a zealot in the crusade against Hinduism, and reintroduced the discriminatory *jizya* tax. Conviction, confrontation, coercion and suppression were his guidelines. At its peak, the army directly or indirectly (through dependants and camp followers) employed a quarter of the imperial population.

From the advent of Islam in India until the present day, there was always the possibility of local spontaneous conflict between Muslims and Hindus. The extent to which rulers and politicians may have played conflicts up, or down, was always bound to vary, but none of them could ever rid India of this inherent communalism.

The British Raj

The British came to India as traders, and their first territorial acquisition in Bengal in 1757 was largely an accidental result of self-defence. That Bengal was the first acquisition was, however, in a geographical sense not an accident: for here was the world's greatest delta, which ocean-going ships could penetrate far upstream, carrying with them their superior ordnance. It was here in the rivers that the problem of inland transport was solved.

The move in self-defence that caused the British to take Bengal had many indirect causes, one of which was the instability of the decaying Mughal empire. This instability created a vacuum into which the British were drawn, as often as not in a proxy war with the French, both sides using local nobles and local feuds as surrogates in their own attempts to wrest the monopoly of trade, and as surrogates for inadequate manpower. The result of 80 years of such activity was that the 'British acquired India in a fit of absence of mind'. The lack of a clear policy and the use of a pragmatic approach are evident in the political map which finally emerged in India (Fig. 6.4). The British had built themselves three major port cities – Calcutta, Bombay and Madras, around which were territories they ruled directly themselves. But 40 per cent of Indian territory and 25 per cent of its population were encompassed in princely states (Coupland 1943), the territories of major and minor nobles which emerged at the collapse of the previous empire, who had treaty obligations with the Crown in external affairs, but who were internally autonomous autocrats. In many ways the British fragmented India politically, dividing in order to rule. But it should also be clear by now that division both territorially and communally was by no means new to India. Under the British these divisions might have been shaped in new ways: but they were always there. As one independence leader observed: 'We divide, you rule'.

British integration relied on all aspects of the integrating forces we have mentioned, but not equally at elite and mass levels. They used superior technology as the basis of coercion where necessary. They relied on the identitive bonds of the British as British to cement the rulers of empire, and they too were forbidden to become landed gentry. The civil service was Europeanized at the highest levels early on, and English instituted as the language of government, supplanting Persian. But the new rulers came from a country which had a rudimentary parliamentary democracy. At some stage they would have to confront questions about the legitimacy of their rule, and the exclusive proprietorship by their group of that right. Racialism was thus inevitable, not so much as an overt policy for future development, but as an

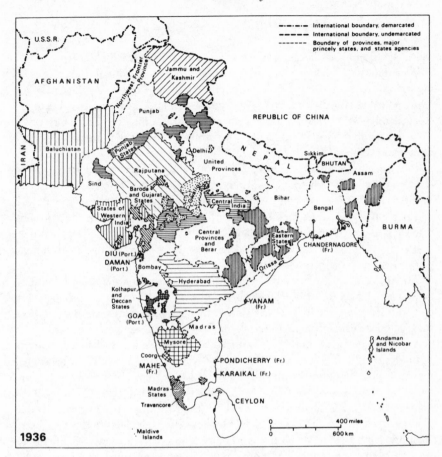

Figure 6.4 Political divisions in South Asia, 1936.
Source: Schwartzberg 1976, and others.

explanation for what had happened. Conveniently, it also stressed the identitive bonds of the rulers and strengthened their adhesion as a group. Although for the majority of the rural masses they did nothing, they nevertheless fostered utilitarian integration by the development of the railways, and by the development in many areas of major irrigation schemes, incorporating millions of people within the command areas of thousands of miles of canals. They also founded new universities in which a new middle-class intelligentsia studied in English.

What they did not do was foster the identitive bonds of the Indian masses as 'Indians'. Partly it was not in their own self-interest; partly they believed in their own propaganda, that India was a sub-continent of many races and tongues.

Independence and partition

With the filtering of Western liberal ideas into India's small emergent middle class, demands for change were made, which were met gradually, starting with democratic elections on very small franchises to town boards. By the end of the 19th century, some elected representatives were allowed on provincial councils (Coupland 1943), though outnumbered by appointees of the Governor ('official members'). But the power of veto remained at the centre, where the Governor-General/Viceroy was answerable to London.

The growing demands in India for more representative government led to the founding of the All-Indian National Congress in 1885. This was above all a middle-class, urban, educated and English-speaking movement: the British had not only infused democratic ideas into India, they had given the slim new middle class the physical and oral means of communication on a pan-Indian basis. The adoption of the qualifier *All-Indian* was a propaganda ploy staking a claim on a perceived future (Rahmat Ali 1942).

The realization that there was a possibility of increasing democratization on a Westminster pattern caused some alarm to farseeing members of the Muslim community. They realized that a simple first-past-the-post system of democracy, if ever entrenched in India, could lead to the interests of the minority community being permanently ignored. It might work well in a culturally homogeneous country such as Britain, where parties could express class interests, but they were doubtful that it could where such conditions did not exist. Because of pressure from the Muslims, the British adopted in 1909 the concept of separate electorates: one roll for the Muslims, one for the others. In provincial elections, there were to be blocks of seats allocated to these different electorates, the minority being given preferential treatment. The scheme, though well intended, wrote communalism into the constitution of India. Obviously the candidate who would appear most attractive was he who could claim to get the greatest concessions from the 'other side'. In the 1920s, Gandhi did not object to the idea of reserved seats *per se*, but he rightly pointed out that the electorate for reserved seats should be universal. In effect all electors could then vote twice, once for candidates for each of the blocks of seats. The effect would have been that though there would be a guaranteed number of Muslim or Hindus in the Councils the candidates would have had to fight a campaign not on sectarian issues but on issues of wider appeal. Could such a system work in Ulster?

During and after the First World War the demands for Dominion status (independence within the Commonwealth like Australia or Canada) grew (Hodson 1969, Phillips & Wainwright 1970, Moon 1961). Gandhi and his philosophy were a key to the pattern assumed. He wanted a non-violent protest, which often involved non-cooperation. To do this he had to have the support of the masses, and in that lay his genius. Though not an official of the party, he transformed Congress from a small, middle-class clique to a much wider movement. Steadily the British conceded more − though always struggling with the contradictions inherent between ultimate responsibility being held in London, while new representative institutions were growing in India. The experience of these new institutions convinced more Muslims that their anxieties for the future were well-founded. Congress had always sought to be secular and multi-communal, but its behaviour locally was often more partisan. To understand this we need to refer back again to the idea of local community, so strong in India. The new leaders might well have been nationalistic: but the masses were sunk still in local perceptions. When they had to be enlisted in the struggle for power, they were told it was for self-determination. But who or what was self? To a Tamil it is Tamils, or perhaps Tamil Brahmins or Tamil non-Brahmins. In Bengal, self meant one's own community, here very clearly either Hindu or Muslim. The Bengali part went unspoken − taken for granted as the starting point. With classic myopia, local differences seemed large, distant ones less important. Thus, later Jinnah could and did appeal to Muslim Bengalis to join his movement as Muslims.

In the 1930s, the Muslim League under Jinnah's leadership campaigned hard for more devolution of power from the centre to the provinces, with the aim of attaining more power locally for the Muslims of the Punjab and Bengal, two mixed provinces in which Muslims were a majority (approximately 55–60 per cent in both: see Table 6.1). In 1935 the Government of India Act actually foresaw a federal future in which the princely states would be involved too. However, the Second World War intervened, and events ran rapidly beyond the ability of either the British or the Indian leaders to control. Realizing that Independence would follow soon after the war, the Muslims had in 1940 proclaimed their goal to be the creation of a separate state, to be known as Pakistan, to be founded in the Indus valley, and to embrace the whole of the Punjab, including eastern Hindu majority districts. The campaigners saw India in regional terms. Bengal was not part of the original Pakistan concept, but the Pakistani camp drew attention to the fact that Bengal, like Pakistan, ought to be able to claim its independence at the end of empire. The Congress leadership, seeing itself as the heir of the British Raj, rejected the demands outright, and tense negotiations began in an attempt to reach a settlement. Basically, the only plans acceptable to the Muslims were based on a weak centre, and reserving the right of secession to the provinces. But Congress wanted a strong centre, and rejected the right of secession.

Here we see the point behind the remark made above about coercion by the masses rather than the elites. Jinnah held very few cards, which was one of the reasons that he was given so little credit by Congress. The Muslim communities were the minority, and not strong in the institutions of the new society, nor strong in trade or banking, nor strong in the civil service. But the masses could be awakened, and what Jinnah could threaten was, simply, anarchy. The often fractious nature of the two communities was openly played upon, with the result that large-scale rioting broke out, particularly in Calcutta in August

1946, but it spread to other areas too. By 1947, the internal law and order situation had disintegrated to the point where it was possible that the British would have no effective government left to transfer to anybody. It was in this atmosphere that the last Viceroy, Mountbatten, reached an agreement with Nehru and Jinnah for the partition of India, something which was acceptable to all only in so far as all could see each other equally miserable and disappointed by the conclusion. Jinnah was miserable, because the logic of partition had been applied within the provinces of the Punjab and Bengal – so he only got the Muslim parts – and hence East Pakistan (now Bangladesh) was formed from just the rural hinterland of Calcutta, but lost the city itself. Nehru was miserable, because he and Gandhi felt that India should never have been partitioned, and that the Muslim League's rejection of Congress's secularism was false. And the British were miserable because they saw the best defence arrangements for South Asia to be within a single state, itself defensible behind the boundaries of British India. They were right – after partition hostility between India and Pakistan has led to each turning to the outside for help – the USA supporting Pakistan and the USSR supporting India.

The real tragedy however was twofold. First, the partition of the Punjab and Bengal provoked some of the largest mass migrations ever known. At least 12 million people moved: some put the figure as high as 16 million. In the first few months the caravans and trains of refugees moved through a land where government, the armed forces, the police, the railway personnel, were being divided, and security was non-existent. In this atmosphere, extremists on both sides perpetrated the most ghastly atrocities (Collins & LaPierre 1975). Whole trains arrived at their destinations with every passenger stabbed or hacked to death. The final death toll is not known, but was perhaps more than a million.

The second tragedy was due to a combination of decades of British procrastination and princely personality. The British had never unified South Asia. The existence of the myriad princely states was but one proof of that. In 1947, the paramount power was to be withdrawn, and from then on in theory the princes could proclaim their independence (which would have led to a Balkanization of India like that at the collapse of the Mughal empire). In practice, they were persuaded that their communications and economies were bound up with the states of India and Pakistan, and that their only real option was to be absorbed into those states. All but three duly aligned themselves on the basis of majority community and contiguity. The most significant of the dissenting three was the state of Kashmir, where a Hindu raja ruled a largely Muslim population. The maharaja wanted independence, and dragged his feet. In October 1947, a force of invading Pathan tribesmen crossed from the Northwest frontier and invaded the state. The maharaja signed a temporary deed of accession with India to gain India's help in repelling the invaders. Within a short time this action had escalated into open warfare between Pakistan and India. On 1 January 1949 a ceasefire, which should have been followed by a plebiscite (which has never taken place), effectively established the line which has partitioned the state ever since, between Azad Kashmir, nominally still independent of Pakistan, and Kashmir in India, which the Indians have incorporated within their republic's constitution. But this issue, more than any other, has continued to bedevil Indo-Pakistani relations since 1947.

It is thus quite clear that by the end of empire in 1947 pan-Indian identitive bonds were not strong enough to maintain the integration of South Asia. For this the Indians may blame the British who divided to rule, keeping princely states apart, and devising separate electorates for the Muslims. But the Muslims blamed Congress, for not in truth being secular at local levels. Casting blame to one side, it is clear now that to expect this sub-continent of creeds and castes, still largely illiterate, and a veritable linguistic Tower of Babel, to have formed a national identity at that time in history was to expect the impossible. As an alternative to identity, coercion was not possible either – except at the fringe over issues like Kashmir. For independence was about self-determination and the rejection of imperial coercion, and in 1947 Congress had reluctantly concluded that negotiated independence for Pakistan was best. That way they inherited a strong centre in the new India, still the largest self-governing unit the sub-continent has ever seen. The real 'surprise' was the creation of the state of Pakistan in two 'wings', separated by thousands of miles of Indian territory, separated by language and script, economically unrelated to each other, and linked only by Islam.

There is plenty of evidence to support the contention that India saw Pakistan in 1947 as a temporary aberration of the political map. South Asia was seen by the government at that time to be the same geopolitical region that the British had dominated. Although the current government of India has stated publicly that it has no designs on Pakistan (Bradnock 1990), there are still regional imperatives that interlock the destinies of the two countries. Both countries, and Bangladesh too, may well wish to keep internal matters to themselves and not to interfere in their neighbours' affairs, but precisely because many issues are regional in a pan-South Asian sense, it is impossible to isolate many issues as purely domestic. There are Sikhs in both Punjabs, who can offer trans-border support to their brethren. There are Bengali Muslims and Bengali Hindus in both Bengals. The Indus river basin is shared by Pakistan and India, the Ganges-Brahmaputra by India and Bangladesh (as well as Nepal and China). And there are Tamils in both India and Sri Lanka, some of the latter being locked in a civil war with the Sinhala majority.

Desite these continuities within the partitioned provinces, new boundary lines were drawn. These could simply have been administrative borders, open to normal trade flows. But because there had been no identitive basis for integrating a new South Asia, utilitarian complementarities were broken in a remorseless hunt for that economic independence which would serve political demands for sovereignty.

Table 6.2   Exports and imports for India and Pakistan, 1984–5.

	Exports to	Imports from
India, Rs million*		
UK	6701	10 188
USA	17 685	16 666
USSR	16 546	18 034
Pakistan	129	157
Bangladesh	932	445
Iran	1340	4849
Pakistan, Rs million +		
UK	2538	5277
USA	3965	11 006
USSR	951	438
India	498	261
Bangladesh	1132	869
Iran	695	1061

* Indian rupees. Source: *A Social and Economic Atlas of India* 1987.
+ Pakistani rupees. Source: *Pakistan Statistical Yearbook* 1986.

There were compelling reasons for 'normal' trade to continue between the successor states. The jute industry of Calcutta needed the growers of East Pakistan, the cotton industry of Bombay the farmers of Pakistani Punjab; Pakistan needed Indian coal, India needed Pakistani wheat. But both this 'logical' economic geography and the technical geography of the irrigation works were sacrificed in the struggles to achieve total independence (Vakil and Rao n.d.). During the Kashmir crisis of 1948, India turned off the water which flowed from its territory, and some of Pakistan's prime lands went brown. This led to a prolonged crisis (Michel 1967) which only ended in 1960 with the signing of the Indus Waters Treaty under the auspices of the World Bank, by which the unified scheme was completely divided, at great cost. Pakistan put an export tax on jute exported from East Bengal to Calcutta. India banned all imports of jute. In 1949, the Indian rupee was devalued along with the pound sterling: but Pakistan did not devalue its rupee. All trade between India and Pakistan ceased. The banks refused even to exchange the two currencies. (See Table 6.2 for current trading position.)

The secession of Bangladesh

In an attempt to develop a new national identity for Pakistan, Jinnah had in 1948 proclaimed Urdu, a language used more by the aristocrats of the West than the peasants of the East, to be the national official language. Urdu is written in the Arabic script, as are all other regional languages of West Pakistan. Those Easterners who were literate mostly used the Bengali script,

Table 6.3 West and East Pakistan: income disparity, 1949–70, (1959–60 prices).

| | GRP per caput | | |
	West	East	ratio
1949–50	345	287	1.20
1959–60	355	269	1.32
1969–70	504	314	1.61

Source: Ahmad UK, 34.

and hence were being asked both to use an alien script as well as an alien language. The first anti-Pakistan riots in Dacca in 1951, which generated the first 'Bangladesh Martyrs', were in protest against the imposition of Urdu.

The history of utilitarian bonding between the West and the East has several twists (Griffin & Khan 1972, Chakravarty & Narain 1986, Wilson & Dalton 1982). Because of the Pakistani–Indian trade war, East Pakistan became drawn into a trade system with West Pakistan, in which the East of the country exported to the rest of the world, the West imported industrial goods and materials, and the balance was completed by the West selling high-priced consumer goods to the East. While in a sense West Pakistan lifted India's blockade, the system that developed was not based so clearly on natural complementarities, and was dominated by Western interests. While the standard of living did slowly grow in the West of the country, it stagnated and declined in the East (Table 6.3). Given the ethnic and geographical difference between the wings, it was inevitable that this too would become a major regional political issue. Pakistan, and particularly its armed forces, was dominated by Punjabis, the largest and most prosperous group of the West. They watched with increasing apprehension the inevitable demands from the East of the country for more equal power sharing, and since the East had the larger populace, if Pakistan remained a democracy under the constitution of the Independence Act (which was basically the 1935 Act) then the East, the Johnny-come-latelies of the Pakistan movement, might dictate to the West, the 'homeland' where Pakistan was first defined.

After a bungled attempt to write a new constitution in 1971, following an election allowed by the military (rather like the recent election that returned Benazir Bhutto), outright rebellion broke out in Bengal. A savage (Punjabi) army response which included large-scale massacres, particularly of intel-lectuals and of Hindus remaining in East Bengal, was followed by waves of refugees fleeing to India, which finally brought war between Pakistan and India (for the third time since 1947) and the proclamation of Bangladesh as a sovereign state in 1972.

Religion alone had not proved a strong enough identitive bond between West and East Pakistan on which to build a polity. The utilitarian bonds were one-sided, leading to exploitation, not mutual benefit. The last recourse was coercion. But at that point the issues involved, particularly the persecution of Bengalis by Punjabis, literally spilt over the borders, and the issue became truly a South Asian, not merely a domestic affair.

By these twists of fate, one of India's *pays* has achieved nationhood.

Regionalism and holism in India and Pakistan

The question is interminably raised: has the division of South Asia into three (Fig. 6.5) terminated the process? Or will Indian Punjab achieve what the extremists demand, their new Khalistan? Is another insurrection likely in Pakistan's Baluchistan? Will the Tamil south ever divorce itself from Delhi?

In India, the most pressing regional problem has been language (Hardgrave 1975, Farmer 1983, Taylor & Yapp 1979, Wilson & Dalton 1982). After Independence in 1947, the demands for self-rule which had been stoked by the nationalist struggle had to be satisfied. These demands took the form of protests for the delimitation of linguistic areas in certain provinces, such as in northern Madras. Here the leaders of the Andhra movement adopted such tactics as fasts unto death, in the Gandhi mould. More than 300 people were killed in rioting. Nehru was at first strongly opposed to changing the administrative map – which was the old provinces and larger princely states, with lesser princely states merged into neighbouring provinces on a pragmatic basis. His view was that this would be to give way to the forces of communalism and regionalism. But after the 1953 events, significantly in the South, he and the government performed a *volte-face*. Now the argument was: if these forces can be accommodated within the constitution, they will have a stake in it: if not, then they will break it. Starting in 1956 in a massive adminstrative reform, India was divided into approximately 15 roughly equal states, each with its own majority linguistic basis, and quite often its own script. In these units, the populace does not find itself unable to communicate with the administrators and educators as once it might have done. Although one should not blame the development exclusively for the subsequent shift in political behaviour, it is also true that the state governments have less and less often been formed of Congress legislators, and instead are more and more of local political groups, such as the DMK, or Dravidian Federalist Party of Tamil Nadu. Even in the central Parliament, the Lok Sabha, regional parties are taking more seats, and the Congress, the only major national party, seems to be withering away. The strong centre which Nehru wanted, and to some extent had, is melting. But in the Indian case this does not necessarily mean the demise of the Union. Many commentators have pointed out that India is still remarkable divided by caste and local faction. This means that in a state such as Tamil Nadu or Andhra Pradesh there are constant struggles between different elements within the state. The state does not define a unity which will voice its

Figure 6.5 Political divisions in South Asia, 1975.
Source: Schwartzberg 1976, and others.

demands for secession. Significantly, the most strident demands have come from the Punjab, where division by caste within Sikhism is weak, and the common identity, though riven by factions, stronger than elsewhere.

Utilitarian bonds have also grown. What India has is size, and the diversity of resources to go with it. Since Independence, successive governments have stressed the development of a comprehensive range of industries, and have pursued a policy of import substitution in a heavily protected environment. There are critics of the efficiency and cost of this industrialization: but India now has more than 200 million urban people, who are in the cash economy, in manufacturing and commerce, in government. There is a large new pan-Indian middle class, with pan-Indian vested interests to protect. They are increasingly proud of national achievements, and no custodians of the Gandhian past of non-violence. Few critics are heard of the cost or size of the armed forces, which now include one of the world's largest standing armies, a 'blue water' navy with two aircraft carriers and nuclear submarine(s), and a large and comprehensive arms industry.

It would appear that, at present, utilitarian and identitive bonds in India are stronger than before, and also more widely appreciated. Yet one cannot assume they will necessarily continue to grow, since a new trading liberalism and lower levels of central government financial support for state governments may both lead again to greater local economic independence and assertiveness.

Pakistan was born as an anti-Congress nation of Muslims. The Muslim League had not had the time that Congress had had to debate before Independence the policies it would pursue afterwards. Perhaps because of this it had drawn fundamentalist clerics and intellectual Marxists of Muslim descent into an unlikely coalition. In India, Nehru lived long enough to set his mould on the new nation and its policies: in Pakistan, Jinnah died soon after Independence with no powerful successor or widely accepted programme of action left behind him to steer the new nation. Regionalism and factionalism have plagued it ever since. Many of the regional problems have international dimensions: the Pathans straddle the border with Afghanistan, and the Baluchs the borders both with Afghanistan and Iran. The country was dominated by feudal landlords on the one hand, and a wave of new urban and educated immigrants (Jinnah was one of them) on the other (Hussain 1979). It had no industry worth speaking of, and had to build new institutions, such as the army and civil service, from the pieces hacked off from the bigger Indian parts. It had no obvious unity except Islam. It has cohesion when exposed to external threat by India, but left to its own devices is riven by regional dissent. The most remarkable feat of its history is that, apart from the loss of Bangladesh, it has survived. It has not done so through identitive bonds: though perhaps there is a new generation that accepts Pakistan as a natural sovereign state. It has done so partly by a policy similar to India's: protected industrialization which has created a new middle class with vested interests. But this has been smaller and more concentrated than in India. It has done so also through coercion, through several periods of army rule, by an army supported hugely by outside funds from the USA. There is no space here to go into the international relations of India and Pakistan in depth (Bradnock 1990, Chapman forthcoming), but it is significant that India has found a true friend in the Soviet Union, and that Nehru's independent non-aligned movement, socialist rhetoric and state planning strained relations with the USA. The Pakistan–China–USA axis that developed fitted American designs for containment, and of course became highlighted during the Afghan war.

Though no one had ambitions to absorb Pakistan, if the country itself fell to pieces, the little bits could soon enter into different arrangements with neighbours. The most important of the bonds that have sustained it since 1947 is the armed forces, supported by external powers. Across the border, in the Punjab, American aircraft types face Russian models. The British desire to see South Asia remain unified – because therein lay its best defence – has been vindicated.

Besides defence, the rationale of a unified South Asia had other merits. In 1946 the Raj governed a sub-continent with a uniform currency, uniform external tariffs, unified postal service, and a commercial and civil legal code which had many common elements. In specified spheres, such as agriculture, considerable powers were delegated to provincial levels. The overall impression is of the kind of commonmarket which Europe is currently trying to achieve in 1989 – except that at its core was the coercion of empire. Since 1947, South Asia has de-common-marketed itself. But the regional imperative cannot simply go away, and recognition of this has resulted in the foundation of the South Asian Association for Regional Co-operation (SAARC). This is years, if not decades, away from rebuilding a common market: but if one day this is achieved it will, one hopes, be done without coercion from the centre.

Conclusions

The aphorism 'nature proposes, man disposes' is applicable to South Asia. Nature has proposed a geopolitical region. Within that region the time which has elapsed between external human shocks has resulted in a continuity of culture despite the detailed complexity of society. This detail is important, but it is the finely patterned cracks in the glaze of an old, cracked plate – yet the plate has survived. The aggregation of this fine patterning into larger hierarchical assemblages portrays a sub-continent of *pays*, blurred only by the metropolitan cities. The only fissure of any real depth is that of religion. It is a tragedy for South Asia that this fissure actually cuts right through some of its strongest regional cultures, in the Punjab and Bengal. In terms of Fig. 6.2 the current borders are 'infrequent'. They do violence to nearly every usual boundary principle except of course one – namely community.

There is a school of thought that says that this has been a history of reactionary politics: that the British gave the nationalists too little and too late – for had they been given Dominion status at the end of the First World War, there would have been no calls for Pakistan. The Congress is likewise accused of offering Jinnah too little, too late, and even in 1946 Pakistan was not inevitable even though the British no longer accepted the responsibility for foisting unity on India. And West Pakistan offered East Pakistan too little, too late. But this is a little simple: counterfactual history cannot prove that had there been in 1919 a great Indian Federation it would have survived.

There had been no spontaneous grass-roots movements for sub-continental integration until this century. Before that, the sheer scale and complexity of South Asia meant that only coercive empire could in any sense (usually slight) unite it. What the 20th century has given the public at large is some conception of the right to self-determination. This 'self' has usually had fairly narrow confines, and regionalism remains a threat to both Pakistan and India. But wider nationalisms are emerging in the age of mass communication and industrialization, although whether the concept of the strong centrist state survives long in the next century is open to question. But the scale of problems, and the advent of large-scale technologies, combine to propel whatever forms of state survive to negotiate with each other those common resource problems (particularly in river basin management) and trading complementarities which they must accommodate to mutual advantage. Apart from resource issues, there are few causes for continuing outright hostility between the current states. Nearly all boundary problems are resolved, and from the nadir of trade embargoes one assumes that things can only get better, except that the size of India so outweighs the other states that they must have their anxieties quietened by Indian diplomacy. The only really major unsolved issue is that legacy of the unfinished business of the British Raj, the ultimate fate of Kashmir.

References

(a) Works cited

A Social and Economic Atlas of India 1987. Delhi: Oxford University Press.

Bayly, C. A. 1983, 1988. *Rulers, townsmen and bazaars: north Indian society in the age of British expansion 1770–1880*. Cambridge: Cambridge University Press.

Bougle, Celestin 1971. *Essays on the caste system*, translated with an introduction by D. F. Pocock. Cambridge: Cambridge University Press.

Bradnock, R. W. 1990. *India's foreign policy* London: Chatham House.

Chakravarty, S. R. & Virendra Narain (eds) 1986. *Bangladesh: history and culture*. Delhi: South Asian Publishers.

Chapman, G. P. *One into three: the geopolitics of South Asia from British Raj to India, Pakistan and Bangladesh*. MSS. Publication forthcoming.

Cohen, S. B. 1963. *Geography and politics in a divided world*. London: Methuen.

Cohn, Bernard S. 1971. *India: the sociology of a civilization*. Englewood Cliffs, NJ: Prentice-Hall.

Collins, Larry & Dominique LaPierre 1975. *Freedom at midnight*. New York: Avon Books.

Coupland, R. 1943. *Report on the constitutional problem in India*. Pt 1: *The Indian problem 1833–1935*, Pt 2: *Indian politics 1936–1942*, Pt 3: *The future of India*. London: Oxford University Press.

Day, W. M. 1949. Relative permanence of former boundaries in India. *Scottish Geographical Magazine* **65**, 113–22.

Dumont, Louis 1970. *Homo hierarchicus: the caste system and its implications*, translated from the French by Mark Sainsbury. Chicago: Chicago University Press.

Farmer, B. H. 1983. *An introduction to South Asia*. London: Methuen.

Griffin, K. & A. R. Khan (eds) 1972. *Growth and inequality*. London: Macmillan.

Hardgrave, Robert L. 1975. *India: government and politics in a developing nation*, 2nd edn. New York: Harcourt, Brace, Janovich.

Hodson, H. V. 1969. *The great divide: Britain–India–Pakistan*. London: Hutchinson.

Hussain, Asaf 1979. *Elite politics in an ideological state: the case of Pakistan*. Folkstone: Dawson.

Michel, A. A. 1967. *The Indus rivers: a study of the effects of partition*. New Haven, Conn.: Yale University Press.

Moon, Sir Penderel 1961. *Divide and quit*. London: Chatto and Windus.

Philips, C. H. & M. D. Wainwright 1970. *The partition of India: policies and perspectives 1935–1947*. London: Macmillan.

Rahmat Ali, C. 1942. *What does the Pakistan Movement stand for?* Cambridge: Cambridge University Press.

Spate, O. H. K. & A. T. A. Learmonth 1967. *India and Pakistan: a general and regional geography*, 3rd edn. London: Methuen.

Spear, Percival 1965, 1970. *A history of India: 2.* Harmondsworth: Penguin.

Taylor, David & Malcolm Yapp (eds) 1979. *Political identity in South Asia*. London: Curzon.

Thapar, Romila 1966. *A history of India: 1.* Harmondsworth: Penguin.

Vakil, C. N. 1950. *The economic consequences of divided India*. Bombay: Vora.

Vakil, C. N. & D. Raghava Rao n.d. *Economic relations between India and Pakistan*. Bombay: Vora.

Wilson, A, J. & D. Dalton (eds) 1982. *The states of South Asia*. London: Hurst.

(b) Other relevant literature

Bowman, Isaiah 1921. *The New World: problems in political geography*. New York: World Book Co.

Brush, J. E. 1949. The distribution of religious communities in India. *Annals of the Association of American Geographers* **39**, 81–98.

The Cambridge economic history of India. Vol.1: *c. 1200–c.1750*, ed. T. Raychaudhuri and I. Habib 1982. Cambridge: Cambridge University Press. Vol. 2. *c. 1757–1970*, ed. D. Kumar and M. Desai 1983. Cambridge: Cambridge University Press.

Charlesworth, N. 1982. *British rule and the Indian economy 1800–1914*. London: Macmillan.

Chatterjee, S. P. 1947. *The partition of Bengal: a geographical study*. Calcutta: Calcutta Geographical Society.

Chaudri, M. A. 1967. *The emergence of Pakistan*. New York: Columbia University Press.

Chen, Lincoln (ed.) 1973. *Disaster in Bangladesh: health crisis in a developing nation*. New York: Oxford University Press.

Griffiths, Sir Percival 1952. *The British impact on India*. London: Macdonald.

Islam, M. Rafiqul 1987. *Ganges water dispute*. Dhaka: Dhaka University Press.

Kirk, W. 1975. The role of India in the diffusion of early cultures. *Geographical Journal* **141**, 19–34.

Lamb, A. 1968. *Asian frontiers*. London: Pall Mall.

Mansergh, N. 1978. *The prelude to partition: concepts and aims in Ireland and India*. The 1976 Commonwealth Lecture. Cambridge: Cambridge University Press.

Menon, V. P. 1956. *The story of the integration of the Indian states*. Calcutta and London: Longman.

Noman, Omar 1988. *The political economy of Pakistan 1947–1985*. London: KPI.

Owen, Sidney 1872. *India on the eve of the British conquest*. Reprinted by Susil Gupta, Calcutta.

Rahman, M. A. 1968. *East and West Pakistan: a problem in the political economy of regional planning*, Occasional Paper No. 20. Cambridge, Mass.: Harvard University Centre for International Affairs.

Rudolph, L. I. & S. H. 1980. *The regional imperative*. Delhi: Concept.

Schwartzberg, Joseph E. 1978. *An historical atlas of South Asia*. Chicago: Chicago University Press.

Schwartzberg, Joseph E. 1985. Factors in the linguistic reorganization of Indian states. In *Region and nation in India*, Paul Wallace (ed.). 155–82. Oxford: IBH.

Tomlinson, B. R. 1979. *The British Raj 1914–1947: the economics of decolonization in India*. London: Macmillan.

Wilcox, Wayne Ayres 1963. *Pakistan: the consolidation of a nation*. New York: Columbia University Press.

Zaman, Munir, *et al.* (eds) 1983. *River basin development*. Dublin: Tycooly International.

7

Separatism and devolution: the Basques in Spain

JAMES ANDERSON

In 1981 Lieutenant Colonel Antonio Tejero of the Guardia Civil held the Spanish Parliament at gunpoint. His objective was to spark off a *coup d'état* by the Spanish army. Elements in the army, a legacy of Franco's highly centralized dictatorship, were opposed to parliamentary democracy and the devolution of some government functions to regional assemblies. They were especially dissatisfied with how the civilian government in Madrid was handling the problem of political separatism in the Basque country. In particular they wanted tougher measures against the militant separatists of ETA, Euskadi Ta Askatsuna (Basque Homeland and Freedom), a clandestine military organization which threatened the unity and territorial integrity of the Spanish state.

ETA, for its part, wanted, and still wants, a separate Basque state for the Basque nation. Its objective is an independent state of Euskadi comprising not only the four provinces which it claims in Spain – Viscaya, Guipuzcoa, Alava and Navarre – but also the three adjoining Basque provinces of Bas-Navarre, Lapurdi and Civeroa in France (Fig. 7.1). This objective is encapsulated in its slogan 'Zazpiak Bat' – 'Seven in One' – and in the graffiti of its supporters '4 + 3 = 1'. Ironically, the strained arithmetic of the equation also points to the deep-seated nature of geographical and political divisions within Euskadi and the consequent difficulty of achieving the objective.

Geography and politics

Geopolitical divisions and the ways in which they have shaped the historic conflict between Basque nationalists and the Spanish state are the focus of this chapter. It traces the development of Basque nationalism which was created at the end of the 19th century – a conservative reaction against the belated centralization of the Spanish state and against the industrialization of the major Basque city of Bilbao. The chapter sketches the ambivalence of the Basques during the Spanish Civil War – their subsequent oppression by Franco's highly centralized regime abruptly ended the brief achievement of devolved government for part of the Spanish Basque country in the 1930s – and outlines the

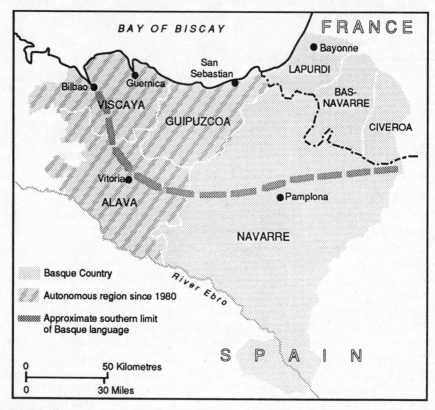

Figure 7.1 The Basque country.

resurgence of a more militant and radical nationalism under ETA's leadership in the 1960s and 1970s and its impact on the Spanish state. Based partly on interviews conducted in the Basque Country[1] the chapter seeks to explain the continuation and intractability of the conflict despite the post-Franco demo-cratization of Spain and the achievement again of devolved government for three of the Basque provinces in 1980.

The main objective is to show how geographical distributions and divisions have been an integral and often crucial aspect of the conflict at different phases in its history. There is not space for a detailed history of the political actors or their ideologies (see, e.g. Heiberg 1982, Jauregui 1986), and the emphasis is on the structural circumstances within which the political struggles took place. Geography is an important element of these circumstances – as it invariably is in struggles over separatism and devolution – but it has to be seen not as separate 'geographical factors' but as part and parcel of economic, social and political processes.

The Basque case clearly has to be understood in terms of its own history and geography, but it is far from being an isolated or entirely unique one. As we shall see, some of its major phases mirrored or were influenced by wider political developments elsewhere in Europe and beyond. While they do not recur in quite the same forms or combinations, the central political and geopolitical issues in the Spanish–Basque conflict also crop up in other conflicts between a would-be nation-state and separate nations in its 'peripheries'. For example, does granting limited regional autonomy simply encourage separatists to demand more, as a Colonel Tejero might argue, or does it weaken support for separatism in contrast to oppressive centralization which gives separatism a *raison d'être*? And for separatists what is the relationship between class and nation, socialism and nationalism? The relationships between class and nation are always important for understanding nationalist movements, but with the general radical turn in the 1960s the relationship with socialism became a highly problematical practical issue for many separatist organizations including ETA (see Hedges 1988). These issues have important geographical dimensions in that class forces and political beliefs and organization vary across territory, most obviously perhaps in contrasts between 'town' and 'country'. Uneven development typically underlies the fortunes of nationalisms, state and oppositional, and the conflicts between them. However the effects of uneven development are complex, and as we shall see the Basque case contradicts an inflated theory of nationalism which views it as a 'progressive' response to 'backwardness' and 'uneven development' (Nairn 1977). Likewise it punctures the simple-minded and pseudo-Marxist notion of 'internal colonialism' in which territory, ethnic or national oppression, and *class* exploitation are conveniently presumed to coincide (Hechter 1975). If they did the conflict would have been settled in the Basques' favour long ago. Nationalist stories are never as simple as nationalists often like to tell them. Geographical distributions and divisions are crucial, but their political implications and how nationalists and others respond to them are much more complex than these would-be general theories recognize.

Intractable conflict

Dubious theory is not simply an 'academic' problem. ETA's opponents, including many Basques, would argue that its understanding of political reality is now seriously flawed, though ETA would make similar counter-charges. The organization was formed in 1959 as a militant youth group breaking away from the then moribund PNV – Partido Nacionalista Vasco – the original party of Basque nationalism established at the end of the 19th century. In the early 1960s ETA allied itself with a series of industrial working-class strikes which were brutally suppressed by Franco. From this it developed a strategy of 'revolutionary war' based on an amalgam of socialist ideas – until then conspicuously absent from Basque nationalism – and a Third World model of national liberation struggle drawn mainly from the armed conflicts in Algeria, Vietnam and Cuba. Its partly Maoist identification of nationalist and socialist liberation rested on the notion that the Basque country was an 'internal colony' of Spain, an idea given wide currency by no less a figure than Jean-Paul Sartre (1976): a flawed idea, as we shall see, but one given credibility by the way Franco's authoritarian state had treated the Basque country ever since his bombing of the ancient Basque capital of Guernica during the Spanish Civil War.

ETA began its military campaign with the derailment of a train in 1961 and gained widespread support in the Basque country and internationally with the Burgos trials of 16 of its activists in 1970. It achieved perhaps its biggest political impact in 1973 when it blew up Franco's Prime Minister and chosen successor Admiral Carrero Blanco: this was probably decisive in upsetting Franco's plans for perpetuating authoritarian rule and certainly helped to pave the way for Spain's democratic transition after Franco's death in November 1975.

However, despite democratization, ETA persisted with its military campaign against the Spanish state, arguing that democracy was a facade and that the state, and particularly the army, was still essentially Francoist. But to most Spaniards ETA was itself a threat to the transition, providing pretexts for officers to stage a coup. Colonel Tejero failed and fear of a coup receded as democratic government became more firmly established; but there remained the more subtle fear that authoritarian repression by the democratic government threatened civil liberties and would prove counterproductive in prolonging the Basque conflict. These fears were shared by a majority of the population within the Spanish Basque country itself – indeed were felt most sharply there – and the region's internal divisions became more marked and bitter with democratization.

As a result of the industrialization process since the 19th century, about half the region's working class was of non-Basque origin, and many Basque as well as non-Basque workers supported the Spanish Socialist Party, the PSOE, rather than Basque nationalist organizations. In this situation the contradictions in trying to marry a socialist strategy, based on the working class, with a nationalist strategy, based on Basques of all classes, were particularly acute. ETA had for long been subject to political divisions for this reason, and the problem became even more acute after Franco's death. Some of ETA's socialist support split off to form Euskadiko Ezkerra – Basque Left – arguing that struggle by a small armed elite, albeit with considerable popular support, was no longer consistent with socialist advance or with mass working-class involvement in achieving nationalist objectives. There was also increasing disagreement about these objectives within the nationalist camp. The moribund PNV, essentially Christian democratic and populist, was revived with largely middle-class support, and its constitutional aspirations were effectively satisfied by the granting of limited autonomy to the new Basque regional assembly in 1980. However the assembly covered only the three provinces of

Viscaya, Guipuzcoa and Alava (Fig. 7.1), but not Navarre (which has a very different history, having been Francoist in the Civil War); and for ETA the shortcomings of autonomy were further underscored by what it saw as the continuing 'occupation' of the Basque country by the Spanish army and police. In its view the PNV, and also Euskadiko Ezkerra, had in practice been 'bought off' by a very limited and partial devolution of state power and had 'sold out' the main objective of a separate state of Euskadi. Thus on top of the historical geopolitical divisions of the Basque provinces there developed major and partly overlapping differences between autonomist and separatist nationalists, between those Basques who prioritized socialist or nationalist objectives, and between those who repudiated or continued to support armed struggle. Furthermore, all in the divided Basque nationalist camp have to compete for the region's 'hearts and minds' against Spanish national parties such as the Communists, the PSOE, and other more right-wing organizations which, in varying degrees, are imbued with a Spanish nationalism which also has considerable influence within the Basque country.

In this political and military battlefield ETA, partly for historical reasons, has retained a strong core of minority support, which fuels and is fuelled by the violent conflict with the Spanish armed forces. The most comparable separatist conflict in Europe is the 'Northern Ireland problem'. There are indeed some similarities (as well as important differences) between the history of ETA with its splits over socialism and armed struggle, its conflict with constitutional Basque nationalism, and the presence of Spanish nationalism within its region, and that of the IRA with its splits – Official and Provisional, the electoral competition between Provisional Sinn Fein and the Social Democratic and Labour Party, and the presence of British nationalism in the Northern Ireland Protestant community (see Hedges 1988; and Pringle in this volume).

As the Basque lawyer Gurutz Jauregui points out, ETA continues to survive with support from 15 per cent of the population and with 50 per cent showing an understanding of it, despite democratization and devolution: 'How can such widespread sympathy and understanding exist? The answer . . . is complex, but it can undoubtedly be found in the "smouldering war" of over 200 years between the Spanish state and the Basque country' (Jauregui 1986, 603).

'Spains' and Basques

Basque nationalism arose from the incomplete national unification of the Spanish state and the coincidence of its belated centralization with industrialization in the latter part of the 19th century. As modern territorial states, most notably England, France and Spain, developed under absolutist monarchies from the 16th century they sought to unify their territories – politically, culturally and economically – in order to secure their frontiers and the loyalty of their subjects, and to boost internal trade and economic development (see

Anderson, 1986). In Spain, however, this historical process of unification was not fully achieved. The present frontiers of the state were established in 1715 but Spain – or rather the 'Spains' in the plural – remained a loose patchwork of distinct regions.

Some of them, such as Catalonia in the northeast, had been powerful medieval kingdoms in their own right, and they retained separate political traditions, a legacy from the long and piecemeal reconquest of territories from the Moors or Arabs between the 8th and 15th centuries. The central region of Castille and the capital Madrid dominated the country, but the incorporation of regions such as Catalonia and the Basque country by the kingdom of Castille had often left local political institutions and loyalties intact, and the central state had contractual relationships with these regions rather than simply imposing its sovereignty. For instance the Basques retained their own legal-administrative system of *fueros*, which included communal ownership of some natural resources, a separate taxation system in the region and their own tariff frontiers. Each year the King of Spain travelled from Madrid to the ancient oak tree at Guernica, the symbol of Basque independence, to sign a contract with the Basque political leaders. They negotiated the region's total tax bill to the central state and controlled the distribution of the tax burden within the Basque country.

In the 18th and especially the 19th centuries regional autonomy had come under increasing attack with the Bourbon kings attempting to achieve a greater degree of centralization and standardization of political institutions, and after Napoleon's invasion of Spain a small liberal bourgeois elite which wanted a unified national market tried to impose a unitary state modelled on post-revolutionary France (Medhurst 1982, 237). The *fueros* system was weakened in the 1830s and public use of the Basque language was restricted, but centralization met stiff resistance, mainly from rural interests opposed to economic integration because they feared open agricultural competition from the rest of Spain. In the Basque country the two 'Carlist' wars of 1833 and 1872, fought under the slogan 'God and *Fueros*', were in part civil wars between these rural conservative interests and urban liberal forces. It was only in 1876 that the latter secured a decisive victory over the former, and with their victory the *fueros* were effectively dismantled.

The strains on the cohesion of the state from the persistence of cultural and political uniqueness in some of its regions were exacerbated by the unevenness of their economic development. There was rapid industrialization in parts of the Basque country and Catalonia from the 1870s but the rest of Spain remained largely agricultural and underdeveloped. The central state intensified its efforts to impose cultural and political unity on the regions, propagating Spanish nationalism and introducing Spanish language primary schools. But to some extent this was counterproductive for it stimulated the development of rival 'regional' nationalisms in a process of reaction and copying. This occurred where economic grievances coincided geographically with distinct regional cultures, most notably in the industrialized regions of Catalonia and the Basque country but also in the underdeveloped province of Galicia in the far northwest. Their unique cultures were directly threatened by 'Spanish-ization' and at the same time cultural uniqueness provided a basis for the creation of separate nationalisms and specifically nationalistic responses to a mixture of cultural, political and economic problems. In underdeveloped Galicia over 2 million people spoke a variant of Portuguese and claimed Celtic origins; in Catalonia some 5 million spoke Catalan, a well-established literary language quite distinct from Castillian Spanish; while about 2 million Basques spoke a language completely different from any other language in Europe. Galicia, Catalonia and a portion of the Basque country would all achieve their own regional parliaments for a brief period during the Spanish republic in the 1930s before Franco reimposed Spanish centralism. However, while each region had the combination of economic grievances and cultural uniqueness which provided a basis for strong nationalisms, their grievances were quite different, the Basque case is not 'typical', and it cannot be simply 'read off' as the result of 'uneven development'.

The creation of Basque nationalism

Basque nationalism arose as a reaction against political integration and against industrialization. Initially its main social base was composed of 'pre-industrial' middle sections of the population of industrial Bilbao – small entrepreneurs and shopkeepers, artisans, clerics and professional people – who were 'squeezed' between the two new classes which formed with industrialization, the big industrial and financial capitalists and the industrial working class. In the words of a Basque historian, nationalism emerged as 'the cry of Basque traditional society destroyed by industrialization and centralism ... the mythification of an archaic, democratic and happy past destroyed by Spain and factories' (quoted in Heiberg 1982, 367).

In this 'destruction' cultural, political and economic factors were closely intertwined. With the dismantling of the *fueros* in 1876 the Basque language went into sharp decline, as the Spanish-language primary schools were established and rapid industrialization led to a large influx of Spanish-speaking workers from poorer regions of Spain to the main industrial centre of Bilbao. Industrialization was based on the massive export of the area's iron ore deposits – within 25 years Bilbao was responsible for about one-fifth of the total world production of ore – and the profits were invested in local steelmaking, shipbuilding and banking. Economic growth and urbanization were spectacu-lar. By 1900 Bilbao's population had mushroomed by nearly 300 per cent. Basque shipowners owned 45 per cent of Spain's merchant fleet, and through the Basque banks a small but very powerful industrial-financial oligarchy in Bilbao (five families owned about half of all Basque capital) gained control of one-third of all Spanish investment capital (Heiberg 1982, 363–4). For instance, it was largely Basque capital which developed Madrid's transportation system and financed about half the country's hydroelectric schemes in the first three decades of the 20th century (Granados 1978).

All this was made possible by the removal of the *fueros* and political integration, but these changes had conflicting implications for different sections of the region's population. Existing class divisions within the region were exacerbated and new ones were created. These divisions were crucial factors in the emergence of Basque nationalism, and they had important *geographical* dimensions, as can be seen in the conflicting reactions to in-migration, customs integration, and the deregulation of iron ore exploitation.

Iron ore deregulation

Under the *fueros* system the rich iron ore deposits around Bilbao had been communally owned and their exploitation was strictly regulated by local municipalities which rented out mining rights on short leases to private operators. The removal of local *fueros* in 1876 meant that private capital (some with British connections) was enabled to gain outright ownership of the deposits and greatly increase the speed at which they were exploited. However the resulting industrialization made Bilbao one of the most polluted places in the world with the highest mortality rate in Europe. While it was predominantly workers and their families who died, the drastic deterioration in the 'quality of life' in Bilbao was felt particularly keenly by the 'pre-industrial' middle sections of the citizenry. They did not have a direct stake in industrialization but suffered from its effects on their environment. They were thus highly susceptible to the nationalist argument that the deterioration resulted from the loss of the *fueros* and from a 'traitorous' Basque oligarchy combining with the Spanish state to trample on the Basque tradition of communal decision-making.

Customs integration

This also had very differential effects, though here the main groups with a grievance were the rural landowners and small farmers. Up to 1876 the region had been outside the Spanish customs area, which stopped at the Ebro River on the southern edge of the Basque country (Fig. 7.1), and hence it was exempt from state customs duties. Integration brought a big increase in tariffs on consumer goods imported to the region from outside Spain, as well as leaving Basque farmers unprotected from competition from other parts of Spain. The urban oligarchy, by contrast, of course welcomed integration. Not only did it get control over the ore deposits, it also got full access to markets throughout Spain and from the 1890s stronger tariff protection from the competition of imported manufactured goods from abroad. Furthermore, two years after the traditional *fueros* were removed the oligarchy won back a new local right to decide on the distribution of the centrally fixed total tax burden for Vizcaya, Guipuzcoa and Alava (the 'Conciertos Economicos') and this enabled it to discriminate against agricultural interests, thereby further widening the division between 'town' and 'country' (Granados 1978). Thus, unlike the smaller Catalan industrialists who wanted to escape Spanish controls, the Basque industrialists and bankers were closely tied to the Spanish state and (with the one significant exception of Ramon de la Sota) they were opposed to Basque nationalism. The rural landowners and farmers, on the other hand, became a crucial part of nationalism's social base along with the 'pre-industrial' sections of Bilbao's population.

In-migration

In-migration from other parts of Spain provided a major source of cheap labour for the industrialists, and in-migrants constituted a majority of the new industrial working class of Bilbao. The Basque country was no longer unambiguously Basque. Among the rich merchants of Bilbao the Basque language had been displaced by Castillian Spanish as early as the 17th century but now the great majority of the population of the region's main city was predominantly Spanish in language and culture. Moreover most workers, including those of Basque ancestry, saw their future as lying with Spain and with socialist rather than nationalist politics. In fact they were spearheading the development of Spanish socialism – Bilbao was the industrial capital not just of the Basque country but of the whole of Spain, Spain's first general strike (defeated by the army) occurred there in 1890, its first socialist newspaper was established there in 1893, and the dominant working-class organizations in Bilbao would be the Spanish Socialist Party, the PSOE, and its trade union affiliate, the UGT.

Basque nationalism was as much a reaction against the influx of Spanish workers and what it saw as the alien and 'Godless' creed of socialism as it was a reaction against industrial pollution and the loss of traditional Basque laws and decision-making practices. The general strike in 1890 was very unsettling for small entrepreneurs. The first Basque nationalist newspaper also appeared in Bilbao in 1893 almost simultaneously with the first socialist paper, and in 1895 the nationalists of Bilbao founded the PNV, its main slogan 'Juan-Goikua eta Lagi-Zarra' – 'God and the Old Laws' – the full *fueros* system as it had existed prior to its weakening in the 1830s.

Building on the remains of the Carlist tradition the PNV under its leader Sabino de Arana-Goiri, himself from an old Carlist family, found fertile ground among people aggrieved by industrialization and integration: initially among the 'squeezed' middle strata of Bilbao, only later in the smaller towns and rural areas where Basque culture was stronger. In 1898 Arana was elected as the first nationalist deputy to the Viscayan provincial assembly in Bilbao with increased support from the urban middle class. That year had seen the final collapse of the last remaining fragment of the Spanish empire and shorn of its overseas possessions the Spanish state became less attractive to many people in the peripheral regions. Nationalist penetration into the Basque countryside however was slow, despite, or perhaps because of, its emphasis on a romanticized rural past.

Basque nationalists had to work harder than most to create their 'imagined community'. Arana, its main creator, faced severe internal obstacles, some of them still obstacles to Basque nationalism today. In contrast to Catalonia, the Basque country has never been a single political unit (though for a brief period in the Middle Ages it was all part of the larger kingdom of Navarre). The four Spanish provinces each had separate *fueros* giving them provincial autonomy from each other, and Navarre in particular had a separate history. In fact Arana had to invent the name 'Euzkadi' for their imagined unity (as he had to invent a national flag, modelled on the Union Jack). Although the Basque language, Eskerra, was a powerful symbol for nationalists it did not extend to the whole of the Basque country, Bilbao being largely outside its area, as we have seen, and also the southern parts of Alava and Navarre (Fig. 7.1). Moreover, the very factors that had enabled the language to survive in rural society – traditionally small-scale peasant communities relatively isolated from each other in mountain valleys – militated against linguistic unification. Unlike Catalan, Eskerra had never developed into a unified literary language.

Rural Basque society had arguably been more democratic than Spanish-speaking areas – Basque nationalists today claim that their region (Navarre again excepted) never experienced feudalism and that there was political equality with *all* Basques considered 'noble'. However, Arana's glorification of a unified Basque past was markedly at odds with the reality in the countryside. Ironically many of the (real) Carlist traditionalists in rural areas saw the new nationalist doctrine as a modern 'urban' fabrication, which indeed it was. Nationalist romanticizing of traditions has less appeal to people still actually *living* them than it has to those who have lost them, as to a large extent the urban Bilbaoans already had. Gellner, for instance, has argued that whereas the 'self-image of nationalism involves the stress of folk, folklore, popular culture ... nationalism becomes important precisely when these things become artificial' (Gellner 1964, 162).

Nevertheless the rural Basques, like the middle strata in Bilbao, had been harmed by Spanish integration, and they too were susceptible to two important planks of nationalist ideology: socialism and 'class warfare' were 'alien' imports from Spain, and so was the anti-clericalism of the Spanish left which ran counter to the deep religiosity of traditional Basque culture. This was particularly telling in rural communities where priests provided the political leadership.

Nationalism and 'uneven development'

Basque nationalism at its inception was reactionary in the full meaning of the word. This contrasts with some of its later, particularly post-1960, manifestations and it is completely at odds with Nairn's (1977) theory of nationalism as a 'progressive' response *against* 'backwardness'. In the 1890s Basque nationalism sought to 'put the clock back' to 1830 and earlier. Strongly influenced by contemporary trends in Catholicism, it saw liberalism as 'satanic'; it saw that liberalism was associated with Spanish centralism; and it was deeply suspicious of modern industrial capitalism (as it happens Arana was the son of a builder of wooden ships who had been displaced by the new iron shipbuilding). It was racist in its emphasis on Basque 'purity' and in its hostility towards Spanish in-migrants (*maketos*) who were seen as tainted with 'Arab blood', unlike the 'pure' Basques who had withstood Arab conquest in their mountain fastnesses. Arana excluded people of Spanish descent from his 'Basque nation', though he also excluded the 'traitorous' oligarchs who sided with Spain – 'The only true Basque is a Basque nationalist'. The latter was a political rather than a biological criterion of *exclusion* – and in the 1960s left-wing nationalists would turn it around so as to *include* in the 'Basque nation' workers of Spanish descent and others who supported their nationalist cause irrespective of their ancestry. But in the early years of Basque nationalism, being Basque in ancestry and language were the important criteria and the one oligarch who supported the nationalists, Ramon de la Sota, industrialist, financier and shipowner, tried to 're-Basqueify' Bilbao by employing only Basques in his Euskalduna (Basque-speaking) shipyard and other enterprises. He helped to fund Arana's PNV which in 1911 established its own trade union wing to combat the UGT and the growth of socialism.

In none of these respects was Basque nationalism exceptional for the time; nor is it the 'exception which proves the rule' for Nairn's general theory. On the contrary, it was very similar to many other late-19th-century nationalisms. In the era of the French Revolution nationalism had been associated with liberalism, democracy, 'modernization' and opposition to *anciens regimes*. But there was a crisis of liberalism after 1870 which resulted in 'a classic era of xenophobia' and anti-democratic nationalisms marked by pseudo-scientific notions of 'racial purity' as a basis for national exclusivity (Hobsbawm 1987, 152–60). In some respects these nationalisms, such as the 'integralist' one in France, were forerunners of nazi and fascist nationalisms. Nairn's mistake is to take the former liberal 'modernizing' nationalisms as standing for nationalism in general, and he compounds the error by applying the theory to the Basque case. Briefly, in his theory of uneven development as applied to Spain, the industrialized regions of Catalonia and the Basque country felt 'held back and exploited by the backward state power controlling them', and in these regions separatist nationalisms arose 'to . . . build middle-class states capable of effective modernization' (Nairn 1977, 185 and 187). In fact this is an accurate depiction of early Catalan nationalism. It continued in the liberal 'modernizing' tradition (by no means all nationalisms were illiberal after 1870), and Catalan industrialists and workers (based mainly on medium-sized textile factories in contrast to the 'heavy industry' and big banks of Bilbao) did indeed see the Spanish state as an obstacle to the economic and social development of Catalonia. But the situation in the Basque country, as we have seen, was very different. There, the very 'modern' Basque industrial oligarchy benefited hugely from its links with the Spanish state; the largely Spanish industrial workforce saw its future lying with Spain for rather different reasons; while to the decidedly 'non-modernizing' nationalism of Arana and his followers Spain (strange as it may seem) was dangerously liberal and progressive!

Uneven development was important in the rise of Basque nationalism but not in the way Nairn suggests. It is important to try to develop general theories of nationalism (see Anderson 1988) but it requires classification and periodization and the recognition of differences as well as similarities.

The Basques under Franco

Basque nationalist aspirations were partially and briefly satisfied during the Second Republic and then brutally squashed by Franco in 1937. Following the centralized dictatorship of Primo de Rivera (1923–30), the republic was established in 1931 and limited autonomy was granted to Catalonia. In elections that year the PNV, led by a Bilbao lawyer, José Antonio Aguirre, re-emerged as the main political force in Viscaya and Guipuzcoa, but its nationalism was still highly traditionalist and hostile towards the republic. However, in a referendum in 1933, 97 per cent of those who voted favoured autonomy and the republic belatedly agreed to the setting up of a regional assembly in 1936. The PNV dominated the new regional government with Aguirre as president, but its support for the republic was at best lukewarm.

Yet within nine months they were engulfed by the Civil War and Francoism. Guernica, the ancient capital, was bombarded by Hitler's airforce on Franco's behalf. Over 1,500 people were killed in what was seen in retrospect as a 'practice run' for the blanket bombing of cities during the Second World War. It was a calculated act against Basque nationalism, for this small city with its famous oak tree was only important as a cultural symbol of the Basques' historic autonomy. Immortalized in Picasso's famous painting of the air raid it would become a major symbol of resistance to Franco. In June 1937 his forces overran the territory of the new regional assembly, the Basque government fled across the border to France, and thousands were killed, executed, imprisoned or exiled.

The Civil War highlighted the divisions and weaknesses of Basque nationalism. Even before that its position was not as strong as the 1933 referendum on limited autonomy might suggest. In the 1936 elections which brought the

Popular Unity government to power in Madrid, the PNV had got only about one-third of the votes in the Basque country, Popular Unity got one-third and so did a pro-Spanish right-wing alliance. When Franco's Spanish nationalists attacked the republic some Basque nationalists argued that it was a purely Spanish matter and no concern of the Basques. Initially the PNV declared neutrality in the conflict. It changed its position to support for the republic some days later, though not in Alava which was overrun by Franco soon after the war started. Here the PNV kept its neutral position, while the fourth Basque province, Navarre, was openly pro-Franco from the start and retained its provincial institutions while Franco was attacking and repressing the Basques of Viscaya and Guipuzcoa.

Basque traditionalism, in its nationalist and its pre-nationalist Carlist forms, was ideologically closer to Franco's Spanish nationalism, also conservatively religious, than it was to the left-inclined republicans with their 'Godless socialism'. Indeed, it was only on the national question, the issue of regional autonomy, and whether Spanish government should be decentralized or centralized, that the Basque nationalism of the 1930s was diametrically at loggerheads with Francoism.

However, Franco's often indiscriminate repression in the Basque country over the next four decades had the effect of transforming the forces of Basque nationalism. It resulted in the bulk of the population becoming more united politically than at any time before or since, though it also exacerbated some of the divisions, and knowledge of it is crucial for understanding the contemporary situation in the region. Viscaya and Guipuzcoa which had opposed Franco, however reluctantly, lost the last remnants of institutional autonomy, whereas neutral Alava and Francoist Navarre retained some autonomy. In Bilbao, while nationalist families were being hounded, the Basque industrial-financial oligarchy retained its loyal and lucrative connections with the central state, though again with the notable exception of the de Sota family which went into exile in England and Argentina, its possessions in Spain expropriated. Franco's repression of Basque culture, and of the region's working class in particular, was, however, to prove counterproductive from the viewpoint of his own Castillian Spanish nationalism and belief in a highly centralized state.

The Basque language – 'fit only for dogs' in Franco's choice phrase – was outlawed, as was Basque folk music. So were their counterparts in Catalan culture, and no newspapers or books could be published legally in Spain in either language. In the Basque case, restrictions on the language had a long history going back to 1876, and earlier to the 1830s, but the enforced cultural assimilation and the imposition of Spanish-language education was more thoroughgoing under Franco. The numbers able to speak Basque continued to decline up to the 1960s, and less than a quarter of the region's whole population now use the language. While it had died out as an everyday language in the southern half of the region (Fig. 7.1), its use within its geographical area is patchy, being mainly confined to the country areas and small towns of its 'core' area of Guipuzcoa. Linguistic oppression does 'work', at least at a cultural level, and the Basque case is similar to some other 'peripheral' or sub-state nationalisms, such as that of Wales, where a major symbol of national distinctiveness is actually weak within its own region or country compared to the dominant language of the state. On the other hand, the oppression generated a strong cultural reaction in the Basque country, particularly in the 1960s and 1970s, as in Catalonia, and this helped to fuel support for Basque nationalism from communities which had long ceased to use Basque themselves (including some Spanish in-migrants whose families had never spoken Basque). With pressure from Basque nationalism there was a very limited relaxation of cultural oppression in the early 1970s – ETA has organized some Basque-language schools, Ikastolas, in the 1960s – and in 1973 some use of the language was allowed in nursery schools.

Not all of the relative decline of the language was due to cultural oppression, however. Some was due to continuing economic development and the in-migration of more Spanish-speakers to augment the region's labour force. The postwar international boycott of Spain had only limited effect, particularly after it was breached by a 'cold war' USA in 1953, and from the late 1950s there was considerable economic growth, much of it in the already industrialized Basque country. In the mid-1960s, Viscaya and Guipuzcoa had the highest *per caput* incomes in Spain, nearly twice the national average; but by now about 40 per cent of household heads in the Basque country were non-Basque in origin.

For most of this period, the main opposition to Franco came from the industrial working class – with trade unions and the illegal Communist Party playing a key role. Basque opposition had, however, peaked in the wake of the victory over fascism in the Second World War and the imposition of the UN boycott in 1946. In 1947 a general strike of 100 000 workers had temporarily united the PNV and socialist groups but this opposition declined, and during the 1950s the main opposition to Franco came from Catalonia. The PNV had become a moribund organization, its exiled and ageing leadership out of touch with events in Spain.

In these circumstances ETA developed the more radical separatist brand of contemporary Basque nationalism. In a series of guerilla operations it transformed the political situation not only in the Basque country but in Spain generally. ETA's military campaign provoked severe repression as it was intended to (Jauregui 1986, 597): a large influx of Spanish military and paramilitary police (the Guardia Civil), arbitrary arrests, torture, summary trials. The ETA's assassination of a police torturer in 1968 led to mass arrests, further torture, and the imposition of a 'state of emergency'. This, together with the cultural oppression, heightened local hostility to the Spanish state, including from non-Basque 'immigrant' workers. The 1970 Burgos trials of 16 ETA activists sparked off massive protest strikes some led by revolutionary groups to the left of the Communist Party. They also resulted in the number of

Guardia Civil in the Basque country being increased to 15 000 (a quarter of the entire Spanish force), and there were large pro-regime demonstrations in Spain by army officers and Franco's Falange party. But ETA had succeeded in putting Franco's regime in the international spotlight and in heightening the internal resistance to Franco in other parts of Spain, particularly Catalonia. In the 1971 Spanish parliamentary elections (for the one-sixth of Cortes members then chosen by popular vote) there was large-scale abstention in the Basque country and elsewhere: in Viscaya province only 33 per cent voted, in the city of San Sebastian only 26 per cent. In 1975, just before Franco's death, over 2000 Basques were in Spanish prisons, and 250 of them had been tortured, according to Amnesty International's conservative estimate. Further state executions of Basques led again to massive strikes, in Catalonia as well as the Basque country. Successful in some respects, ETA's orientation on the working class and on armed struggle was, however, highly contradictory.

Nationalist resurgence and 'internal colonialism'

The reasons for the resurgence and radicalization of Basque nationalism in the 1960s were rooted in the particular circumstances of the region. But, as with the different character of Basque nationalism in the 1890s, they were related to wider contemporary trends. There was a general international resurgence of separatist and devolutionary nationalisms in the 'peripheries' of advanced industrial countries during the 1960s and 1970s – for example in Northern Ireland, Scotland and Wales (see Anderson 1989), in Brittany and Quebec, and in Flanders and Wallonia in Belgium – and most were more radically 'left-wing' than their antecedent nationalisms. They were confronted by some of the same problems and presented with some of the same opportunities. These revolved around increasing 'internationalization' – economic, cultural and political. On the one hand, this 'internationalization' was seen as eroding regional cultures and reducing local economic and political power, on the other, it was seen as increasing the potential viability of small states. For instance, the growth of supra-state bodies such as the European Community or NATO provided an 'umbrella' which gave small states some of the benefits (e.g. a large 'internal' market, an adequate 'external' defence) which in the 19th century had been confined to large- or medium-sized states. Conversely, 'peripheral' nationalists could increasingly argue that medium-sized states such as the United Kingdom or Spain were no longer independent economic or military units. Belonging to them was now less attractive, particularly when shorn of former empires. If tiny Luxembourg could have the political independence to deal directly with the European Parliament in Brussels, why not Scotland or Brittany? Furthermore, with political decolonization overseas, many small colonies were now independent states. If Dahomey (1960) or Gambia (1965) could have seats at the United Nations, why not Wales or the Basque country?

149

The success of anti-colonial nationalism encouraged the more radical 'peripheral' nationalists. They borrowed the anti-imperialist rhetoric and in some cases the strategy of anti-colonial struggles and sought to combine them with a more socialist orientation in recognition of the need to come to terms with working-class aspirations and political power. Anti-imperialism and socialism were neatly if somewhat fraudulently combined in the influential theory of 'internal colonialism' in which cultural-national and class òppression were presumed to coincide (e.g. see Hechter 1975, 30–4).

In the Basque case the workers, Basque and non-Basque alike, had suffered from Franco's repression, and for much of the postwar period they constituted the main opposition to Francoism. Even before any theoretical elaboration ETA recognized that the national and class struggles had somehow to be united and it was this which led to its radical redefinition of nationalism and the 'Basque nation'. Where the traditional nationalism of the PNV was socially conservative, Catholic and racist towards Spanish-descended workers, the new nationalism had to come to terms with an increased Spanish component in the working class, considerable intermarriage between Basques and non-Basques, and a further decline of the Basque language. In consequence, ETA's nationalism became non-confessional, despite the continuing importance of Catholicism in Basque culture, and rejected 'race' and language criteria of membership in the 'Basque nation' (Jauregui 1986, 593). In its more fully political and less exclusive redefinition, the 'Basque nation' included everyone in the region who opposed Franco's Spanish state and who thereby supported the Basque nationalist cause or could be won to it.

'Internal colonialism' was developed to unite the national and the class struggles theoretically, and it was influential because it reproduced nationalist ideology and obscured the contradictions between them. Typically it 'swept them under a carpet' of pseudo-Marxist rationalization. Hechter, its main Anglo-Saxon proponent, implies that it derives from Lenin and Gramsci but they used the term 'internal colony' in very different senses, both from each other and certainly from Hechter (Hechter 1975, 8; Lenin 1964, 568; Gramsci 1957, 28). In fact, 'internal colonialism' derives from 'dependency theories' about the 'exploitation' of colonial or neo-colonial countries in the 'periphery' of the world economy by metropolitan countries in the 'core'; and the transfer to a qualitatively different context compounds the theories' original inadequacies – their tendency to obscure class divisions and dynamics within the 'periphery', to over-externalize 'blame' to the 'core', and to reduce class relations to spatial relations between 'core' and 'periphery' (see, e.g. Munck 1985, 12–15). The (albeit incomplete) territorial unification of the state means that the economic and cultural differences between so-called 'internal colonies' and 'cores' are generally not nearly so great as those between metropolitan countries and separate colonies or former colonies overseas, nor is there the same coincidence or causal connection between cultural oppression and economic exploitation. Indeed, the concept of 'exploitation' in 'internal colonialism' often refers to oppression rather than to the extraction of an economic surplus, despite the theory's claimed Marxist parentage; and, as in 'dependency theory', 'exploitation' is often seen as a relationship between 'horizontally' delimited territorial groups rather than between 'vertically' differentiated social groups or classes which have varying geographical distributions.

However, as Jauregui (1986, 596) notes, Francoism had 'virtually converted ETA's colonial mirage into a reality'; and Jean-Paul Sartre (1976), with a more sophisticated version of 'internal colonialism' than Hechter's, supported ETA's contention:

> Euskadi is a colony of Spain ... The forcible suppression of the Basque language is cultural genocide ... the Basque wage earner is ... a colonized worker ... not merely exploited, as the Castillian worker is exploited, who wages a 'chemically pure' class struggle, but deliberately super-exploited in that he ... receives a lower wage ... despite the over-industrialization ... there are two essential factors in a classical example of colonialism: pillage, fiscal or other, of the colonized country and super exploitation of the workers ... 'Spain' super-exploits the Basques *because they are Basques*. (Sartre 1976, 159–64, emphasis in original).

However, Sartre himself has already said (161–2) that Spanish in-migrants were also 'super-exploited', and the allegedly lower wages than in Madrid and other Spanish cities may not be comparing like with like given their different occupational structures. In any case the notion of 'super-exploited colonized workers' has to be set against the fact that in the mid-1960s *per caput* incomes in Viscaya and Guipuzcoa were nearly twice the Spanish average and large numbers of Spaniards were choosing to migrate to jobs in the 'colony' (see above). His 'fiscal pillage' refers to discriminatory state taxes and tariffs which meant that the Basque country was subsidizing less productive parts of Spain.

It is not unusual, of course, for there to be some cross-subsidization between rich and poor regions of a state, but accurately measuring the *net* balance of all the financial flows is often difficult, and Sartre's view of a productive Basque 'colony' being dragged down by a more backward Spain has similarities with Nairn's incorrect explanation of Basque nationalism's creation. But where Nairn thought that Basque employers wanted to be free of Spain for this reason, Sartre is closer to the mark in seeing that Franco's centralist policy involved 'the complicity of the large employers of Biscay and Guipuzcoa'. However, he calls them 'collaborationists whose centralism spells ruin to the Basque economy', which on the face of it seems even more implausible. Collaborationists in their own economic ruin? Whatever the fate of the workers, 'the large employers' profited hugely from 'centralism', as we have seen, and the Basque country not only remained Spain's leading industrial region but experienced significant growth during Franco's rule.

Sartre was motivated by a commendable opposition to Franco (and to the strong centralist tradition in his own country); existing state frontiers corresponded 'to the interests of the dominant classes and not to popular aspirations'; Basque independence could 'only be obtained by armed struggle' (Sartre 1976, 155 and 169). He was right in emphasizing the inadequacy of a 'chemically pure' class struggle which failed to engage with the national question (though even this notion of 'chemical purity' is suspect for where or when can workers afford to ignore the state and politics?). But, interestingly, he does not deal with the splits in ETA beyond contrasting its heroic armed struggle with 'conservative' defections from 'the anti-colonialist struggle ... to wage, with the Spanish workers, "the chemically pure" class war' (Sartre 1976, 169–70). This formulation hardly does justice to the various groups expelled from ETA by its more militaristic wing, and it completely skates over the reasons for all the splits and the problems of combining a working-class struggle for socialism with an armed struggle for national independence by a clandestine group. For instance, one requires openness, democracy and active mass involvement to succeed, the other requires secrecy and military command structures. A clandestine military elite is likely to become isolated from the mass of workers, and its support is often confined geographically to relatively small 'core' areas. There can also be very direct clashes of interest if military action destroys workplaces and jobs or, even worse, results in workers inadvertently being killed, as happened when ETA bombed a nuclear power station. Furthermore, workers in the Basque country, of whatever ancestry, had a real interest in making common cause with workers in the rest of Spain. They often faced the same problems and the same employers, and to a much greater extent than is generally the case in 'real' colonial situations. In short, the geopolitical complexities of the Basque country fail to live up (or down) even to Sartre's sophisticated version of 'internal colonialism'. The theory is counterproductive to the cause of separatist nationalisms, as it is for anyone trying to make analytical sense of them.

After Franco

With socialist defections and expulsions ETA became more militaristic and 'Third Worldist'. According to Jauregui, the rhetoric of 'internal colonialism' only 'served as ... minimum ideological support to the armed struggle', in contrast to ETA's early contribution in redefining the 'Basque nation' and debating a range of political and cultural issues: 'The great contradiction between a highly developed social and economic reality and a third world-style revolutionary strategy still exists ... To all intents and purposes since 1970 ETA has been ideologically dead' (Jauregui 1986, 598). This judgement may be harsh but certainly ETA was not equipped to respond to the changed situation after Franco's death. Its response was to deny that anything had really changed.

In 1975 the King of Spain granted limited legal recognition to the Basque and Catalan languages; in 1976 Viscaya and Guipuzcoa were granted concessions on taxation; and in 1977 ETA's boycott of Spanish parliamentary elections left it politically isolated – over 80 per cent of the Basque country electorate voted, in marked contrast to the large-scale abstention of 1971. In 1978 the new Spanish constitution introduced a regionally devolved state structure to promote political stability; in 1980 the new Basque assembly got overwhelming approval in the Basque country; and in 1981 Tejero's 'anti-devolution' Francoist coup attempt was a farcical failure (though this was by no means a foregone conclusion at the time).

ETA, probably more than any other single organization, could take credit for forcing devolution on Spain. The Basques, together with the Catalans, encouraged and 'pulled along' weaker regional movements such as those in Galicia and Andalusia, and the principle of limited regional autonomy was extended to the whole country partly to 'dilute' special treatment for the Catalans and Basques.

But ETA's threadbare Third Worldism meant it was not theoretically equipped to benefit from the more complex political situation which it had helped to create, and the PNV was the main beneficiary. When the obvious enemy, Francoist centralism, was replaced by the more subtle 'regionalism as reform' (Hebbert 1987), the divisions within Basque nationalism, and between nationalists and centralists, together with the related geographical contrasts, all intensified, as can be seen in the electoral statistics between 1977 and 1984. In 1977 centralist parties did well in Alava and Navarre, nationalist ones in Viscaya and, especially, Guipuzcoa. The 'centralist' Communist Party, despite its long tradition of struggle in the Basque country, failed to get any seats – a salutary warning that ignoring nationalist aspirations in the 'periphery' can be interpreted as support for the state nationalism of the 'core'. Devolution altered but did not diminish Basque nationalism.

ETA may have been 'ideologically dead' but by the 1979 elections it was linked to a new separatist coalition of leftist groups, Herri Batasuna – sometimes translated as 'United People' (typifying nationalist wishful thinking). It won (but did not take up) three parliamentary seats and the PNV won seven. In 1980 HB won 11 seats in the new 60-seat Basque assembly, benefiting from a big swing towards nationalist parties (42 seats in total) and away from centralist ones. The swing was boosted by protest against industrial decline in the Basque country and also by central government encouragement of the constitutional nationalists of the PNV as a means of weakening support both for the separatists of ETA-HB, and for the socialist opposition PSOE. The PNV got 25 seats, Euskadiko Ezkerra 6, and the PNV was handed an absolute majority by HB refusing to take up its 11 seats. This was effectively repeated in 1984 when the PNV won 32 seats in an enlarged 75-seat assembly (EE won 6, PSOE 19, CP9) and HB with (a relatively reduced) 11 seats again refused to attend (like Sinn Fein it only participated in local councils). It saw acceptance of devolution as 'selling out' a separate independent Euskadi. HB's non-attendance effectively allowed autonomist nationalists to monopolize assembly power, and lost it some support. Yet HB still managed to get 15 per cent of the vote in 1984. PSOE got 23 per cent, CP 9 per cent, and EE 8 per cent while the PNV got 42 per cent. As Sartre (1976, 168) had in a sense correctly predicted, the democratization of Spain had greatly increased the proportion of Basque nationalists 'allied to the oppressor ... and content with concessions'.

The concessions are quite limited: 'sovereignty devolved but not divided' (as it would be in a fully federalist state structure), in order to integrate Spain and undercut separatism (Hebbert 1987, 242). On the other hand, the 'halfway house' between a unitary and a federal state generates continuing confrontation between the 'centre' and the 'periphery' which is all grist to the nationalist mill. It may not prove a lasting solution and it is possible that European integration will lead to a reassertion of centralism (Hebbert 1987, 248). Either way ETA and HB still have everything to fight for. Democratization changed the context of the conflict, but democracy *per se* cannot solve it for the conflict is about the institutional and territorial framework within which democracy should take place.

The impacts of geography

The conflict is 'about geography', and we have seen how shifting geographical distributions and divisions have been an integral element in all its main historical phases. The Basque case highlights the main political issues involved in separatism and devolution, and while its particular combinations and outcomes cannot be 'read off' to other conflicts it exemplifies many of the ways in which geography presents opportunities and obstacles to the contending political forces.

In summary, the impacts of geography can be seen at several levels. National conflicts are influenced by their wider international context, whether, as in the Basque case, it is the influence of late-19th-century illiberalism and ethnic xenophobia, or the anti-colonialism of the 1960s and the increasing internationalization which, perhaps paradoxically, increased the potential viability of small states and regenerated and radicalized separatist nationalism. At the level of the would-be nation-state, we saw that incomplete and belated homogenization generated oppositional nationalism in 'peripheral' regions. The state's response oscillated between centralist repression and regionalist concessions, the former damaging its international standing and civil liberties in the state as a whole, the latter, while stopping well short of separatist demands, altering the structure of the state itself.

But it is within the 'peripheral' region that geography's impact is most telling. The region, or rather some parts of it, are the main site of the conflict which is why *internal* geopolitical divisions are so important. Contrary to what its nationalists might like to think, there is no simple polarity of the 'periphery' versus the 'core'. Instead we typically find a variety of internal divisions which crucially weaken nationalism: in the Basque case historical divisions between provinces, between 'town' and 'country', and between linguistic, ethnic, class and other groupings, all of which have varying geographical distributions. There are parts of the Basque country – particularly the small cities and more rural areas where the indigenous culture is strongest – in which separatists have very substantial, sometimes majority, local support. But other parts – most notably the whole southern edge of the Basque country – are almost totally integrated into Spanish culture and imbued with Spanish nationalism; and in between there are large 'intermediate' areas where local space is shared.

These different geographies and the different political responses to them preclude easy generalization. Geographers might welcome general theories which incorporate geography in their causal explanations, but we saw that 'internal colonialism' was counterproductive both for theoretical understanding and as a guide to practical politics. It was also clear from the Basque case that 'uneven development' as an explanation of the rise of nationalism is at best a crude over-generalization. But geography is no less important for that. Areas with deep-rooted separatist traditions constitute problems for the state which an appeal to democratic majority decisions cannot solve, though they can bring pressure to bear on the often 'war-weary' people in the main conflict areas. Conversely, the fact that other parts of the region are integrated, or partially integrated, into the dominant political culture of the state means that the separatists cannot achieve their objectives by peaceful means either. The structural circumstances encourage both sides to resort to physical force. It is this which gives the little wars of peripheral nationalism their intractability. They are largely 'civil wars' within the 'peripheral' region, and their violence reflects the weakness as much as the strength of separatist nationalism.

Note

1 My thanks to the following – none responsible for the viewpoint of this chapter but all helpful in providing information: Jose Miguel Abando, Javier Arzalluz (President, PNV), Manuel Escudero (PSOE), Pilar Gore, Carlos Gorostiza (PSOE), Vicente Granados, Gurutz Jauregui, Maria Moisa, Juan Okinena (Herri Batasuna), Hugh Phillips, Pedro de Sota (great grandson of Ramon de la Sota) and Ramon Tamames.

References

Anderson, J. 1986. Nationalism and geography. Chapter 6 in *The rise of the modern state*, J. Anderson (ed.), 115–42. Brighton: Harvester.
Anderson, J. 1988. Nationalist ideology and territory. Chapter 2 in *Nationalism,*

self-determination and political geography, R. J. Johnston, D. Knight and E. Kofman (eds), 18–39. London: Croom Helm.

Anderson, J. 1989. Nationalisms in a disunited kingdom. Chapter 3 in *The political geography of contemporary Britain*, J. Mohan (ed.), 35–50. London: Macmillan.

Gellner, E. 1964. Nationalism. Chapter 7 in *Thought and change*, 147–78. London: Weidenfeld & Nicolson.

Gramsci, A. 1957. *The modern prince and other essays*. New York: International Publishers.

Granados, V. 1979. The nationalist question within the Spanish state: the case of Catalonia and Euskadi. Unpublished MS, Centre for Urban and Regional Studies, University of Birmingham.

Hebbert, M. 1987. Regionalism: a reform concept and its application to Spain. *Environment and Planning C: Government and Policy* **5**, 239–50.

Hechter, M. 1975. *Internal colonialism: the Celtic fringe in British national development, 1536–1966*. London: Routledge & Kegan Paul.

Hedges, C. 1988. Problems in combining labour and nationalist politics: Irish nationalists in Northern Ireland. Chapter 7 in *Nationalism, self-determination and political geography*, R. J. Johnston, D. Knight and E. Kofman (eds), 102–16. London: Croom Helm.

Heiberg, M. 1982. Urban politics and rural culture: Basque nationalism. Chapter 9 in *The politics of territorial identity*, S. Rokkan and D. W. Urwin (eds), 355–87. London: Sage.

Hobsbawm, E. 1987. *The age of empire: 1875–1914*. London: Weidenfeld & Nicolson.

Jauregui, G. 1986. National identity and political violence in the Basque country. *European Journal of Political Research* **14**, 587–605.

Lenin, V. I. 1964. *The development of captialism in Russia*. Moscow: Progress.

Medhurst 1982. Basques and Basque nationalism. Chapter 8 in *National separatism*, C. H. Williams (ed.), 235–61. Cardiff: University of Wales Press.

Munck, R. 1985. *Politics and dependency in the Third World: the case of Latin America*. London: Zed.

Nairn, T. 1977. *The breakup of Britain*. London: New Left Books.

Sartre, J.-P. 1976. The Burgos trials, Appendix A in *A case for the Balkanization of practically everyone: the new nationalism*, M. Zwerin (ed.). London: Wildwood House.

156

8

Separation and integration: the case of Ireland

DENNIS PRINGLE

Religious differences, compounded by differences in national identity, have long been a source of communal tension and conflict in Ireland. The first section in this chapter outlines the historical background to this conflict, and explains how separation (in the form of partition between Northern Ireland and the Republic, and also between both parts and Britain) was adopted in an attempt to satisfy disparate demands. Total separation between the two groups, however, proved impossible, with the result that significant numbers found themselves stranded as a minority in a state dominated by the other group. The second and third sections of the chapter consider the extent to which the majority and minority communities have subsequently remained separate or integrated at a more local level in Northern Ireland and the Republic respectively. Relations between the two groups are clearly more strained in Northern Ireland than in the Republic: the final section considers the extent to which this may be attributed to the higher degree of integration found in the Republic.

Integration and separation may be viewed as the opposite poles of a continuum, although it is doubtful whether either extreme is actually found in reality. It is difficult to conceive of situations in which two communities in close proximity could remain totally separate. Conversely, if they were to be totally integrated they would, by definition, cease to remain separate and would form a single community. In practice a balance tends to be struck between these two extremes. It is suggested that this balance may be conceptualized as operating on at least four 'levels': spatial, social, ideological, and demographic. At the lowest level, spatial integration simply entails the use by both groups of the same space; social integration implies social interaction or even co-operation between the two groups, although each may attempt to minimize non-essential contacts with the other group; ideological integration refers to the emergence of shared ideas and common identities; whilst demographic integration may arise if the two groups inter-breed. Unless rules are adopted to share the offspring of such unions between the two groups, demographic integration may eventually result in total integration of the two groups, or the assimilation of one group by the other.

157

The historical background

Ireland was formally brought under English crown control in 1171 when Henry II, backed by a large army, successfully secured the submission of the Gaelic nobility and the Anglo-Norman barons (who had invaded Ireland two years previously with armies of their own). However, by the early 16th century, effective crown control was confined to the Pale – a small area in the east centred on Dublin. The Tudor kings and queens of England, fearing that Ireland might be used as a base to launch attacks on England by England's continental rivals, consequently embarked on the reconquest of Ireland. This continued sporadically throughout most of the 16th century, and generally entailed planting land confiscated from rebellious Gaelic or Gaelicized Norman leaders with loyal English subjects. The number of settlers from England, however, remained fairly small.

By the end of the 16th century most of Ireland, with the exception of Ulster (which remained the most Gaelic and rebellious part), had been brought under effective English control. The eventual defeat of the Ulster Gaelic chieftains in 1603 at the end of a long war, followed by their flight in 1607, created the conditions for the Plantation of Ulster which was initiated shortly afterwards. The Ulster Plantation proved (from an English or British point of view) to be highly successful. Ulster, in the course of the 17th century, was gradually transformed into the most British part of Ireland through the large-scale migration of settlers from England and, more especially, Scotland. The new Ulster landlords found it relatively easy to attract land-hungry Scots as tenant farmers, especially after the area became politically more stable in the second half of the century.

Further longlasting changes occurred following two other political upheavals in the 17th century: the Cromwellian wars in the 1640s, and the Williamite wars in the 1690s. Both resulted in large-scale confiscation of land from those who supported the losing side, followed by grants to soldiers and adventurers who had supported the victors. Given that most of the Gaelic and Gaelicized Norman nobility had the misfortune to support the losing side in both wars, the net effect of these confiscations was a major transfer in landownership from the native Irish to new English landlords. However, these changes in landownership, which had their greatest impact in Leinster and Munster, were not associated with a large-scale influx of migrants, as had occurred in Ulster.

By the beginning of the 18th century, Ireland was inhabited by three fairly distinct groups of people: the 'native Irish' (including Gaelicized Normans and other culturally assimilated groups); the 'new English', who were numerically fairly small but who controlled most of the land and political power in the colony; and the 'new Scots', who were more numerous but were mainly confined to Ulster. These three groups were reflected by religious differences. Ireland had been relatively unaffected by the Reformation in the 16th century, and consequently most of the 'native Irish' remained Catholic; England had broken away from the Catholic Church, hence many of the English settlers were Anglicans (i.e. Church of Ireland); whereas Scotland had been strongly influenced by Calvinism, and consequently most of the Scottish settlers were nonconformists. Presbyterianism became the dominant religion amongst the Scots in Ulster following its introduction from Scotland in the 1630s.

There would appear to have been relatively little intermixing between these three groups, each of which appears to have been content to remain separate. Although a series of penal laws, which discriminated against non-Anglicans in general and Catholics in particular, were passed in the early 18th century, their prime function was probably to defend the privileged position of the Anglican landowning elite (or 'Protestant Ascendancy'), rather than to force other groups to conform religiously (or integrate). Likewise, the other groups apparently made comparatively little attempt to proselytize.

By the latter part of the 18th century, frustrations caused by resentment against both the domination of the Dublin Parliament by the Protestant Ascendancy, and by Westminster's treatment of Ireland as a whole, led to demands by a group calling themselves the United Irishmen for unity (or integration) between 'Protestant, Catholic and Dissenter' and separation from Britain. The United Irishmen, who initially gained most of their support from the Presbyterians in Ulster, were effectively the founders of Irish republicanism: a political movement represented today by the IRA (Irish Republican Army). Most Ulster Presbyterians, however, for reasons discussed below, are now staunchly unionist and vehemently anti-IRA.

Following the defeat of the United Irish rebellion in 1798, the British government recognized that reforms were required to tackle the political crisis. The Irish Parliament was consequently persuaded to disband, and Ireland was more fully integrated into the British state by the Act of Union (1800), under which Ireland became an integral part of the United Kingdom.

Political unification was reinforced by integration at other levels throughout the 19th century. For example, improvements in transportation, associated with the industrial revolution, reduced the travel time between Ireland and Britain, whilst the gradual growth of state intervention did much to eliminate cultural differences (e.g. English became the language of education in the state-initiated national schools). However, a number of factors, not least of which were a number of basic geographical considerations, combined to limit the level of integration. Ireland's location relative to the core of the British state – both peripheral and separated by sea – discouraged population movements from Britain to Ireland and hence lessened the impact of British cultural influences within Ireland, whilst the apparent sparsity of mineral resources (especially high-grade coal) severely restricted the potential for industrial development. Ireland became increasingly integrated into the British economy, but as a periphery providing unprocessed agricultural goods and cheap labour. Resentment of this peripheral position and of its social consequences – unemployment, poverty, famine, and large-scale emigration – was a major factor underlying the growth of Irish nationalism and eventually an upsurge in separatism in the middle and late 19th century (Pringle 1985).

The situation in Ulster was somewhat different. In contrast to most of the rest of Ireland, the 19th century was a boom period in east Ulster. Belfast developed rapidly as a major industrial city, based upon textile, shipbuilding and engineering industries, in much the same manner as other industrial cities in England and Scotland in the 19th century. Much of this prosperity, however, was dependent upon free access to Britain and the empire. The raw materials used by Belfast's industries had to be imported, whereas the major part of their output was exported. Separation from Britain would have meant economic disaster in Belfast. This fact was fully appreciated by industrialists and workers alike: Irish nationalism, with its separatist aspirations, consequently found little support. In terms of national outlook, the people of Belfast and the surrounding area (or at least its Protestant majority, including the Presbyterians) had been fully integrated into Britain by the end of the 19th century and regarded themselves as British. Ulster Protestants, in response to the growth of Irish nationalism, became ardently unionist.

The nationalist–unionist cleavage corresponded closely to a religious divide between Catholics and Protestants. Nationalism did not consciously exclude Protestants – indeed the concept of the Irish nation being comprised of people of all religions is one of the key tenets of Irish nationalism in general, and Irish republicanism in particular – but in order to highlight the separate distinctiveness of the Irish nation *vis-à-vis* Britain, Irish nationalists emphasized and glorified Ireland's Gaelic heritage (i.e. language, folklore, culture, and so forth). Protestants, however, due to the lack of integration in previous centuries, found it difficult to identify with the Gaelic Irish nation defined by the nationalists. Irish nationalism, because of its Gaelic emphasis, consequently tended to become coterminous with Catholicism.

Protestants of different denominations also tended to coalesce in the face of the perceived common threat posed by the growth in social power of the Catholic Church, following the removal of the last of the penal laws in 1829. In the absence of a strong secular Catholic middle class, the Catholic clergy were perceived to exert an exceptionally strong influence over the minds of the Catholic people, who formed a substantial majority in Ireland as a whole. This influence became increasingly significant after 1884 when the extension of the franchise resulted in large numbers of previously disenfranchised Catholics gaining the right to vote. The social power of the erstwhile Protestant Ascendancy, following the Act of Union and the Churches Act (1869), had, meanwhile, all but disappeared by the end of the 19th century. Presbyterian resentment of the Protestant Ascendancy in the 18th century was consequently transferred to a growing concern about the possibility of a Catholic Ascendancy in the 19th century. Protestants of all denominations therefore sought common cause in the face of the perceived Catholic threat, and in particular turned to Britain and to unionism as the guarantor of religious freedom.

By 1920 the level of conflict between nationalists and the British authorities, and between unionists and nationalists, was so great that separation became the only feasible solution. In effect, a three-way separation was introduced by the Government of Ireland Act (1920) and the Anglo-Irish Treaty (1921):

(1) Nationalist demands for separation from Britain were partly satisfied by granting independence to 26 'southern' counties with an overwhelming nationalist majority. The new state was initially called the Irish Free State, but following a further severance of links with Britain and the Commonwealth in 1948 it was officially renamed the Republic of Ireland.

(2) Given unionist opposition to the threat of being dominated within an all-Ireland state by nationalists and the Catholic Church, six counties with a combined unionist majority were separated from the rest of Ireland to form Northern Ireland, which remained part of the United Kingdom.

(3) A partial separation occurred between Northern Ireland and Britain. Although Northern Ireland remained part of the United Kingdom, and continued to send MPs to Westminster, it was granted a significant degree of local autonomy. Elections were held periodically to elect MPs to a local Parliament (which met from 1932 onwards at Stormont on the outskirts of Belfast). The Northern Ireland government was granted considerable powers over internal affairs, with very little interference from Westminster. The original reason for this partial separation from Britain may have been to provide a mechanism for unification with the rest of Ireland, and complete separation from Britain, if a majority within Northern Ireland were in favour of such a change. This option, however, was very quickly rejected by the Northern Ireland unionist majority.

Partial separation had never been a unionist demand. In fact, unionists were initially opposed to both the separation of the Free State from Britain and to the separation of Northern Ireland from the Free State, but they came to accept both as necessary compromises. However, they also quickly came to appreciate the power which partial separation from Britain conferred upon them. The activities of the Stormont government were consequently a major source of grievance amongst Northern Ireland's nationalist minority, prior to the abolition of Stormont and the introduction of 'direct rule' from Westminster in 1972.

The following sections consider the implications of these separations for integration between nationalist and unionist, Catholic and Protestant, communities within Northern Ireland and the Republic of Ireland respectively.

Northern Ireland

When first created, Northern Ireland had a 2:1 Protestant:Catholic majority. Given the events which preceded partition, religious affiliation, national identity and political allegiances were generally very closely interrelated: most Protestants regarded themselves as British and unionist, whilst most Catholics regarded themselves as Irish and nationalist. The national question was by far the most important issue in formal politics.

The same is true today: the major cleavage in Northern Ireland politics is still between unionists and nationalists, although there are secondary internal divisions on both sides. The unionist majority is strongly in favour of maintaining the link with Britain, but there are internal differences of opinion over the optimal balance between separation from and integration with the rest of the United Kingdom. Some unionists would like to see Northern Ireland more fully integrated into the United Kingdom whilst others would prefer the reintroduction of a regional Parliament, possibly with a degree of 'power-sharing' guarantees for the minority. The nationalist minority, on the other hand, favours complete separation from Britain and unification with the Republic, but there are considerable differences of opinion within the minority as to how unification should be achieved and about what form a united Irish state would take – most Northern nationalists see unification as much more than a simple extension of the Republic of Ireland. Unionists, needless to say, are totally opposed to unification: if 'abandoned' by Britain (a perpetual unionist fear), most unionists would probably opt for an independent Ulster rather than contemplate living within a united Ireland.

Given that unionists are unlikely to have a change of heart, and given that nationalists are unlikely to form a majority within Northern Ireland in the immediate future, the likelihood of a united Ireland must be regarded at present as, at most, a distant possibility. The persistence of the national question as the dominant issue in Northern Ireland politics therefore requires some explanation. Why, for example, are party politics in Northern Ireland not centred to a much greater extent around class issues, as in Britain?

The persistence of the national question can perhaps be better understood if the internal politics of Northern Ireland are viewed in a broader perspective, using what is sometimes referred to as a 'double minority' model (Douglas and Boal 1982, Poole 1983, Stewart 1977, Whyte 1978). Catholics are in a minority within Northern Ireland, but viewed from an all-Ireland perspective Protestants are also a minority – in fact, in Ireland as a whole they are outnumbered by Catholics by approximately 4:1. Northern Ireland Protestants are consequently extremely apprehensive about the possibility of a united Ireland, as such a change would transform them from forming a strong majority into forming a weak minority. This has engendered what is sometimes referred to as a 'siege mentality', in which the perceived need to preserve separation from the Republic outweighs all other considerations.

Table 8.1 Religious affiliation in Northern Ireland.*

Year	Roman Catholics	Other denominations
1911	430 161 (34.4%)	820 372 (65.6%)
1926	420 428 (33.5%)	836 133 (66.5%)
1937	428 290 (33.5%)	851 455 (66.5%)
1951	471 460 (34.4%)	899 461 (65.6%)
1961	497 547 (34.9%)	927 495 (65.1%)
1971	559 800 (36.8%)	960 300 (63.2%)
1981	586 400 (38.6%)	940 700 (61.5%)

* The figures for 1911–61 are from the Censuses of Population, as summarized by Vaughan & Fitzpatrick 1978. A large number of respondents did not state their religion in 1971 and 1981, so the figures stated for these years are as estimated by Compton & Power 1986. These estimates also take account of the low response rate in 1981.

Under such an outlook, Northern Ireland Catholics (most of whom aspire to a United Ireland), are regarded by the Protestant majority as an internal threat. Catholics consequently found themselves excluded from positions of authority within the Northern Ireland state apparatus, simply because (in the eyes of the unionist authorities) they had to be treated as potential saboteurs. Catholics, as a permanent minority, consequently not only found themselves excluded from any effective say in the government of the state in which they lived, but also found themselves discriminated against with regard to employment opportunities and many other forms of benefit controlled by the state. Many Catholics came to regard the Northern Ireland state as unreformable, and therefore tended to look towards a united Ireland, and the removal of their minority status, as the only possible way of achieving social justice.

Poole (1983), noting that where there is a minority there is also a majority, argues that the conflict in Northern Ireland may also be examined from a 'double majority' perspective. The fact that Protestants form a majority within Northern Ireland gave them control over the state, whilst the fact that Catholics within Northern Ireland were part of an all-Ireland majority has provided them with a sense of strength and moral justification. Nevertheless, irrespective of whether the stress is placed upon the strength provided by majority status, or apprehension and grievance provided by minority status, the net effect of the 'Irish dimension' is that the national question has been kept at the top of the political agenda in Northern Ireland. All other issues, such as social justice, tend to be interpreted in Catholic–Protestant nationalist–unionist terms.

The situation is exacerbated by what Compton (1976) has referred to as the 'demographic irritant' – i.e. the fact that the Catholic birthrate in Northern Ireland is significantly higher than the Protestant birthrate. This has served to intensify Protestant fears that they will eventually be 'outbred' by Catholics and be voted into a united Ireland. This threat was more imaginary than real until the 1960s because the higher Catholic birthrate was counterbalanced by a higher rate of Catholic emigration (Compton 1982). In fact, the percentage of Catholics remained remarkably stable between 1901 and 1961, varying between 33.5 and 35.2 per cent (Table 8.1). Since 1961, however, emigration rates have tended to converge, resulting in a gradual increase in the percentage of Catholics. The exact figures are unknown, partly because of a partial IRA-instigated boycott of the last census in 1981, but the percentage of Catholics in Northern Ireland in the early 1980s was estimated by the New Ireland Forum to be 43 per cent. Compton (1985) puts the figure more conservatively, and probably more accurately, at 37–8 per cent. Either way, the fear of being eventually outnumbered serves to intensify Protestant apprehensions, although the earliest date currently predicted for a Catholic majority in Northern Ireland is 2020.

There is also what might be termed a 'spatial irritant'. Protestants form a majority in Northern Ireland as a whole, but the distribution of Protestants and Catholics is uneven (Fig. 8.1). Many parts of Northern Ireland have a local Catholic and nationalist majority, including two of the six counties (Fermanagh and Tyrone). Protestants are generally in a strong majority in the greater Belfast area (i.e. areas within about 50 km of Belfast city centre), with the exception of the main Catholic enclave in west Belfast. However, there is a strong distance decay component in the size of the Protestant majority, with the result that most areas close to the border with the Republic have a strong Catholic majority (e.g. south Armagh, south and west Fermanagh, Derry west of the Foyle). When partition was initially introduced, the intention had been to redraw the border between Northern Ireland and the Free State to correspond more closely with the national aspirations of communities in the border region. However, views on how the border should be redrawn differed markedly and repartition became such a sensitive issue that the governments of Britain, Northern Ireland and the Free State signed a tripartite agreement in 1925 ratifying the existing border drawn along county boundaries (Fanning 1983).

The uncertainty caused by the delay in ratifying the location of the border had long-term ramifications. Many nationalists assumed that the Boundary Commission would transfer so much territory from Northern Ireland to the Republic that Northern Ireland would become unviable, and that unionists would consequently agree to a united Ireland. Partition, in other words, was regarded by nationalists as merely an interim measure. Nationalists within Northern Ireland began to look towards Dublin rather than to Belfast, and nationalist-controlled local authorities, including Fermanagh and Tyrone county councils, passed motions recognizing the Dublin government. This, of course, did little to assuage unionist fears that the Catholic minority was bent upon the destruction of the Northern state and the enforced incorporation of unionists in an all-Ireland state.

The Belfast government responded to the crisis caused by the minority

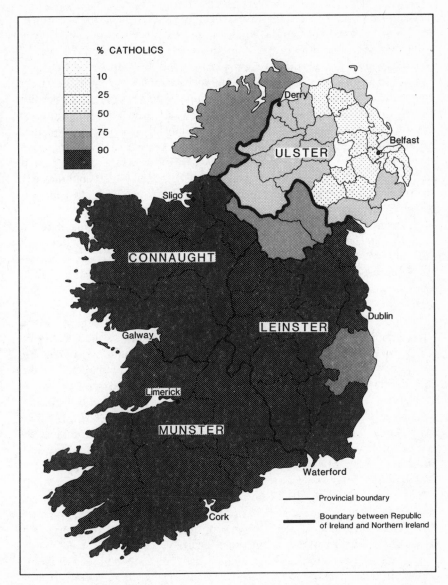

Figure 8.1 Religious affiliation in the Republic of Ireland by county and in Northern Ireland by district council area, 1981.
Sources: Census of Population, Central Statistics Office, Dublin; Compton & Power 1986.

forming local majorities by introducing local government 'reforms', the net effect of which was to manufacture unionist 'majorities', through gerrymandering, malapportionment, and various other electoral abuses, in areas with a local nationalist majority. Given that local authorities determined the allo-

165

cation of important scarce resources, including housing and local authority employment, control over the local authorities provided unionists with a powerful mechanism for compensating for the higher Catholic birthrate. By allocating jobs and housing to Protestants, and by depriving Catholics, unionist councils were able to 'encourage' Catholics to emigrate. Local government abuses, not surprisingly, became a major source of grievance amongst the Catholic minority and reinforced the belief that the Northern Ireland state was unreformable. Most of the demands made by the Northern Ireland Civil Rights Association in the 1960s, for example, centred on abuses in local government. These demands were met by reforms in local government and by the centralization of housing allocation by the early 1970s, but the belief amongst Catholics that Northern Ireland is unreformable would appear to persist.

Given the level of distrust, fear and antagonism between the majority and the minority, frequently reflected in outbreaks of violence (although usually only involving small minorities on both sides), relations between the two communities have been characterized by a high degree of separation. This separation takes a number of forms, but the most visible is probably residential segregation.

Residential segregation has long been a feature of life in Northern Ireland, but it is generally much more pronounced in the larger towns and cities. Poole (1982), in a comparative study of 26 towns and cities, found that Belfast had the highest degree of segregation, and that the degree of segregation was correlated with urban size. Only four towns (Belfast, Armagh, Lurgan and Derry) had a segregation index larger than 50 (where 100 is the maximum possible value) but Poole noted that, given their comparatively large size, these towns contain a substantial majority of the total urban population. At the other end of the settlement continuum, Harris (1972) reported a fair degree of residential integration in an in-depth study of a rural area referred to as Ballybeg, but detailed a higher degree of separation at the social, ideological and demographic levels. People on both sides of the divide appeared conscious of a latent conflict, but adopted a complex set of behavioural rules to ensure that the conflict remained latent. Integration at the spatial level, in other words, was facilitated by separation at the other levels.

Urban segregation, especially in Belfast, has been analysed by a number of geographers (e.g. Evans 1944, Jones 1956 and 1960), but the most detailed study so far is by Poole and Boal (1973). This examines residential segregation in Belfast in early 1969 (i.e. immediately prior to the outbreak of the present 'troubles') at a number of scales, including individual streets. Poole and Boal found a very high degree of segregation: in almost half of the streets in the city, 97 per cent or more of the inhabitants were of the same religious denomination, whilst two-thirds of the total households in the cities lived in streets which had a minority of less than 10 per cent. Protestants appeared to be less willing to live in Catholic streets than the converse: only 1 or 2 per cent of the

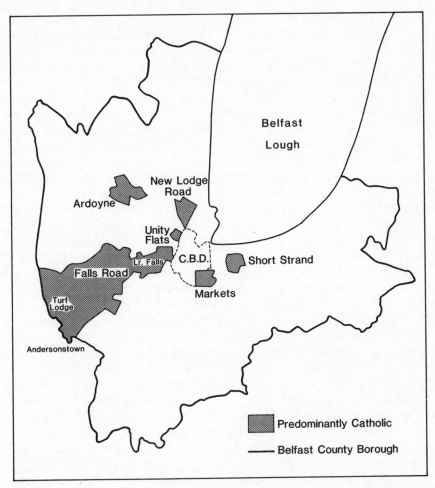

Figure 8.2 The main Catholic areas in Belfast, 1969. Large parts of the city are predominantly Protestant, but the unshaded part of the map includes mixed areas (especially in parts of the north and the south of the city) and some non-residential areas (e.g. Bog Meadows, an area immediately to the south of the main Catholic sector).

total Protestant households in the city lived in streets with a Catholic majority, whereas approximately one-quarter of the total Catholic households lived in streets with a Protestant majority. Overall, however, the distribution was markedly bimodal, with very few streets having what could meaningfully be called a mixed population. Locationally, the predominantly Catholic streets formed six clusters (or ghettos), although one, centred on the Falls Road, was much larger than the others and contained 70 per cent of all Catholic households in the city (Fig. 8.2).

Following the onset of communal violence in 1969, Belfast became even

167

more segregated as minority households on both sides of the religious divide moved to areas where they would form part of the local majority. The first large-scale moves were a direct result of violence, when several Catholic homes in Bombay Street on the edge of the Falls enclave were burnt by Protestant rioters from the nearby Shankhill Road in 1969. By 1970, however, people were beginning to move either because of direct intimidation or, more often, a perceived threat of violence. Protestant evacuation of the mixed New Barnsley estate in 1970 set the precedent for a massive movement in 1971 when communal conflict was at its greatest. More than 2000 households (representing about 1 per cent of the total population of the city) moved in a three-week period following the introduction of internment in August 1971. The Northern Ireland Community Relations Commission Research Unit estimated that about 60 per cent of these were Catholic households (NICRC 1971). By 1972, the percentage of households living in streets with less than a 10 per cent minority had increased from 66 per cent to 76 per cent (Boal *et al.* 1976). The remaining 24 per cent lived in 'mixed areas', most of which had a significant Protestant majority and were mainly middle class (Boal 1982).

Residential segregation in Belfast, as noted by Boal (1969) in a classic study of a small area straddling the Shankill–Falls divide (including the ill-fated Bombay Street), is characterized by a high degree of territoriality. Protestant areas, especially in the summer 'marching season', are marked by loyalist marches and bunting; more permanent markings include gable-end wall paintings, slogans relating to the Queen (favourably), the Pope (unfavourably) and various paramilitary organizations, and curbstones painted red, white and blue. Catholic areas are similarly marked with territorial identifiers, although the wall slogans are naturally the opposites of those in the Protestant areas.

Territoriality is also evident in movement patterns. Boal found that people on both sides of the Shankill–Falls divide generally avoided entering the other group's territory. Protestants close to the divide generally preferred to walk to the Protestant Shankill Road to catch a bus to the city centre, rather than take the shorter route to the Catholic Falls Road; while Catholics in the Falls area normally took a circuitous route through the city centre if visiting friends in the Ardoyne, rather than risk taking the direct route through the Shankill. Separation, in other words, did not simply entail living in separate areas: it extended, in large measure, to almost all forms of human activity, including morning newspapers taken and support for football teams (Glasgow Rangers and Glasgow Celtic were obvious foci for Protestant and Catholic support respectively, but support for Liverpool (Protestant) and Everton (Catholic) still retains a sectarian dimension in Belfast which has probably more or less disappeared in Liverpool itself).

Residential segregation and territoriality in Belfast clearly indicate a high degree of separation at the spatial level. This, by itself, would probably result in a high degree of separation at the social, ideological and demographic levels, but in the Northern Ireland context these forms of separation are reinforced by other forms of segregation. The most controversial are probably segregation in education (which tends to be blamed on the Catholic minority) and segregation in employment (which tends to be blamed on the Protestant majority).

Northern Ireland, like the Free State, inherited a *de facto* religiously segregated educational system in which the national (i.e. primary-level) schools were mostly controlled by the clergy of the locally dominant religion. Secondary education was mainly provided on a fee-paying basis by religious institutions (diocesan schools, religious orders, Presbyterian colleges, etc.), and catered mainly for the middle classes (Murray 1983). The first Minister of Education in the Northern Ireland government, Lord Londonderry, commissioned a committee in 1921 to investigate the creation of a non-denominational state education system, but the clergy on both sides were initially unwilling to surrender their control. The Protestant clergy eventually agreed to the surrender of most of their schools upon condition that the curriculum would include Bible studies without 'instruction as to any tenet which is distinctive of any particular religious denomination' (Buckland 1979, 263). This, however, was unacceptable to the Catholic hierarchy, who regarded 'the interpretation of sacred Scriptures by private judgement', without reference to instruction from the (Catholic) Church, as tantamount to Protestantism. The Catholic Church consequently retained control over what were officially referred to as 'voluntary' schools, whilst most of the Protestant schools became 'controlled' or more simply 'state' schools.

The impact of segregated education upon Protestant–Catholic relations is difficult to assess. On the one hand, it is frequently argued that its impact is minimal because both types of school teach a common syllabus, and the prime concern of the vast majority of teachers on both sides is the education and welfare of their pupils. Although each side suspects the other of engaging in some form of nefarious political brainwashing, it is probably only an extremely small minority of politically motivated teachers who consciously do so. On the other hand, segregation permits the reproduction and reinforcement of cultural values and attitudes towards the other group without any need for critical assessment or re-evaluation. The schools are by no means the main source of misinformation about the other group, but the mere fact of being segregated, coupled with separation in almost every other sphere of life, permits the development and perpetuation of myths which feed communal fear and eventually violence.

These myths are perpetuated in adult life by a high degree of segregation in employment. Protestants and Catholics tend to be employed in different occupations: shipbuilding, the aircraft industry, and engineering, for example, are traditionally Protestant sources of employment, whilst deep-sea dockers and construction workers are more likely to be Catholic. Prior to reforms in the early 1970s, public sector employment, including the Northern Ireland Civil Service, local government workers and the police, was very heavily dominated by Protestants. The bias in the public sector possibly reflected to some extent a reluctance by Catholics to seek employment in the apparatus of a state to whose very existence they were opposed, but there would also appear to be strong circumstantial evidence of unionist attempts to exclude Catholics from positions in the state apparatus where they could do damage: Catholics, for example, were even more underrepresented in the higher grades in the public sector than in the lower grades. Viewed from the perspective of the Catholic minority, this simply reinforced the belief that the Northern Ireland state was anti-Catholic (as opposed to anti-nationalist) and unreformable, and strengthened the determination to seek social justice through national reunification.

In the private sector, there would seem to be a preference by both Protestant and Catholic employers to 'look after their own' (Barritt & Carter 1972), although the decision was very often forced upon employers by the reluctance of workers to work with members of the other religion. Protestant domination of the shipbuilding and engineering industries in Belfast, for example, seems to have owed much to the early organization of skilled workers into exclusive trade unions in the mid-19th century, whilst the Orange Order (an exclusively Protestant organization) seems to have fulfilled a similar role for unskilled workers (Patterson 1980). Given that the local economy was disproportionately under the control of Protestants, the net effect has been a traditionally much higher rate of unemployment amongst Catholics, which has only served to fuel feelings of religious discrimination amongst the minority.

Other factors would need to be considered in a full account of segregation in employment (including, for example, demographic factors, and the reluctance of some workers to seek employment in establishments located in the other group's territory). However, irrespective of the causes, it is obvious that there is in fact a high degree of separation in employment, although separation in employment is much less marked than residential separation, which, in turn, is much less marked than separation in education. Also, following local government and other reforms in the late 1960s and early 1970s, the indications are that separation in employment may now be less marked than in the past.

Spatial separation provides short-term security for both sides by virtue of the avoidance and defence functions noted by Boal (1972 and 1976); it also reduces the minority's longer term fears of being assimilated and losing its group identity by providing a suitable context for ideological reinforcement. However, reinforcement may be a two-edged sword: in addition to reducing fears of being assimilated, reinforcement may also permit erroneous myths about the other group to be perpetuated. Each group's image of the other is based upon stereotypes which are continuously reinforced without the correcting influences of personal experience. Misunderstanding leads to fear, and eventually to further conflict. The short-term security provided by separation, in short, may well lay the foundations for further long-term conflict.

170

The causes of communal violence in Northern Ireland are complex (e.g. see Murray 1982), but the hypothesis that segregation may be a contributory factor would seem to be supported by empirical studies of violence in Northern Ireland since the late 1960s. Poole (1983), for example, found that eight out of nine towns having more than 500 Catholics living in areas more than 90 per cent Catholic were characterized by high levels of violence, whereas all 18 towns having fewer than 500 Catholics living in segregated ghettos were characterized by low levels of violence.

The Republic of Ireland

Separation of the Free State from the United Kingdom partly satisfied the aspirations of many nationalists, but the solution was far from ideal for two reasons.

First, the degree of separation from Britain was not as complete as many nationalists desired. The Irish Free State remained part of the British Commonwealth and, under the terms of the Anglo–Irish Treaty, members of the Free State Parliament had to swear an oath of allegiance to the King (Fanning 1983). A substantial minority argued that the terms of the Anglo–Irish Treaty should not have been accepted and, within months of gaining 'independence', the Free State found itself plunged into a civil war between pro-Treaty and anti-Treaty factions. The pro-Treaty forces initially gained ascendancy, but the anti-Treaty supporters later emerged as the dominant faction in southern politics.

Second, separation between Northern Ireland and the Free State was a source of considerable grievance to nationalists. Partition not only failed to satisfy the aspirations of nationalists left on the wrong side of the border with Northern Ireland, but also the aspirations of very many nationalists in the South who desired an independent Irish state embracing the whole island.

Although the population of the new state was overwhelmingly Catholic and pro-nationalist, it included a small Protestant and unionist minority (plus even smaller numbers of other religions). Not all Protestants were opposed to independence – indeed several played a prominent role in the independence movement – but separation from Britain was regarded with concern. A substantial number of Protestants responded to their new circumstances by adopting an extreme form of separation – emigration either to Northern Ireland or to Britain – but most had deep roots in the areas where they lived and opted to come to terms with the new state. The remainder of this section focuses upon the relationship between the majority and minority communities within the Republic.

Relations between the minority and majority have generally been fairly amicable, especially when compared with the situation in Northern Ireland. In particular, there has been very little violent conflict between the majority and minority since the early 1920s, when, because of the breakdown in law and order during the civil war, isolated Protestants were intimidated, attacked and, in several instances, murdered by the IRA (Kennedy 1988). This absence of conflict is accompanied by a high degree of integration, especially at the spatial and social levels, although some elements of separation are also present, especially at the ideological and demographic levels.

The minority is almost totally integrated in many aspects of day-to-day life. For example, there is no residential segregation, as such, between Catholics and non-Catholics in the Republic. Non-Catholics are more numerous in some areas than in others, but this is rarely the product of a conscious attempt to separate for religious reasons: in rural areas it is usually a function of landholding and inheritance (i.e. areas traditionally having a large percentage of Protestant farmers tend to retain a high percentage of Protestants due to the farms being retained within the family); in urban areas it is usually a function of social class – Protestants are overrepresented in the more affluent sections of society and are therefore overrepresented in high-status areas, although within such areas they are totally interspersed with high-status Catholics.

Catholics and non-Catholics are also reasonably integrated with respect to employment. As in any society, certain occupations are confined to members of a particular religion (e.g. priest, rabbi, etc.). There are possibly more such occupations in the Republic than in most west European countries: many schools and hospitals, for example, which elsewhere might be under secular state control, are under religious control (both Catholic and non-Catholic). Such institutions naturally tend to recruit applicants who conform with the ethos of the institution in question, although the successful applicants need not necessarily be members of the 'correct' religion. Segregation is less pronounced in the private sector. Although small businessmen may show a tendency to 'look after their own', religious affiliation would appear to have very little bearing upon the allocation of jobs in places of employment not under direct religious control.

The minority has also been integrated fairly effectively into the mainstream of southern Irish politics. Although non-Catholics are probably more pro-British than the population as a whole, and may even harbour a certain degree of nostalgia for the 'old' United Kingdom, there is no overt unionist movement in southern politics. Non-Catholics join and support the same political parties (most of whom officially favour a united Ireland) as the Catholic majority, although non-Catholics tend to favour parties which adopt a more liberal stance on the national question and on social issues. For example, Fine Gael – the 'pro-Treaty' party – traditionally gets more support from non-Catholics than Fianna Fail – the 'anti-Treaty' party and largest party in the state since the early 1930s. Despite comprising a very small minority, Protestants have on occasions achieved high office: Douglas Hyde and Erskine Childers, for example, both served terms of office as President (i.e. head of state).

172

Although politically integrated, the Protestant minority has adopted a strategy of separation in other spheres of life in an attempt to avoid being totally assimilated by the Catholic majority at the ideological level. The most obvious form of separation in this regard is in church-related activities (e.g. charitable organizations, boy scouts, etc.). However, church-related activities in the Republic extend, as noted above, into the spheres of education and the health services. Although in receipt of state funding, the management of most schools in the Republic is controlled by either the Protestant or Catholic clergy, or religious orders. Education is consequently denominational and religiously segregated, although not as rigidly as in Northern Ireland.

Although separation provides a potential mechanism for the maintenance of a distinctive identity, it is not always a viable option, due to the small size of the Protestant minority. Separation is only possible if there are sufficient numbers within easy travelling distance to maintain a separate existence. The absolute size of the minority is more important in this respect than its size relative to the majority. Protestants have consequently found it much more difficult to maintain a separate existence in rural areas (where, with the exception of counties bordering on Northern Ireland, the absolute number of Protestants is small) than in the larger urban areas. Protestant schools and churches have been forced to close in many areas, while many Protestant churches are only kept open on a rotating basis – i.e. several churches in an area share the same clergyman who attends a different church each week. In the absence of separate schools, non-Catholic parents are forced to send their children to a local 'Catholic' school, unless they are affluent enough to send them away to a boarding school (which entails a form of double separation, from Catholics and their own families).

In situations where separation is not a viable option, Protestants and other non-Catholics find themselves faced with enormous pressures to conform. A substantial portion of a child's third year at a Catholic-controlled national school, for example, is allocated to religious lessons in preparation for the Catholic rite of Holy Communion. Non-Catholic parents of children attending such schools have the right to request their children to be exempted from religious classes, but this option is not always taken because it could create problems for the child amongst his or her peer group by emphasizing that he or she is different. In the absence of alternative non-Catholic schools, it is generally simpler to allow the child to receive a Catholic training.

In the absence of marked spatial and social separation, and declining levels of separation at the ideological level, the likelihood of integration at the demographic level (and hence the total elimination of a distinctive minority) has increased. Intermarriage has made major inroads on the size of the Protestant minority in the Republic (Table 8.2). In the past the partners in a mixed marriage were obliged by the Catholic Church, under the Ne Temere decree, to bring their children up as Catholics. This is no longer enforced, but unless a couple makes a conscious decision to bring their children up as

Table 8.2 Religious affiliation in the Republic of Ireland.*

Year	Roman Catholics	Other denominations
1911	2 812 509 (89.6%)	327 177 (10.4%)
1926	2 751 269 (92.6%)	220 723 (7.4%)
1936	2 773 920 (93.5%)	194 500 (6.6%)
1946	2 786 033 (94.3%)	169 074 (5.7%)
1961	2 673 473 (94.9%)	144 868 (5.1%)
1971	2 795 596 (93.9%)	182 652 (6.1%)
1981	3 204 476 (93.1%)	238 929 (6.9%)

* These figures are based on Census data published by Vaughan & Fitzpatrick 1978. The increase in the number of people classified as 'other denominations' in 1971 and 1981 is mainly due to an increase in the number of people not stating any religion. The number of Protestants continued to decline during this period.

non-Catholics, and to send them to a non-Catholic school, the net effect, given the dominance of the Catholic majority, is much the same. However, this assimilation is not entirely a one-way process. The power and influence of the Catholic Church in Ireland has declined markedly over the last 25 years due to the impact of secularism, thereby creating (from the perspective of the minority) a more acceptable middle ground.

Discussion

The absence of overt conflict in the Republic between the majority and minority contrasts markedly with the high level of inter-group violence in Northern Ireland. Given the high degree of integration in the Republic, compared with a high degree of separation in Northern Ireland, the case studies would appear to support the arguments of those who advocate integration as a solution to communal conflict. This conclusion, however, requires a number of qualifications.

The first qualification is that the situations in Northern Ireland and the Republic differ with regard to much more than simply the degree of integration. The relative size of the minority, for example, is markedly different, with obvious implications for the nature of group relations in the two countries. In the Republic, the minority is extremely small and getting smaller. It therefore tends to keep a low profile to avoid attracting hostile attention from the majority. The majority, for its part, does not perceive the minority as a threat and therefore refrains from putting overt pressure on the minority to conform, thereby creating a suitable environment for peaceful coexistence.

In Northern Ireland, on the other hand, the minority is large, and getting larger, and is very strongly perceived by the majority as a threat, especially when viewed in an all-Ireland context. The minority in Northern Ireland is also strong enough to 'put up a fight', and therefore does not have to assume a cowering attitude. The 'defensive' measures taken by the majority (e.g. electoral abuses and discrimination) have only served to intensify the demands of the minority for the type of change (a united Ireland) most feared by the majority. The fact that the minority in Northern Ireland sees itself as part of an all-Ireland majority has provided further impetus to these demands.

The second qualification relates to time scale. Integration may provide a better long-term solution to communal conflict, based upon the development of mutual understanding between the groups and the elimination of the differences which underlie the conflict, but in the short term, given the existence of conflict, integration (especially spatial integration) might actually exacerbate the situation by maximizing the number of inter-group contacts and therefore the opportunities for violence. Spatial separation, in contrast, by satisfying people's need for security, could conceivably facilitate better inter-group relations in the long term by helping to defuse the conflict in the short term. However, the potential provided by spatial separation for the reinforcement of stereotypes must be regarded as a cause for concern in the long term.

Thirdly, even though integration may provide a better long-term solution, it may be beneficial to retain some degree of separation, especially in situations where a very small minority is fearful of being totally assimilated by the majority. The relative success of group relations in the Republic, for example, surely owes much to the fact that, generally speaking, the minority has not been forced to integrate or conform (although some exceptions arise where Catholic doctrine has been enshrined in civil legislation – as, for example, with regard to divorce), without actually being formally excluded.

Finally, even if it is deemed desirable, integration cannot easily be imposed from 'above'. Integration is dependent upon a desire to integrate, or at least upon an absence of opposition to integration. However, integration at the ideological level is likely to be perceived by the minority as an attempt to force it to conform; whilst, at a spatial level, if conflict already exists, it may be perceived by both sides as entailing unacceptable risks. Attempts to create religiously integrated housing estates in Belfast in the 1960s, for example, failed because, as soon as the finely balanced equilibrium was upset (as it invariably was), the local minority felt threatened and moved out. Today, housing policy in Belfast recognizes the need to provide security: housing estates are segregated and physically separated by 'peace walls', whilst housing design would appear to reflect a perceived need to provide 'defensible space' (Dawson 1984).

If conflict exists, integration will only be possible over a long period of time. There would appear to be a limit to what may be achieved to encourage integration by social engineering and public policy at local level. Integration at local level requires a favourable 'environment', and attempts to foster integration should therefore focus upon trying to resolve the underlying conflict at the appropriate level. In the specific instance of Northern Ireland, the key to better communal relations is to seek a solution to the national conflict which would be acceptable to all interested parties. Various options – a united Ireland, devolution, independent Ulster, further integration with Britain, etc. – entail varying degrees of integration with and separation from Ireland and Britain. Each option has its own advocates and detractors, but none seems capable of breaking the deadlock. More consideration should perhaps be given to the possibilities provided by integration into an even larger political entity, such as that envisaged for 1992 by the Single European Act.

References

Barritt, D. P. & C. F. Carter 1972. *The Northern Ireland problem: a study in group relations*. London: Oxford University Press.

Boal, F. W. 1969. Territoriality on the Shankhill-Falls divide in Belfast. *Irish Geography* **6**(1), 30–50.

Boal, F. W. 1972. The urban residential sub-community: a conflict interpretation. *Area* **4**(3), 164–8.

Boal , F. W. 1976. Ethnic residential segregation. In *Social areas in cities*, D. T. Herbert and R. J. Johnston (eds). Vol. 1: *Spatial processes and form*, 41–79. Chichester: Wiley.

Boal, F. W. 1982. Segregating and mixing: space and residence in Belfast. In *Integration and division: geographical perspectives on the Northern Ireland problem*, F. W. Boal and J. N. H. Douglas (eds), 249–80. London: Academic Press.

Boal, F. W., R. C. Murray & M. A. Poole 1976. Belfast: the urban encapsulation of a national conflict. In *Urban ethnic conflict: a comparative perspective*, S. E. Clarke & J. L. Obler (eds). Chapel Hill, N.C.: Institute for Research in Social Science, University of North Carolina.

Buckland, P. 1979. *The factory of grievances: devolved government in Northern Ireland 1921–1939*. Dublin: Gill & Macmillan.

Compton, P. A. 1976. Religious affiliation and demographic variability in Northern Ireland. *Transactions of the Institute of British Geographers* **1**(4), 433–52.

Compton, P. A. 1982. The demographic dimension of integration and division in Northern Ireland. In *Integration and division: geographical perspectives on the Northern Ireland problem*, F. W. Boal & J. N. H. Douglas (eds), 75–104. London: Academic Press.

Compton, P. A. 1985. An evaluation of the changing religious composition of the population in Northern Ireland. *Economic and Social Review*, **16** (3), 201–24.

Compton, P. A. & J. P. Power 1986. Estimates of the changing religious composition of Northern Ireland local government districts in 1981 and change in the geographical pattern of religious composition between 1971 and 1981. *Economic and Social Review* **17**(2), 87–106.

Dawson, G. M. 1984. Defensive planning in Belfast. *Irish Geography* **17**, 27–41.

Douglas, J. N. H. & F. W. Boal 1982. The Northern Ireland problem. In *Integration and division: geographical perspectives on the Northern Ireland problem*, F. W. Boal & J. N. H. Douglas (eds), 1–18. London: Academic Press.

Evans, E. E. 1944. Belfast: the site and the city. *Ulster Journal of Archaeology* **7**, 25–9.

Fanning, R. 1983. *Independent Ireland*. Dublin: Helicon.

References

Harris, R. 1972. *Prejudice and tolerance in Ulster: a study of neighbours and strangers in a border community*. Manchester: Manchester University Press.

Jones, E. 1956. The distribution and segregation of Roman Catholics in Belfast. *Sociological Review* **4**, 167–89.

Jones, E. 1960. *A social geography of Belfast*. London: Oxford University Press.

Kennedy, D. 1988. *The widening gulf: northern attitudes to the independent Irish state, 1919–49*. Belfast: Blackstaff Press.

Murray, R. 1982. Political violence in Northern Ireland, 1969–1977. In *Integration and division: geographical perspectives on the Northern Ireland problem*, F. W. Boal & J. N. H. Douglas (eds), 309–31. London: Academic Press.·

Murray, D. 1983. Schools and conflict. In *Northern Ireland: the background to the conflict*, J. Darby (ed.), 136–50. Belfast: Appletree Press.

Northern Ireland Community Relations Commission Research Unit 1971. *Flight: a report on population movement in Belfast during August, 1971*. Belfast: Northern Ireland Community Relations Commission.

Patterson, H. 1980. *Class conflict and sectarianism*. Belfast: Blackstaff Press.

Poole, M. 1982. Religious residential segregation in urban Northern Ireland. In *Integration and division: geographical perspectives on the Northern Ireland problem*, F. W. Boal & J. N. H. Douglas (eds), 281–308. London: Academic Press.

Poole, M. 1983. The demography of violence. In *Northern Ireland: the background to the conflict*, J. Darby (ed.), 151–80. Belfast: Appletree Press.

Poole, M. & F. W. Boal 1973. Religious residential segregation in Belfast in mid-1969: a multi-level analysis. In *Social patterns in cities*, Special Publication No. 5, B. D. Clarke & M. B. Gleeve (eds), 1–40. London: Institute of British Geographers.

Pringle, D. G. 1985. *One island, two nations? A political geographical analysis of the national conflict in Ireland*. Letchworth: Research Studies Press.

Stewart, A. T. Q. 1977. *The narrow ground: aspects of Ulster, 1609–1969*. London: Faber & Faber.

Vaughan, W. E. and W. E. Fitzpatrick 1978. *Irish historical statistics. Population 1821–1971*. Dublin: Royal Irish Academy.

Whyte, J. 1978. Interpretations of the Northern Ireland problem: an appraisal. *Economic and Social Review* **9**(4), 257–82.

9

Involuntary incorporation: the case of Israel

STANLEY WATERMAN

Petty bourgeois behavior, our way of life all these years, will be the official code of behavior for now on. 'Grab what you can'. And now it will be accompanied more and more by the tom-toms of a dim cultic tribalism. Blood and land and passion and intoxicating slogans, Betar and Massada, the whole world is against us, wars of poverty and defilement, fanaticism along with dark fears, oppression of the mind in the name of stirring visions, and over everything will float the cry 'the haters of Israel will suffer'. (Amos Oz, quoted in Aronson 1987, 61).

Introduction

The story of modern Israel is one in which two peoples claim sovereignty over the same piece of territory at the same period in history. One is a people with a long-established identity who achieved a renewed association with their ancient homeland through a modern European nationalist movement. The identity of the other people has only recently been shaped, catalysed in great part by the events of the past 40 years, during which they have become detached from their homes and homeland.

Thus, Israelis and Palestinians are destined to live in close mutual proximity in a land which they both consider to be exclusively theirs. Although the Jews are the majority in the Israeli state and in the areas occupied by that state, the non-Jewish inhabitants – those who are Israeli citizens and those who live in the Occupied Territories of Judaea, Samaria and Gaza – form part of a more extensive ethnic grouping, the Arabs, who dwarf the Israelis numerically in the broader regional context (Soffer 1983). This fact received special emphasis during the 1950s and 1960s, when the focus of the Israeli–Arab conflict was the hostile relations between Israel and its Arab neighbours. This differs from the perspective of the 1970s and 1980s, during which the direct confrontation between Israelis and Palestinians within Palestine/Eretz-Yisrael (the Land of Israel) has been emphasized.

This complex interrelationship of varying majority–minority conditions between Arabs and Jews in Palestine contributes to many of the tensions between Israelis and Palestinians, and between Israel and the surrounding Arab states. While Israel controls the West Bank and Gaza and the inhabitants of those territories, by virtue of a military occupation that has existed since June 1967, the Arabs are regarded by many Israelis as an alien people, as a Fifth Column, hostile to the Jewish state and not to be trusted. 'Israeli' Arabs, citizens of the state for over 40 years, have increasingly come to identify with Palestinian national ideals and to see themselves alienated in their homeland, in which they have always lived, by a state which claims them as full and integrated citizens.

Although Jewish and Arab societies in pre-state Palestine existed side by side, there was only a minimum of contact between the two peoples. Even though there was little ethnic mixing, the British only agreed to the partition of Palestine under considerable pressure (Fraser 1984, Waterman 1987). Yet, in retrospect, it seems that the partitioning was only a means of giving formal expression to the separation of and the continuous conflict between the peoples and the separate economic, cultural and social systems that already existed. The *de facto* acceptance of the armistice agreements of 1949 by Jews and Arabs was an acceptance of a division of space rather than a sharing of space. The operational issues were the timing of the partition and where the dividing line between the Jewish and Arab parts should run. The UN partition plan, accepted by the Zionists and rejected by the Arabs, was naive in the extreme. British Palestine was to be divided into a Jewish and an Arab state. Each state would include a large minority of the other group (Cohen 1983). In addition, the plan included an international zone around Jerusalem and corridors to allow free access to different parts of both states and to free ports. The plan assumed normal relations between the states in a period when normal relations between the Arab and Jewish communities appeared to be increasingly unattainable and even unthinkable.

Involuntary incorporation

In the pre-state period, almost the only mixing that occurred between Arab and Jew was in the towns and cities. Even there, the degree of social contact was minimal, as the traditional towns were divided into distinct quarters, for each of the various communities (Ben-Arieh 1984). Residential segregation was and remains almost complete (Kipnis & Schnell 1978, Ben-Artzi 1979 and 1980, Waterman 1989), and although these settlements are referred to as 'mixed towns', the extent of mixing depends on the scale of study and the viewpoint of the observer. The segregation is not restricted just to Jews and Arabs, for separation of the non-Jewish settlements, primarily by religious community, is also the norm, and separation among the Jews on the basis of religious orthodoxy also occurs (Shilhav 1983, Shilhav & Friedman 1985). Cultural differences kept communities apart, and even where cultures bore

179

general similarity, as with some Muslim Arabs and some Sephardi Jews, religious factors continued to act as a barrier. Apartness between Jew and Arab has been the norm since the earliest Jewish settlements in Palestine, even though long-established families, both Jewish and Arab, often proudly remark on their contacts with the other over the decades (Eliachar 1983).

In the Zionist colonization of Eretz-Yisrael, pioneering focused on the rural areas, and it was here that separateness between the groups was most complete. It was here that, in ideology at least, the Jews were most determined to break the shackles that tied them to their European origins. It was here that the building of a new Jewish society was most vividly felt. The first effort to 'go it alone', as it were, almost caused the new colonies (*moshavot*) to end in ruin (Weintraub, Lissak & Azmon 1969). Some seven years after the first *moshava* had been 'successfully' launched, the financial and technical assistance of Baron Edmond de Rothschild had been called in to rescue the settlements from their almost certain demise (Weintraub, Lissak & Azmon 1969). Although in the decade which followed, during the consolidation of the *moshavot*, Jewish labour was not the only labour which was employed, the effective use of Arab labour (which had become quite common) was weakened by the demands of Jewish socialists who had immigrated to Palestine during the second *Aliyah* (immigration wave) of 1905–14 and before. Their demand was for Jewish labour to be employed on Jewish projects in the light of their self-perception as rebuilders of the Jewish people. When the members of the third *Aliyah* of the early 1920s organized the elitist labour battalions of the Zionist movement, promoting self-resurrection through self-labour, the divorce from Arab society had become almost complete.

The development of a separate Jewish economy reinforced the residential segregation that had been apparent by this time. The struggle for Jewish labour continued through the 1930s with the development of the port of Haifa by the British authorities, and the growth of industry in the adjoining Haifa Bay region (Shapira 1986), in which the dominance of Jewish labour was almost total. By the mid-1930s, the Jewish sector of the economy was as separate from the Arab sector as was possible in a British colony organized as a unitary state; Jewish society had already been so for longer. Politically, this segregation was marked by the 'disturbances' of 1936–9, and by the willingness of many of the Zionists to accept partition in order to achieve the dream of a Jewish state (Rose 1971, Waterman 1987). The separation of Jew and Arab in Palestine was thus primarily the result of internal cohesive forces at work inside the Zionist community.

That the Zionists tended to ignore the Arabs is not altogether surprising; the so-called 'Jewish problem', relating to the status of the Jews within Eastern Europe, was very real to the Jews. Zionism was a political ideology motivated to normalize the position of the Jews in relation to other peoples in the world. That the state of Israel later continued to ignore the plight of the Arabs is also unsurprising. The Zionists had always perceived Palestine as an empty land, devoid of indigenous inhabitants. Moreover, after the Holocaust of the Second World War, the Jewish problem had become a nightmare, and finding a home for the Jewish survivors became the focus for the Zionist community. Mass migration brought hundreds of thousands of Holocaust survivors to Israel, to be followed by equally large numbers of migrants from countries of the Middle East and North Africa. Besides an ideological reason for the lack of attention that Zionists paid to the Arabs, there was very simply too little time to give much thought to other people. Since the late 1940s, inertia has played a major role, in that the general situation between Arabs and Jews failed to change. Further factors have been the constant opposition and hostility displayed by the Palestinian and other Arabs to Israel over the decades.

The idea of a Jewish state matured politically in the second half of the 1930s (Fraser 1984, Rose 1970 and 1971). It was only a matter of the timing and the shape of the borders that would enclose the Jewish state that were in question. The UN partition plan of 1947 divided the area west of the Jordan river into an Arab and a Jewish state. This plan was rejected out of hand by the Arabs as illegal, consisting of a trespass on the sovereignty of original inhabitants, and a denial of the Palestinians' natural right to self-determination (Kattan 1988). It was an unreal plan which assumed normal diplomatic relations between the two states, something which could not have been further from the real situation. Fear and hatred were mutual. It is little wonder that the negotiated armistice lines which gave Israel its first 'permanent' appearance in 1949 were a far cry from what the majority of the members of the UN General Assembly had voted for in November 1947.

A major consequence of the war fought between Israel and her Arab neighbours between 1947 and 1949 (in Israeli parlance, the War of Independence or the War of Liberation) was the exodus of most of the Arab population from areas controlled by Israel. Whether this occurred as part of an organized expulsion by the Jews, was directed by the Palestinian Arab leadership or other Arab leaders, or was the result of a benign or a malign lack of interest by Israeli politicians and military commanders to prevent it from happening, is a moot point. The three processes probably operated simultaneously. By the end of 1948, only 160 000 Arabs remained in Israel (Mossa 1988).

These 'Israeli Arabs' were in a state of shock. Cut off from the rest of their people, from their ostensible leaders, they had suddenly become a small minority in a state built around an ideology that did not include them as an integral part of it, that took no real interest in them other than to see them as a threat to security, and that was about to discriminate against them actively and passively. The incorporation of these Arabs into the Jewish state was unavoidable, but was desired by neither side (see Smooha & Peretz 1982, 466).

In the 1950s and 1960s, during the first quarter-century of Israeli statehood, little was done to enhance the status or wellbeing of most of the non-Jewish population of the state. This was in sharp contrast to the Jews, for whom Jewish immigration was the life-source of the new state. Immigrants were needed for a variety of tasks in the building of the new state and nation. In addition to the general need to increase the number of Jewish citizens in the state, there was also the need to people all parts of the country, especially in border areas, in towns and cities, and to settle and farm the land and establish new villages.

The new *status quo* was the working *status quo*. Few stopped to contemplate the morality of peopling a country at the expense of another people. Vacated space was regarded as vacant space, irrespective of how that empty space had been created. The absorption of Jewish immigrants remained the motivating ideal of Israel, with all its difficulties, until after the Yom Kippur War of 1973 (Waterman 1979).

In this ideal, there was little place for the Arabs of Israel. They were an encumbrance upon the Jewish state. Arabs could neither contribute to the refurbished Jewish identity being worked out for the new state nor could they readily identify with the state itself. A sizeable proportion of the remaining Arab population consisted of 'homeland' or 'internal' refugees, persons who had been dispossessed of their lands and homes and had sought refuge within the borders of the new Israel (Al-Haj 1986 and 1988, Hassan 1988). They lived in towns and villages that were looked upon either as security threats (as in the case of villages along the former border with the Jordanian-occupied West Bank – the so-called 'Green Line') or as obstacles which prevented the realization of the Zionist dream of making all the Land Jewish.

It was too awkward to expel the Arabs after the War of Independence, for events which occur in the course of hostilities cannot usually or readily be repeated during periods described as peacetime. Moreover, the state of Israel was established on democratic principles, so that all its inhabitants – in theory, at any rate – must be entitled to the same rights as citizens and liable to the same obligations. This, however, posed a dilemma for the new Israelis. Rights such as the franchise and obligations such as payment of taxes provided no great moral difficulty for the Jews *vis-à-vis* the Arabs or even for the Arabs themselves. But the right or obligation to serve in the army was more than even a democratic Israel in a hostile Middle East could contemplate (Shamir & Sullivan 1985).

It was not simply that Arabs in Israel were excused from compulsory military service. Defending the Jewish state from its Arab enemies was an obligation perched on the highest rung of the ladder in Israeli society. By making *compulsory* military service primarily a Jewish affair, the state only acted to emphasize further the exclusive Jewish character of the state and alienate the Arab population (Lustick 1980). The continued reference to the Jewish and Arab sectors within society only underlined the differences. And none of this was unselfconsciously done. Arabs in Israel remained under the rule of a military governor until the middle 1960s; it took almost 20 years of statehood before these Israeli citizens could move as freely within the confines of their state as their Jewish counterparts. Nevertheless, the Israeli authorities consistently referred to the Arab citizens of the state as 'Israeli Arabs', as if this new-found identity had been adopted by the Arab citizens themselves. Indeed, Smooha (1980) has pointed out that one of the failures in Jewish–Arab relations in Israel has been the inability to create an 'Israeli' identity with which Arabs could identify. The government did not wish for a real integration or absorption of the Arabs. In fact, they received support for the preservation of their separate identity; parochialism, as in the Ottoman Empire, was encouraged!

Almost everything that was being accomplished in the new state was designed to maintain and even to increase levels of separation between Arab and Jew. The new towns and villages that were founded were established initially as wholly Jewish settlements, as were new neighbourhoods in the established towns and cities. The incorporation of the Arabs into Israeli society was an incorporation of no alternative. It was involuntary on the part of both Arab and Jew. Functional incorporation had to occur so as to ensure the relatively smooth running of the state even though moral and physical separation continued to exist. The Arabs were incorporated into the Israeli economy, through the workplace and the system of tax collection, and into society in general (much less completely) through the educational system, especially near its upper end, in the universities. Yet, even these examples of functional incorporation were not seen in a favourable light by the majority of Jews, many of whom felt that they had little in common with the Arabs, and the little spatial integration that has occurred, as in the migration of Arabs from Arab Nazareth to the Jewish new town of Upper Nazareth, has resulted more from the need to find a solution to an acute housing shortage than from trends of social integration (Doron 1988).

The main driving force of Israeli society during the 1950s and 1960s had been the rejuvenation of the Jewish people in the Jewish state through the absorption of the Jewish diaspora into the pragmatic socialist-Zionist model; but there was a market change following the Yom Kippur War of October 1973.

There are three benchmarks in the chronology of Israel in the second stage of its development: 1967, 1973 and 1977. In 1967, as a result of the Six Day War, Israel conquered the territories and inhabitants of Judaea and Samaria (the West Bank), and Gaza, along with those of the Sinai Peninsula and part of the Golan Heights (Fig. 9.1). These lands were taken in the heat of war, with little consideration at the time given to the political, moral and social consequences of the actions. In the case of Sinai, most of the local inhabitants were nomads; in the Golan, all the local population fled, with the exception of four Druze villages in the north. However, in Gaza and the West Bank the Israeli conquest brought 800 000 Arabs under direct Israeli rule.

This act had several effects. First, Israelis and Palestinians once more came into direct contact, this time without the British or Hashemite Jordanians as

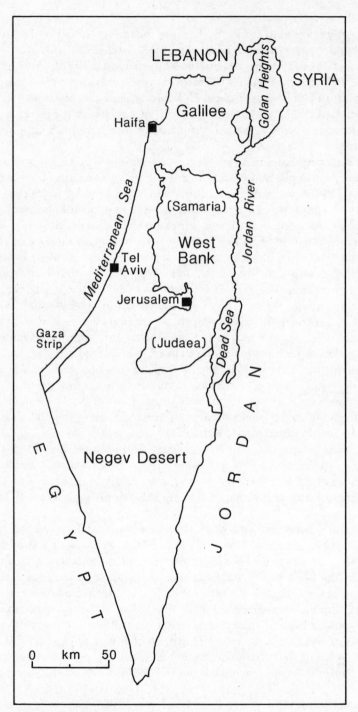

Figure 9.1   Israel and the Occupied Territories.

barriers or go-betweens. But this was not contact between equals, for the Jews were the controllers and the Arabs the controlled.

The Arabs of the West Bank and Gaza were able to renew contacts with 'Israeli Arabs' (or, as they were referred to, the '1948 Arabs'), with consequences which were far from simple (Grossman 1988). On the one hand, genuine family reunions took place, as did genuine political contacts. However, the initial contact was not the happy reunion that many had expected and dreamed of. The Israeli Arabs regarded themselves as superior and more secure in their position than their 'non-Israeli' counterparts. Although contacts were renewed, there was no free migration from one to the other. Intermarriage rates have remained very low and even villages which had been bisected in the 1949 armistice agreement between Israel and Jordan remained divided, as the inhabitants of one side were Israeli citizens whereas those on the other lived under the military rule of an occupier. The intimation here is that Israeli Arabs did at least develop a partial separate identity which distinguished them from the brethren from whom they had been separated.

A longer term consequence, and one which took almost two decades to develop fully, was the emergence of a genuine feeling of Palestinian nationhood and national aspiration in which the Israeli conquest and occupation ('liberation' in the Israeli lexicon) acted as catalysts. This national identity has not simply been restricted to the inhabitants of the Occupied Territories but has been adopted by an increasing number of Israeli Arabs who have lived as Israeli citizens for over 40 years (Smooha & Peretz 1982). (It is, perhaps, a significant observation that the Arabs of the West Bank and Gaza have lived under Israeli rule – though not as citizens – for longer than had the Israeli Arabs at the time of the Six Day War.) If the Palestinian Arabs have been able to cement a developing national identity during this period, why should many Israeli Arabs not have adopted a similar, if not identical, identity during the same period (see Smooha & Peretz 1982, 466 and 474)? This question should be examined in the light of their status as Israelis, a status that had not really been encouraged to the full by Israeli society and the Israeli authorities between 1949 and 1967, and with reference to the stage which they had reached on the axis of modernization.

One of the most significant changes to occur with the conquest of the West Bank and Gaza was that it altered the numerical relationship between Arab and Jew in Palestine (Fig. 9.2). While the Arabs were but a small minority (initially about 20 per cent, declining rapidly during the three years of mass Jewish immigration to around 10 per cent, they were not perceived as a group which endangered the integrity of the state despite their irredentist potential. This, of course, is related to the fact that Palestinian Arab nationalism, as distinct from pan-Arab nationalism, was then in its infancy. It was relatively difficult to identify with an entity that had not previously existed, or with nationalist feelings for a people that had not yet fully come into existence.

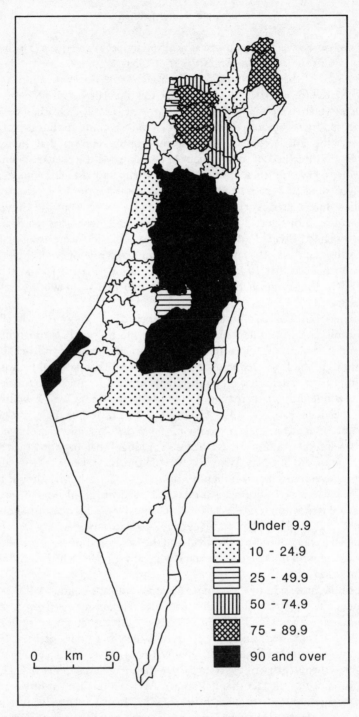

Figure 9.2 Israel and the Occupied Territories: non–Jews as a proportion of the total population, 1988.

Between 1967 and 1973, Israel rode on the crest of a wave. After the surprise attack on Israel by Egyptian and Syrian forces in the Yom Kippur War of October 1973, the descent into the real world was sharp and steep. Israel was no longer perceived as invincible; Palestinian identity could now grow with greater vigour alongside Arab pride. But 1973 also brought another change.

The Zionist coin had two sides, together representing the 'renewal of the Jews in their Land'. Whereas absorption of immigrants and the creation of a new Israeli nation from the Jewish people represented the 'people' side of the Zionist coin and guided Israeli society during its first two and a half decades, the appeal of 'people' yielded to the appeal of 'Land' around the beginning of the 1970s. This change in emphasis, though apparent from 1968 and always present even when Palestine had been partitioned between Arab and Jew, became considerably more marked after 1973, ingrained into government policy after the defeat of the Labour-led coalition in the 1977 elections, catalyzed by the peace treaty with Egypt in 1979, and crystallized by the withdrawal from the northern Sinai settlements in April 1982. Although the Zionists had always stressed 'the Jewish people in the Land of Israel' and had recognized the necessity of the struggle for control and ownership of the Land, this had been allowed to take second place to the need to *re-create the people in their Land*. Only in the 1970s did the land issue take over as the principal moving force of Zionism.

Although the first unauthorized attempt to settle the West Bank by Jews took place in the spring of 1968, and the first acquiescence to settler pressure by the government occurred soon after, the movement gathered momentum after 1973 (Aronoff 1985, Newman 1985). Although the most successful of the 'Land' movements – Gush Emunim – had been spiritually influenced by the outcome of the Six Day War, it was only from 1974 that the messianic mission of this organization began to make itself felt in settlement terms. This movement, and others that agreed with or supported its aims, gloried in the historic rights of the Jewish people over the whole Land of Israel. Gush Emunim adopted an aggressive settlement policy, initiating action and prompting reaction from the government of the time which was headed by Yitzhak Rabin. No sooner had the government decreed the dismantling of an illicit settlement than another arose. Gush Emunim's supporters were punctilious in not coming into violent conflict with the country's leading national institution, the army; however, this did not prevent them from pressing its claims as near to the brink of actual physical confrontation as was possible.

It is not as if the government of the time did not have a settlement policy of its own for the Occupied Territories. The official policy, such as it was, was governed principally by pragmatism, and not by emotion, by considerations of defence first and then by the notion of historic rights. It was based on the so-called Allon Plan, drawn up in 1967, which stressed the old socialist-Zionist ideal of settling border areas with rural settlements. Thus *kibbutzim* and *moshavim* were founded in the Jordan valley, atop the Golan Heights, and on the coast of northeastern Sinai. All of these regions were peripheral and all devoid of settlement, or sparsely settled by indigenous populations. Jewish settlement prior to 1974 expressly avoided areas densely settled by Arabs. In contrast, Gush Emunim's efforts aimed at settlement throughout and over the whole of the Land of Israel, irrespective of who else lived there.

After the Likud electoral victory of 1977, the aims of the government and those of the settlement activists converged. Within the Jewish Agency, the body responsible for Jewish settlement in Israel, the land settlement portfolio, which had always been held by a member of the Labour Party, was now shared with a member of the Herut Party. The central credo of Herut was settlement throughout historic Israel – on both sides of the Jordan river. While the establishment of Jewish settlements on the East Bank (the kingdom of Jordan) was obviously a political impracticality, settlements throughout all parts of the West Bank was not. Moreover, through control of the agriculture and housing ministries, the Begin government had the practical means at its disposal to put its political plans into effect.

Israeli settlement activity in the West Bank thus took on a new form. It was ranked highest on the list of the government's priorities. The plans were comprehensive, and included villages and towns, and other settlements of an urban nature. The settlements were spread throughout all parts of Judaea and Samaria. There was a radical shift away from rural settlements based on agriculture to settlements based on industry, or to those that simply had little more than dormitory functions. In this context, the exurban settlements in those parts of the West Bank within easy commuting range of Tel Aviv or Jerusalem had a two-pronged political aim. Not only did they satisfy the old Herut desire for settlement throughout the Land of Israel, but by providing cheap and spacious residential units that were virtually unobtainable within Israel proper, they were meeting the materialistic demands that had once more come to characterize many in the Jewish population of Israel, a characteristic that had been overshadowed by the 70-year-long, but temporary, hiatus brought about by socialist-Zionist ideas and dreams that were ill-suited to the long-term materialistic desires of the Jewish people (Kellerman 1987). This fits in with the process of gentrification and Americanization of the landscape of Israel proper that has been observed primarily from the 1970s (Waterman & Bar-Gal 1987, Gonen 1989). Of course, it may also be that there is an inherent belief that the settlement effort of the 1980s resembles the settlement effort of the 1930s and 1940s, when Jews succeeded in designing the future shape of the state by establishing their presence in the landscape through the erection of settlements in a semi-official manner.

The policy was thereby designed to attract further support within Jewish society to the policies of right-wing nationalist political parties. The number of Jewish residents in the Occupied Territories had reached 60 000 by 1986 and perhaps 80 000 today. Although this represents only about 2 per cent of Israel's total Jewish population, it is a proportion which did not exist at all some two decades ago. The ratio of Jews to Arabs (residents and refugees) in the West Bank is approximately 1:14 and to Arabs in all of the Occupied Territories about 1:22 (Soffer 1989).

In some cases, a modern road system has been constructed which links Jewish settlements solely and directly, bypassing Arab villages and towns. Where the arteries that link the Jewish settlements pass close to or through Arab settlements, tensions have risen measurably. In both cases, the symbolism is clear. These roads, built by Jews, for Jews, either bypass or consciously ignore the existence or the needs of the Arabs.

Settlement is more than just a matter of mere numbers. Even when there is no agriculture, settlements require land for buildings and roads. Land requirements have often been substantial because of the marketing procedures for the region, in which purchasers are promised single-family dwellings within easy commuting distance of Tel Aviv and Jerusalem – a compensation for living on the frontier. Land has also been required to provide the access to the new Jewish settlements by road. The settlements must be connected to the national electricity and water grids. Land must also be provided for military sites, and the functions of the army have become much more concerned than before with the protection of the settlements and the settlers.

It has been estimated by Meron Benvenisti, probably the most objective observer of events and processes on the West Bank, that Israel now controls 36 per cent of the land and resources on the West Bank (Benvenisti 1987, 37; *Economist* 25 April 1987, 26). This control has been obtained by legal methods, although it is doubtful whether these methods could be termed fair. By using existing Jordanian or British law, the Israeli authorities have acquired control over state lands; some land was acquired by private purchase in the earlier years of the Israeli administration; other private lands have been acquired by using a series of promulgations and ordinances available to the ruling authority. When many of these methods were challenged successfully in Israel's independent court system by Arab owners, the Israeli authorities, under the tutelage of a senior government attorney with responsibility for land transfers, conducted a thorough search of land law and land titles for loopholes and errors in order to promote the aims of the government. Benvenisti has noted that the Israeli incorporation of the West Bank – inevitable in the circumstances, not only in terms of ownership and control, but in investment and infrastructure – is such that even if it were the express will of the majority of the Israeli population (which it is not), it would be extremely difficult, if not impossible, to make a complete withdrawal from all the lands occupied in 1967.

Add to this control over more than a third of the land area of the West Bank the emotional attachment of many of the Jews to the region which, it is often effectively argued, is the most historically Jewish in the whole Land of Israel, together with the economic interdependence of Arab and Jew (Newman & Portugali 1987), and the apparent permanence of the Israeli presence throughout the whole Land of Israel should become more readily apparent.

Epilogue

In the Israeli–Arab conflict in general, and the Israeli–Palestinian dispute in particular, the political dimension is of paramount importance if we are to speak in terms of 'conflict resolution', 'a just and lasting solution to conflicting legitimate claims' and 'peace'. Meanwhile, the traditional processes grind on and the struggle of two nationalisms for control of the same territory continues.

The Zionist movement did not create a colonial society in the style of the British Raj in India, or even in the style of Europeans in Kenya, Rhodesia or Algeria. Yet, in many ways, Israeli society and the Zionist movement which envelops it can be regarded as a pioneering settler society, but on a large scale, involving hundreds of thousands and even millions, and with a time span of over a century. The act of settlement and the continuing desire to establish a Jewish presence throughout the Land of Israel as a whole still spearhead Israeli policies.

Although what most readily springs to mind in this context is the active struggle for land in the Occupied Territories of the West Bank (Judea and Samaria) and the Gaza Strip, the struggle for territorial control is no less severe in those parts of the Land of Israel that form an integral part of the Jewish state. This is especially so in northern Israel – Galilee – where the establishment of over 30 'lookout' settlements (*mitzpim*) by the government settlement agencies, and the unapproved building of houses and extensive planting of olive groves by the Arab inhabitants, are very clear physical expressions of this deep-seated competition.

Throughout the course of the past century, the different varieties of Jewish and Arab nationalism have tried to ignore one another while simultaneously acknowledging each other's presence through stressing each other's very threat as a rival. Thus, Israel has been unwilling or unable to recognize the emerging nationhood and nationalism of the Palestinian Arabs with their accompanying demands for political expression, and their modernization and growing middle-class desires. The attempt to incorporate the Arabs into the Jewish state as full and equal citizens, a continuing experiment extending now over 40 years, was doomed to fail because of the very fact that Israel was founded as a nation-state with which Arabs, with an increasingly clear identity of their own, could not identify. Conversely, the Arabs failed to appreciate either the scale or the permanence of the Zionist effort, especially after the Holocaust, even though they were constantly reminded of this permanence in the recurring wars between Israel and the Arab states, and by the continuing state of conflict between Israelis and Palestinians.

Among the consequences of this inability to appreciate the reality as represented by the other side have been the rise in the level of active competition between Arab and Jew over that most basic of national resources – land; increased Arab attempts to express their national identity more clearly; and a growing attempt by Israeli Arabs to release themselves from their partial and involuntary incorporation into Israeli society.

Writing about a region as volatile as Israel/Palestine is a hazardous occupation. Events are likely to overtake the unfortunate writer as the ink dries on the page. The *intifada*, or popular uprising against Israeli rule on the West Bank and in the Gaza Strip which began in December 1987 and which still continues at the time of writing, is likely to serve as a catalyst for the changes that began to occur when Israel entered the Occupied Territories as an occupying or liberating force in June 1967. Although initially out of the control of the Palestine Liberation Organization and in the hands of local organizing groups, the PLO has succeeded in playing the *intifada* card to its full advantage, declaring a Palestinian government-in-exile and achieving a modicum of recognition as the major Palestinian mouthpiece among Western governments. Whether this will lead to an autonomous Arab area within a Jewish-dominated Palestine, an Arab federation or confederation involving Palestinian Arabs and Jordan, or an independent Palestinian state, is anyone's guess, and the accuracy of the guess will depend on the courage or foolhardiness of the politicians who will eventually have to negotiate a settlement or face the unsavoury consequences. Whatever the eventual settlement plan, it appears that the process of change has been set in motion in recent months.

From the viewpoint of October 1989, the cycle of divide or share appears to be moving once more towards a division of space, a partition of Palestine among the two principal competitors. Whether this actually happens depends to a great degree on whether both sides are prepared to share either sovereignty or territory, the will for which has been distinctly missing in the past. And yet, with the increasing stridency of Jewish settlers in the Occupied Territories on the one hand, and the increasing number of urbanized Arabs in the state of Israel who are an integral part of the Israeli economy – and even its society – on the other, the solution of partition seems in fact to be less likely.

References

Al-Haj, M. 1986. Adjustment patterns of the Arab internal refugees in Israel. *International Migration* **3**, 651–74.

Al-Haj, M. 1988. The Arab internal refugees in Israel: the emergence of a minority within the minority. *Immigrants and Minorities* **7**(2), 149–65.

Aronoff, M. 1985. The institutionalisation and co-optation of a charismatic, messianic, religious–political revitalisation movement. In *The impact of Gush Emunim*, D. Newman (ed.), 46–69. Beckenham: Croom Helm.

Aronson, G. 1987. *Creating facts: Israel, Palestinians and the West Bank*. Washington, DC: Institute for Palestine Studies.

Ben-Arieh, Y. 1984. *Jerusalem in the 19th century – the old city*. Jerusalem: Yad Izhak Ben-Zvi.

Ben-Artzi, Y. 1979. The intra-urban migration of Arabs in Haifa. *Horizons in Geography* **4**, 27–38 (in Hebrew).

Ben-Artzi, Y. 1980. *Formation of a residential pattern and change of residence among the Arabs in Haifa*, Middle East Research Publication Series, (N.S.) 1 (in Hebrew). Haifa: University of Haifa.

Benvenisti, M. 1987. *The West Bank data base project. 1987 report*, Jerusalem: the Jerusalem Post.

Cohen, S. B. 1983. *Israel's defensible borders: a geopolitical map*, Paper No. 20. Tel Aviv: Jaffee Center for Strategic Studies.

Doron, Y. 1988. Geographical perspectives on Arab–Jewish relations in the Nazareth mountains. Unpublished MA thesis, Department of Geography, University of Haifa.

The Economist 25 April 1987. The West Bank, 23–6.

Eliachar, E. 1983. *Living with Jews*. London: Weidenfeld & Nicolson.

Fraser, T. G. 1984. *Partition in Ireland, India and Palestine: theory and practice*. London: Macmillan.

Gonen, A. 1989. Obstacles to middle-class suburbanization in Israel. *Contemporary Jewry* **10**, in press.

Grossman, D. 1988. *The yellow wind*. New York: Farrar, Strauss & Giroux.

Kattan, H. 1988. The Palestinian problem: a Palestinian point of view. In *The Middle East*, M. Adams (ed.), 569–87. New York & Oxford: Facts on File Publications.

Kellerman, A. 1987. *To become a free nation in our land*. MonoGeoGraphy 5. Haifa: Department of Geography, University of Haifa (in Hebrew).

Kipnis, B. A. 1989. Geographical perspectives of peace alternatives for Israel. In *War, peace and geography, seminar abstracts*, S. Waterman and N. Kliot (eds). Haifa: University of Haifa.

Kipnis, B. A. & I. Schnell 1978. Changes in the distribution of Arabs in mixed Arab–Jewish cities in Israel. *Economic Geography* **54**, 168–88.

Lustick, I. 1980. *Arabs in the Jewish state – Israel's control of a national minority*. Austin: University of Texas Press.

Mossa, H. 1988. The geographical distribution of Arab homeland refugees in the Galilee region. Unpublished MA thesis, Department of Geography, University of Haifa.

Newman, D. 1985. Gush Emunim in society and space. In *The impact of Gush Emunim*, D. Newman (ed.), 1–9. London: Croom Helm.

Newman, D. 1989. Overcoming the psychological barrier: the role of images in war and peace. In *War, peace and geography, seminar abstracts*, S. Waterman and N. Kliot (eds). Haifa: University of Haifa.

Newman, D. & J. Portugali 1987. Israeli–Palestinian relations as reflected in scientific literature. *Progress in Human Geography* **11**, 315–32.

Rose, N. 1970. The debate on partition 1937–1938: the Anglo-Zionist aspect. I: The proposal. *Middle Eastern Studies* **6**, 297–318.

Rose, N. 1971. The debate on partition 1937–1938: the Anglo-Zionist aspect. II: The withdrawal. *Middle Eastern Studies* **7**, 3–24.

Shamir, M. & J. L. Sullivan 1985. Jews and Arabs in Israel. Everybody hates somebody, sometime. *Journal of Conflict Resolution* **29**, 283–305.

Shapira, A. 1986. The struggle for 'Jewish Labour' – concept and consequences. In

References

Conflict and consensus in Jewish political life, S. A. Cohen and E. Don-Yehiya (eds), 92–100. Ramat-Gan: Bar-Ilan University Press.

Shilhav, Y. 1983. Communal conflict in Jerusalem – the spread of Ultra-Orthodox neighbourhoods. In *Pluralism and political geography*, N. Kliot and S. Waterman (eds), 100–13. London: Croom Helm.

Shilhav, Y. & M. Friedman 1985. *Growth and segregation – the Ultra Orthodox community of Jerusalem*. Jerusalem: Jerusalem Institute for Israel Studies (in Hebrew).

Smooha, S. 1980. Control of minorities in Israel and Northern Ireland. *Comparative Studies in Society and History* **22**(2), 256–80.

Smooha, S. & D. Peretz 1982. The Arabs in Israel. *Journal of Conflict Resolution* **26**, 451–84.

Soffer, A. 1983. The changing expression of majority and minority and its spatial expression – the case of the Arab minority in Israel. In *Pluralism and political geography*, N. Kliot and S. Waterman (eds), 80–99. London: Croom Helm.

Soffer, A. 1989. Demography and the shaping of Israel's borders. *Contemporary Jewry* **10**, in press.

Waterman, S. 1979. Ideology and events in Israeli human landscapes. *Geography* **64**, 171–80.

Waterman, S. 1987. Partitioned states. *Political Geography Quarterly* **6**, 151–70.

Waterman, S. 1989. Residential segregation in Israel: a practical approach. Paper prepared for the Annual Meeting of the Association of American Geographers, Baltimore, Md.

Waterman, S. & Y. Bar-Gal 1987. Values, society and landscapes in Israel. Paper presented at the IBG Social Geography Study Group Conference, University College London.

Weintraub, D., M. Lissak & Y. Azmon 1969. *Moshava, Kibbutz, Moshav*. Ithaca, NY: Cornell University Press.

10

Imposed separation: the case of South Africa

ANTHONY LEMON

> The apartheid policy has been described as what one can do in the direction of what you regard as ideal. Nobody will deny that for the Natives as well as for the European complete separation would have been the ideal if it had developed that way historically. (H. F. Verwoerd 1948, 234).

Apartheid represents an extreme response to the problems of ethnically divided societies. It seeks to create a divided social and political space which coincides with officially defined ethnic divisions at personal, local and national scales. The necessity for a degree of economic integration has always been recognized, but attempts have been made to minimize even this, largely through programmes of industrial decentralization (Bell 1973).

The roots of apartheid grew out of British-inspired, colonialist traditions of segregation (Christopher 1983). The government formed by Smuts and Hertzog in 1933 elaborated and entrenched the segregationist policies of its predecessors, notably by removing African voters from the common role in the Cape (the only province where they enjoyed this position) and by passing a new land Act which effectively laid the foundations for the Bantustan policies of the 1950s.[1]

The propagation of apartheid by Afrikaner nationalists in the mid-1940s was a response to what they perceived as a growing threat of liberalism and integration. Wartime industrial expansion had increased labour demands, pulling large numbers of Africans to the cities, and industrialists were beginning to stress the value of semi-skilled Africans in manufacturing employment. Smuts' United Party government appeared slowly to be recognizing the need for reform of influx control and the migrant labour system, urged on by the findings of several official bodies (South Africa 1941, 248; 1943, para.8; 1946, para.11). Liberals in the English-language universities and the South African Institute of Race Relations were increasingly demanding the abandonment of white supremacy in favour of a policy of black political participation, racial integration in the cities, and a common society based on shared values, a common Christian faith, English as a *lingua franca*, and a universal education system designed to further this vision (Giliomee 1987, 364).

The National Party came to power in 1948 after an election which it had depicted as a stark choice between liberalism and apartheid. Apartheid ideologues believed that the greater the range of contact in an open society, the greater the friction as blacks and whites competed for homes, jobs, access to services and amenities, and political power. Black numbers posed an obvious long-term threat to white power and privilege in such an open society. Nationalists were anxious to protect that power and privilege, as well as the Afrikaner nation and its culture, but their political, intellectual and religious leaders were also concerned to demonstrate the moral basis of apartheid and refute the charge that they were mere racists. Thus they readily embraced the 'cultural idealism', or cultural pluralism, which was gaining official acceptance during the Smuts government of 1939–48. By maintaining the indigenous social structure of Africans in semi-autonomous political entities, Nationalists argued that Africans would enjoy greater opportunities than if they had to compete with whites in a common society.

There is no mistaking the sense of purpose of Nationalist governments after 1948. Moved by 'a most rational, most passionate, most radical will to restructure the world according to a vision of justice', in the words of a critical Afrikaner historian, they carried out a radical restructuring of South African society in less than one generation (de Klerk 1975, 241). Spatial reordering of society and polity, and of economy where practicable, was necessarily fundamental to this apartheid planning, and the thoroughness of the process led to its being dubbed 'the most ambitious contemporary exercise in applied geography' (Smith 1982, 1).

The implementation of apartheid

The whole apartheid edifice rests upon the Population Registration Act of 1950 which requires the classification of all South Africans as white, coloured (mixed race), Indian or Bantu (African). For the coloureds such classification has always been particularly arbitrary, in so far as they range from dark-skinned people indistinguishable from Africans to light-skinned people indistinguishable from whites, many of whose own claim to racial 'purity' is questionable. Culturally, coloureds are mainly 'brown Afrikaners' in terms of their home language and, for many, religion. Indians now mainly speak English at home, but most are Hindus or Muslims; for them integration at the level of intermarriage would be rare even in the absence of imposed segregation and apartheid.

Separation has been imposed at three spatial scales. The micro-scale, commonly termed 'petty apartheid' in South Africa itself, involves the segregation of personal action space in the use of services and amenities. Its rationale was supposedly the avoidance of friction between culturally incompatible groups. In practice only the susceptibilities of whites were considered:

for 'petty apartheid' purposes the African majority was lumped together with coloured and Indian minorities, and offensively defined by what they were not, as 'non-whites'. But Africans were regarded as the major threat: as apartheid was implemented at other spatial scales and African population numbers in 'white' areas declined, the perceived need for micro-scale segregation was expected to decrease.

In practice, economic imperatives ensured that African numbers continued to grow, yet the gradual dismantling of 'petty apartheid' which has occurred has not been accompanied by a noticeable increase in friction. Indeed, the continuing absence of such friction in public places is remarkable given the rising anger and frustration among urban blacks in the 1980s. Early reforms at the micro-scale included the desegregation of post offices and the opening of some parks and theatres to all races in the 1970s. Many such matters are the responsibility of municipal authorities rather than central government, and geographical variations in the dismantling of 'petty apartheid' reflect white attitudes in the areas concerned. In conservative districts, long-established practice may well outlast the removal of signs, while the signs themselves have been restored in some Transvaal towns where the right-wing Conservative Party won control in the October 1988 local elections. Some aspects of 'petty apartheid' depend upon the policy decisions of private entrepreneurs, but in many cases these too will be sensitive to local variations in the opinion of whites as the major customers. Even state bodies move at different speeds in the implementation of reform; South African Railways displayed characteristic conservatism by desegregating only a small proportion of coaches on its trains (in practice usually those hitherto reserved for 'non-whites'!) from 1985 onwards.

More fundamental to apartheid is meso-scale segregation, particularly of residential areas. This is achieved primarily through 'group areas' legislation and related measures. If it is true, as social geographers have argued, that social distance is correlated with spatial distance (Peach 1975), then South Africa's enforced urban social segregation does indeed provide an effective instrument for maintaining and in some cases accentuating group divisions. It is not difficult to see why this should be so.

In the first place, much voluntary association takes place at the level of the neighbourhood or suburban community, through sports and social clubs, churches and other organizations. Even where, as in many churches, there is a desire for more inter-racial contact, this is made difficult by transport and other problems in the 'apartheid city'. Joint worship or social events thus require careful planning and are unlikely to occur often; when they do, the very character of apartheid society may render them contrived or self-conscious (Lemon 1987, 54). Residential segregation also provides a territorial basis for segregated schools, which are regarded by most whites as a critical element in their way of life, and for segregated health and welfare services. At a political level, group areas provide a basis for apartheid frameworks in both local and, under the 1983 constitution, national government. These issues will be considered further below.

At the national scale a basis for the segregation of Africans already existed in the form of the reserves. Cultural idealism found its expression in the Bantu Authorities Act of 1951, which reinforced the position of chiefs and elders and thereby weakened that of urban-trained intellectuals. African cultural development was to be directed towards the reserves and around tribal tradition. A degree of autonomy in the reserves was to compensate for the denial of political rights outside them in 'white' South Africa. To lend greater credibility to the reserves as administrative entities, a limited degree of territorial consolidation was gradually undertaken, and they were re-christened Bantustans, and subsequently homelands. Dr. H. F. Verwoerd, who is regarded as the prime architect of apartheid and became Prime Minister in 1958, was only grudgingly persuaded to accept the possibility of full independence for the homelands as the ultimate logic of his grand design (Giliomee 1985).

Economically, the reserves constituted a pathetically inadequate basis for separate development. Originally intended as subsistence areas for Africans not involved in the modern economy, analogous to reserves for Aborigines in Australia and for North American Indians, these scattered and fragmented areas were amongst the least accessible and least developed in South Africa, and their existing infrastructure was negligible. Although they included some fertile agricultural land and were mainly located in the better watered eastern half of the country, they occupied a peripheral position in the South African space-economy. Slowly increasing population pressure on the land did not lead to the innovation and intensification of agricultural practices which Boserup (1965) has described in other areas, but rather to an increase in the number of Africans seeking jobs in 'white' areas. By the mid-1950s most of their population of 3.6 million was already at least partially dependent on outside earnings or remittances from family members working as migrant labourers in the mines or on white farms.

The Tomlinson Commission put forward a detailed plan for the socio-economic development of the reserves, whereby they would be developed so as to carry 8 million people with only partial dependence on labour migration (South Africa 1955). Proposals were made for land-use planning and land reform, irrigation, commercial agriculture, afforestation, intensive mineral surveys, the establishment of manufacturing and the creation of towns. These proposals created a dilemma for apartheid planners; to implement them in full would have been prohibitively expensive, yet to do significantly less would undermine the moral basis of the whole apartheid design, leaving the reserves as mere labour reservoirs, increasingly overpopulated areas which offered negligible opportunities, economic or political, for meaningful African advance. As we shall see, this is in effect what happened, despite the partial implementation of many of the Tomlinson proposals.

The Commission also proposed major changes in South Africa's political geography. These included the ultimate removal of all Africans from west of the 'Eiselen line' (so named after the administrator who devised it in 1955), leaving only whites, coloureds and a small number of Indians to live and work in the western and central Cape. In 1955 some 180 000 Africans, mostly temporary migrants, lived west of this line. The Tomlinson proposal was based on the absence of Africans in the area concerned when white settlement began in the 1650s. It was adopted as official policy in 1962, and only finally abandoned in 1985, when the policy of giving preference to coloured over African labour west of the Eiselen line was also ended.

More fundamental was Tomlinson's recommendation that the existing reserves be consolidated into seven blocks or 'heartlands' around 'historico-logical' (*sic*) centres. This proposal, which was in any case rendered impracticable by its demand for the incorporation of the British High Commission territories of Basutoland, Bechuanaland and Swaziland into South Africa, was rejected outright by the government. Instead, additional land was added to the reserves in terms of the 1936 Native Land Act, which became the basis of the government's homeland consolidation policies in the 1970s. Some further consolidation was effected in terms of the van der Walt Commission proposals in the 1980s, but much fragmentation remains (Fig. 10.1), above all in KwaZulu, which will have 15 sections even after 'consolidation'.

This, then, is the political and economic basis of homeland 'independence' which began with the Transkei in 1976 and continued with Bophuthatswana (1977), Venda (1979), and Ciskei (1981). The other six homelands, or 'national states', as they are now officially called, are self-governing in most respects, but all except KwaNdebele, the last to be created and one of the most impoverished, have resisted the offer of 'independence'. The situation is unclear in KawNdebele, where political instability has led to reversals of policy; its authorities have been told by Pretoria that they must demonstrate popular support for independence, but all the evidence suggests that this will be impossible (McCaul 1987, TRAC 1987). The homelands have inevitably created bureaucracies with vested interests, and have helped to perpetuate tribal awareness among rural Africans. But some 60 per cent of Africans are now functionally urban, and for most of them the common experience of oppression has come to outweigh the sense of tribal identity which apartheid has sought to foster.

The consequences of apartheid

Urban social segregation

The segregation of Africans was provided for in the Natives (Urban Areas) Act of 1923. Apartheid policies subsequently sought to impose ethno–linguistic zoning within African townships which housed several tribal groups, especially in the Transvaal, but with limited success (Pirie 1984a).

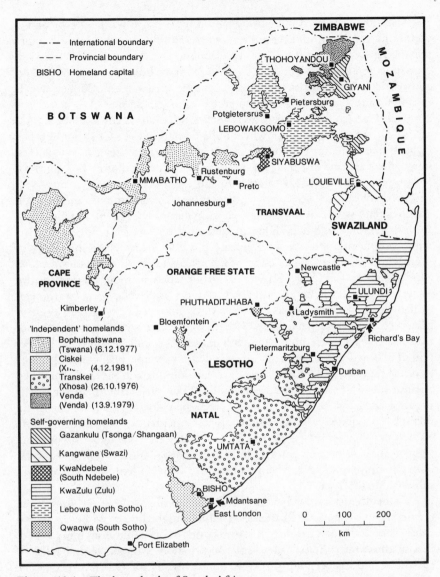

Figure 10.1 The homelands of South Africa.

Those South Africans officially classified as coloured (3 million), Indian (0.9 million) or white (5 million) are housed today in some 1700 racially exclusive residential areas. Rezoning in terms of the Group Areas Acts of 1950 and 1966 has involved the relocation of over 125 000 *families*, primarily coloureds and Indians, and an unknown, possibly even greater, number of Africans who have been moved to make way for the designation, implementation and expansion of coloured, Indian and white group areas. In many cases people were

199

physically better housed but emotionally impoverished by the destruction of their homes and community, and remoteness from the environment in which they had grown up. In some cases race zoning has actually exacerbated over-crowding and squalor. The hardships caused have been widely documented, and particularly traumatic cases have become well known: Sophiatown in Johannesburg where Trevor Huddleston worked among Africans facing removal; District Six in Cape Town where the coloured community was the victim; Grey Street in Durban where Indians retained their CBD but lost their right to live there until this was restored in 1983; and Pageview in Johannesburg where Indians lost their businesses as well as their homes (see e.g. Pirie 1984b, Hart & Pirie 1984, Lemon 1976 and 1987, Western 1981).

One result of such social engineering has been the creation of a recognizable apartheid city with a distinctive spatial formation (Davies 1981 and Fig. 10.2). Both the amount and desirability of land allocated to each race group reflect white dominance and the intermediate position in the ethnic hierarchy of Indians and coloureds. The design of the apartheid city is planned to endure, allowing space for future growth of group areas in their allotted sectors. Wherever possible natural features such as rivers, steep valleys and escarpments or man-made barriers such as industrial or commercial belts or railways have been used to separate group areas. 'Islands' of one race within an area occupied by another have been eliminated, and segregation indices approach 100 per cent, if live-in domestic servants are excluded. The whole plan is even designed to discourage movement of people of one group through the area of another. African townships are characteristically found on the periphery of the city in the least attractive sector(s); in many cases their design and location permit them to be quickly cordoned off in an emergency (Adam 1971, 123). Sometimes they may be close to factories where their inhabitants work, but frequently their location enforces long commuting journeys which are costly both for those who make them and for the state and employers who must subsidize them.

Apartheid cities not only reflect but also reinforce the social formation, restricting even the limited transition which might otherwise occur from a situation of divided or conflict pluralism to one of open pluralism more akin to that in the United States. Meso-scale segregation is thus a central pillar of apartheid, and has been left relatively untouched by the reform process. The principal exception to date is economic: the 1984 Group Areas Amendment Act has resulted in the opening up of increasing numbers of CBDs to trading by all races.

In the 1980s, however, the government has faced unprecedented pressures for substantive reform or repeal of group areas legislation. These arise from the housing market itself with the response of white vendors and estate agents and black home-seekers; the recognition of this reality by the judiciary; and a growing challenge from some white city councils and major business firms (Lemon 1989a).

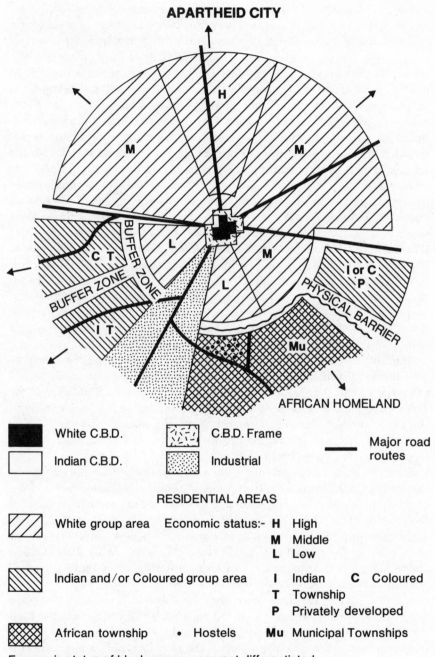

APARTHEID CITY

H

M   M

BUFFER ZONE

BUFFER ZONE

C T

I T

L

M

L

I or C
P

PHYSICAL BARRIER

Mu

AFRICAN HOMELAND

| | White C.B.D. | | C.B.D. Frame | | Major road routes |
| | Indian C.B.D. | | Industrial | | |

RESIDENTIAL AREAS

	White group area	Economic status:-	**H**	High
			M	Middle
			L	Low
	Indian and/or Coloured group area		**I** Indian	**C** Coloured
			T Township	
			P Privately developed	
	African township	• Hostels	**Mu** Municipal Townships	

Economic status of black group areas not differentiated
Domestic servant quarters not shown

Figure 10.2 Apartheid city.

The implementation of group areas has produced an inequitable distribution and an artificial scarcity of land, and has greatly impeded freedom of choice for the growing black middle class who frequently find it impossible to buy housing commensurate with their living standards and aspirations (de Vos 1986). Whereas an estimated surplus of 37 000 housing units for whites existed in 1985 – a reflection of low natural population increase and the beginnings of an exodus – the estimated shortages for other groups were 52 000 for coloureds, 44 000 for Indians and 538 000 for Africans outside the homelands (ibid.) As a result, the average price of land and buildings in white areas is considerably lower than that of comparable properties in coloured, Indian and African areas. In such circumstances it is hardly surprising that blacks have taken matters into their own hands, moving into white areas even it it means paying a substantial premium to vendors and estate agents. Pockets of integrated residential settlement have become characteristic of most larger cities; examples include Hillbrow, Mayfair, Doornfontein and Yeoville in Johannesburg (de Coning, Fick & Olivier 1986), Clairwood and Greyville in Durban, Korsten and North End in Port Elizabeth, and Woodstock, Salt River and Observatory in Cape Town. Growing numbers of elite blacks are also purchasing or occupying luxury homes in affluent Sandton (Johannesburg), Constantia and Newlands (Cape Town), and along Durban's beachfront (Pirie 1987). In Johannesburg, particularly, business firms are buying houses for their black executives in the affluent northern suburbs.

More liberal local authorities such as East London, Durban, Pietermaritzburg and Sandton have not only accepted these changes *de facto* but also pressed for varying degrees of *de jure* change. Meanwhile, the strict application of the 1966 Group Areas Act has been increasingly compromised by judicial rulings, and the Attorney General of the Transvaal actually announced in 1986 that he had not of late been instituting any prosecutions in terms of the Act (de Coning, Fick & Olivier 1986).

In response to these pressures, the Constitutional Committee of the President's Council was asked to consider possible consolidation and revision of group areas and related legislation. Its report not unexpectedly embraced the concept of 'local option', proposing procedures for local application to make existing group areas open to all races, and for developers to apply for open status in the case of new residential areas (South Africa 1987, Lemon 1989a). The report recommends that local authorities should give particular attention to creating open residential areas in or near CBDs, which would in effect be to legalize the *status quo* in the areas mentioned above. It also gives some attention to related issues, including schools and the franchise at local government level, revealing in the process the extraordinary labyrinth of interconnected issues which arises when the rambling edifice of apartheid is subject to piecemeal tampering rather than fundamental reform.

Piecemeal tampering is clearly the most that can be expected in the foreseeable future. President Botha has repeatedly reiterated his commitment to residential segregation and the preservation of an own-community life for the different population groups (Lemon 1989a). The 1989 Free Settlement Areas Act makes limited provision for the creation of open areas, but the Group Areas Amendment Bill would, if passed, tighten controls everywhere else; at the time of writing the President's Council has referred it back for reconsideration and amendment. The government undoubtedly fears that more widespread residential integration would lead to the development of cross-cutting social cleavages which could ultimately threaten the preservation of a distinct Afrikaner culture. More immediately it fears that bolder reform would strengthen the extreme right-wing Conservative Party which became the official Opposition in 1987 (Lemon 1989b). An unspoken but real fear must concern the effect of widespread ethnic residential mixing in enabling the spread of unrest and violence to white suburbs, hitherto almost totally insulated from the realities of life in African townships.

Underlying such fears is the fundamental thinking of the Nationalist ruling elite, which remains group-bound. This is reflected in its approach to constitutional change at all levels. Group areas constitute the territorial basis for the exercise of 'own affairs' by the coloured, Indian and white houses of the tricameral Parliament. They are also the basis of 'primary local authorities' (PLAs) in which it is intended that each group should administer its own affairs at local level (Todes & Watson 1985, Heymans & Totemeyer 1988). It is these PLAs which nominate members of the new multi racial Regional Services Councils whose responsibilities include the upgrading of infrastructure in those areas – effectively black areas – where the need is greatest (du Toit 1988). Imposed separation at the local level thus remains critical to official planning, and no major retreat from it is likely.

The 'homeland' periphery

It is difficult to overstate the importance of homeland policies on the lives of Africans. The combination of high natural population growth (currently around 2.5 per cent p.a.), restricted out-migration and the forced removals of 3 million 'surplus' people to the homelands since 1960 (Platzky & Walker 1985) has left most parts of the homelands impoverished, undermining the role of agriculture as a major source of support and precluding meaningful development. Industrial decentralization programmes have enjoyed very limited success, and it is the homeland bureaucracies themselves which offer almost the only attractive employment prospects within these territories. Migrant labour and 'frontier commuting' – daily movement across homeland borders to jobs in 'white' areas – are the major sources of employment, and both have been responsible for internal population shifts within the homelands. Peri-urban squatter areas, resettlement camps, industrial growth points and homeland 'capitals' on virgin sites have all transformed settlement patterns.

Table 10.1 Arable land, production and income in the homelands, 1985.

Homeland	Arable land per household (ha.)*	Commercial production (R'000)	% of GDP	Subsistence production (R'000)	% of GDP	Agricultural production per household (R p.a.)*	Agricultural income as % of household income*
Bophuthatswana	1.4	22 400	1.9	30 000	2.6	183	5.4
Ciskei	0.6	2 964	0.7	16 600	3.9	157	6.6
Gazankulu	0.6	3 540	1.5	20 310	8.8	231	15.7
Kangwane	0.5	8 500	7.9	9 100	8.5	235	6.9
KwaNdebele	0.5	800	1.5	1 500	2.9	48	1.3
KwaZulu	0.8	75 000	7.1	133 000	12.5	285	8.7
Lebowa	1.0	12 000	2.2	33 000	6.1	125	7.3
QwaQwa	0.2	2 000	1.8	1 990	1.8	114	4.2
Transkei	1.5	26 700	2.0	137 000	10.1	327	31.2
Venda+	0.8	9 141	4.6	17 100	8.7	341	22.8

* These figures relate to *all* homeland households, including those which are officially or functionally urban. They would be up to twice as high if urban households were excluded, but there is no reliable statistical basis for doing this for individual homelands.
+ Production figures for Venda relate to 1984.
Source: Development Bank of Southern Africa, cited in Cobbe 1986.

Some 12.7 million people, 44.7 per cent of the African population, lived in the homelands in 1985. Of these, five-sixths are officially classed as rural, but this proportion includes substantial peri-urban squatter populations. In practice 7–8 million people, or 50–60 per cent of the homeland population, live in a rural environment today, whereas the Tomlinson Commission estimated that the land could support only 1.8 million people. As a result, most homelands have an average of less than two hectares of arable land per rural household (Table 10.1), and many households are landless. The contribution of agriculture to the combined GDP of the homelands has decreased from 28 per cent in 1977 to less than 11 per cent in 1984, as the limited growth of other sectors has left agriculture behind. Average agricultural production per rural household was worth only R400–480 in 1985 (R4 = £1). Even this is inflated by the increasing share of homeland agricultural production accounted for by agribusiness in the hands of corporations; if this is excluded, the household average drops to around R300 p.a.

In such circumstances the term 'subsistence agriculture' is misleading. Most African farming is certainly for subsistence purposes, but few families grow enough to feed themselves. Agricultural earnings provide barely 20 per cent of total income for the average rural household. The rest consists of migrant workers' remittances, the earnings of the relatively small number of rural household members who have jobs within the homelands or within commuting distance of their homes, and, for the poorest families, pensions and charitable handouts.

The depressed state of the South African economy in the early 1980s was felt most acutely in the homelands, whose role as labour suppliers expands or contracts according to demand in the core areas of the space-economy. Thus the number of migrants and commuters requisitioned by regional development boards fell from 1 302 586 in 1983 to 1 046 183 in 1985; a further 251 887 Africans were recruited from the homelands by the Chamber of Mines in 1985 (SAIRR 1986, 164 and 1987, 730–1). This latter figure has remained relatively stable, but the overall decline in the context of a growing labour market has meant acute poverty for many more homeland families. The few jobs on offer at homeland labour bureaux have tended to go to those who happen to be on the spot when a requisition arrives. For the rest, the only hope is to seek work directly in urban areas. Although the repeal of racially discriminatory influx control legislation in 1986 has theoretically made this easier, the use of racially neutral squatter, slum and health controls over land and housing discourages rural workseekers (Hindson 1987). Those already living in urban areas are anyway in a better position to take what jobs are available.

Many homeland families have moved to those parts of the homelands which are within commuting distance of 'white' metropolitan areas, especially Durban and Pretoria; Third World urbanization is thus displaced across homeland borders by apartheid (Lemon 1982, Murray 1987).Some 1.5 million squatters live in the greater Durban area alone, most of them within the

borders of KwaZulu. Nearly one-third of Bophuthatswana's total population lives in townships north of Pretoria and the adjoining squatter areas
of the Winterveld, where many non–Tswana endure persistent ethnic discrimination and harassment by the Bophuthatswana authorities in order to
remain within reach of actual or potential employment. Ciskei has experienced a similar movement of population to the sprawling township of
Mdantsane, linked by a commuter railway to East London. Towns exercis-
ing a lesser attraction on homeland population include Pietermaritzburg,
Newcastle, Ladysmith and Richard's Bay (from KwaZulu), Rustenburg
(from Bophuthatswana), and Pietersburg and Potgietersrus (from Lebowa)
(Fig. 10.1).

Labour from these metropolitan supply areas is increasingly replacing the
hitherto predominant migrant labour. Cobbett (1987) believes that the current
decentralization plan with its nine development regions (Fig. 10.3) is intended
to further this trend. Recognizing at last the necessity of African urbanization,
the state's new strategy, based on a report of the President's Council, entails the
establishment of residential areas near deconcentrated industrial areas on the
peripheries of metropolitan centres (South Africa 1985). The strategy divides
South Africa into nine development regions which straddle homeland
boundaries.

The uneven distribution of the deconcentration points so far announced
clearly reflects perceived development demands (Fig. 10.3). They include
Tongaat on the north Natal coast, an Indian growth point under an earlier
industrial strategy, and the new coloured city of Atlantis north of Cape Town.
Natal's needs are also served by the designation of Pietermaritzburg and its
neighbouring African areas, together with a point north of Tongaat in
KwaZulu.

Botshabelo, 65 km east of Bloemfontein, is the only deconcentration point
in the Orange Free State. It began as a resettlement camp for non–Tswana
(mainly Sotho) people who had been moved out of the Thaba 'Nchu district
of Bophuthatswana, but is now receiving both the natural increase of
Bloemfontein's African townships and a large influx of people displaced by
mechanization on white farms, as well as an illegal influx from Lesotho.
Botshabelo is perhaps the single most dramatic testimony to the tangible
results of imposed separation; since 1979 it has been transformed from barren
veld to a sprawling settlement with a population approaching 500 000, with
few urban facilities and minimal employment opportunities. Its male workers
either commute daily to Bloemfontein or weekly to the Orange Free State
goldfields.

The remaining deconcentration points are all in the southern Transvaal,
South Africa's industrial heartland which accounts for 40 per cent of the
country's GDP. They include Babelegi which already has three-quarters of
Bophuthatswana's manufacturing jobs, the township of Garankuwa which
acts as a dormitory for Pretoria, the non–Tswana township of Soshanguve

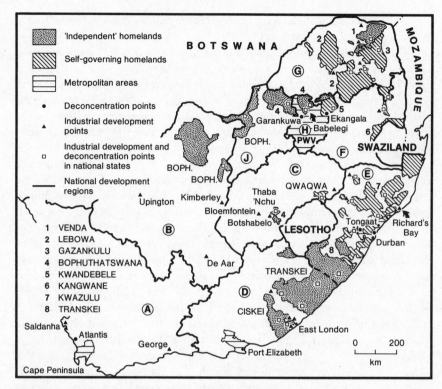

Figure 10.3   Foci for industrial development in South Africa.

which has a similar function, the 'white' town of Brits which is strategically positioned between Bophuthatswana's Odi 1 and Odi 2 districts (the former including the Winterveld), and Bronkhorstspruit-Ekangala northeast of Pretoria together with a nearby point in KwaNdebele. Ekangala, a new township with only 5 500 people in 1985, is destined for particularly rapid growth, and there have even been suggestions that it should absorb the whole natural increase of Soweto's 1.5 million people. Unless the adjacent industrial estate of Ekandustria can match such growth, this would imply a massive increase in the scale of ultra-long-distance commuting. This is already the hallmark of the KwaNdebele homeland itself, which has become a second and much more distant base for those seeking to find somewhere to live with their families within daily reach of work in Pretoria and even distant Witwatersrand towns.

The uneven distribution of these deconcentration points is partly balanced by the distribution of 48 industrial development points, 28 of which are located in the homelands. In practice, only a handful of these can be expected to grow significantly; undisclosed priorities agreed for infrastructural spending are likely to be an influential determinant. Although it is the remotest

207

development points which enjoy the highest incentives, the likelihood is that few will attract much industry.

The state's motives in pursuing this decentralization policy have been the subject of a lively debate. At one level it is clearly attempting a new form of influx control, seeking to direct the inevitable process of African urbanization in order to minimize the socio-political repercussions. Quite simply, Africans in Botshabelo or KwaNdebele are politically less threatening than if they were added to Soweto or the Rand townships. Cobbett *et al.* (1987) link decentralization to a fundamental political restructuring which they see as the basis for a federal or confederal constitution, a view which seems consistent with the second- and third-tier constitutional reforms outlined below. Their case for the new strategy benefiting the interests of capital is harder to sustain. Tomlinson & Addleson (1987) show that the state's regional policy assists only that small segment of capital (some of it drawn from Taiwan and Israel) which benefits from decentralization concessions, whilst influx control and the costs of homeland 'development' slow down growth. While capital may not always understand what is required for its survival and profit maximization, there is no reason to suppose that South African capital is misjudging its own interests when it calls for free spatial mobility of capital and labour. Only in the indirect sense that the strategy is intended to underpin the continuation of white domination, and therefore allegiance to capitalism, can the latter be regarded as a beneficiary: and this only to the extent that capitalist interests would suffer under a black majority government, which is by no means certain.

Whatever its motivation, the state's current response to the inevitability of African urbanization is creating a new settlement geography at great cost in human terms. To this must be added the more developed of the homeland capitals such as Mmabatho, Bisho and Ulundi, places which owe their very existence to apartheid, and where substantial parts of the development budgets of their respective homelands are spent to create the iconography of statehood. Nothing could better symbolize the vested interests which are now present in the homelands, and which will constitute a stumbling block both to the negotiation of fundamental political change and to post-apartheid planning. It will not be easy to dismantle the urban and political geography which apartheid has created, however artificial was its conception.

Apartheid planning, white domination and the interests of capital

Apartheid has been in transition since the late 1970s, but it is doubtful that even the architects of state policy are clear about the desired end product of transition. Not only do they seldom articulate their motives, but much of their policy is probably formulated reactively, and constantly adapted in the light of past failures, new pressures and changing perceptions. It is frequently the case that the implications of policies are 'neither well thought out nor clearly perceived by those who make them' (Tomlinson & Addleson 1987, xv).

Apartheid has from its inception been characterized by a central contradiction between imposed spatial separation in the social and political spheres in the context of unavoidable economic integration which could only move in one direction as the South African economy developed. This did not preclude certain critical aspects of apartheid from serving the needs of capital. Above all, the homelands (and neighbouring countries) served as a reservoir of migrant labour which could be paid wages below the costs of family survival because of the cushion provided by subsistence agriculture (Wolpe 1972); however this system long predated the introduction of apartheid *per se* in 1948, and it is doubtful that its strengthening thereafter greatly benefited capitalist interests. Other aspects of apartheid, such as job reservation, favoured white labour at the expense of white capital, and indeed the latter was sufficiently strong in the agricultural sector to ensure that job reservation was never applied on white farms. It also gained from an agreement between the Chamber of Mines and the South African Agricultural Union which reserved certain parts of the homelands for the labour needs of particular employers, such as the Natal sugar industry which monopolized recruitment in Pondoland, northern Transkei (Leys 1975, Lemon 1984).

Merle Lipton's masterly analysis has shown that the standard question as to whether economic growth shores up or erodes apartheid is too crude (Lipton 1985). Capitalists in South Africa have never been wholeheartedly or unanimously in favour of apartheid. In its early years of government, the National Party relied on Afrikaner farmers and blue-collar workers for the bulk of its electoral support (hence the political strength of agricultural capital), while industrial and mining capital, still overwhelmingly controlled by English-speakers, was more closely associated with the United Party, and later the Progressive Party, whose links with Harry Oppenheimer and Anglo-American were well known (Hackland 1980). The situation gradually changed with the growing embourgeoisement of Afrikaners and the growth of Afrikaner capitalist interests, both of which processes were actively assisted by the state. Meanwhile the entrenchment of Nationalist political power made capital realize the necessity of co-operation with Nationalist governments.

At the same time the greater sophistication of the South African economy required increasing numbers of skilled workers, and the interests of capital began to shift towards a free, mobile, competitive labour market. Industry was also becoming more capital intensive, with labour costs declining as a proportion of total costs, while it became increasingly obvious in certain sectors of manufacturing that low wages constrained the domestic market. Exceptionally rapid economic growth during the 1960s and early 1970s accentuated the impracticability of imposed spatial separation. The resultant pressures for reform flowed *both* from the changing interests of capital *and* from growing popular resistance, symbolized above all by the 1976 Soweto riots, which themselves reflected the heightened contradictions of the apartheid state in the face of increasing black urbanization and occupational mobility unmatched by political change.

Although capitalist interests wanted socio-economic change, they were more ambivalent about fundamental political change, and remain so, fearing for the future of capitalism itself under black rule. The strength and persistence of popular resistance in the years 1984–6 appeared to persuade some business leaders to ask more fundamental questions, and some of them met leaders of the African National Congress in Lusaka in September 1985. During 1984–6, spokesmen for Afrikaner business organizations moved closer to their English-speaking counterparts, although not to the point of joining the Lusaka meeting, which they felt would assist the ANC strategy of isolating the government politically. Since 1986, business activism has noticeably waned as repression of popular resistance by the police and the army has brought outward calm to the townships. Increased sanctions have so far drawn business closer to the state in a common effort to overcome external pressures, although the comprehensive mandatory sanctions long sought by the ANC could well persuade business of the necessity for negotiation.

Both capital and the state fundamentally seek order and stability in a period of economic restructuring and social change. However, the state is also concerned with constitutional restructuring designed to increase its legitimacy with blacks, and this may or may not accord with the short-term interests of capital. At the national level, the state has moved towards an increasingly centralized structure in which top bureaucrats, technicians and the military have gained influence and which seeks to absorb co-opted elements (including blacks) from outside the National Party.

In terms of formal constitutional reform, however, the state is focusing initially on the second and third tiers. In 1986, it replaced elected white provincial councils with multiracial nominated executive committees seen as facilitators of the official concept of 'power sharing' in the administration of 'general affairs' at the second tier of government (Heymans 1988). The introduction of multiracial provincial government, with a possible subdivision of the vast Cape and Transvaal provinces into three, now seems possible (Heunis 1987).

At the local level, there is a new division between responsibility for the so-called 'own affairs' of each ethnic group and what are deemed by the 1983 constitution to be 'general affairs'. The former are the responsibility of 'primary local authorities' (PLAs), which are ethnically defined and based on group areas and townships. These authorities elect representatives to multiracial 'regional services councils' (RSCs) which are to be entrusted with 'general affairs'. Voting strength on the RSCs depends on consumer power rather than population, and is thus heavily biased towards whites, although early experience suggests that most decisions are taken with a degree of consensus. The most critical responsibility of RSCs is to use their revenues, derived from taxes on the business sector, for the upgrading of coloured, Indian and especially African areas. The state hopes that the tangible results of what is proving to be a substantial redistribution of wealth at local level will buy legitimacy of both RSCs and PLAs. The October 1988 local elections were seen by both the state and extra-parliamentary organizations as a test for such legitimacy. The government even made it illegal to call for a boycott, and attempted to reduce supposed intimidation by introducing a system of 'prior' voting, which enabled electors to cast votes up to a fortnight before polling day. These tactics failed; registration levels were low amongst Africans – only 347 000 of an estimated 1 million eligible adults in Soweto – and there was no contest in many constituencies. Countrywide, a mere 400 000 Africans actually voted.

Despite the multiracial character of RSCs and the new provincial councils, the government's constitutional thinking remains entirely group-bound. The fundamental objective is to share power without losing control. This appears to be based on the conviction that only a government enjoying majority Afrikaner (or at least white) support 'can successfully orchestrate all the technocratic skills and abilities that serve the material welfare of everyone in the country' (Giliomee 1987, 381). In its increasing emphasis on socio-economic needs ahead of political rights, Pretoria's approach is, curiously, coming to resemble the 'dictatorship over needs' characteristic of eastern European regimes which justify repression by claiming for a bureaucratic oligarchy an indispensable role in addressing socio-economic needs (ibid., Feher *et al.* 1983).

Territorial reordering and a negotiated settlement

Many see the state's current approach as leading towards regional federalism which is intended to prevent national democratic forces from mobilizing against the central state (Cobbett *et al.* 1987, 24). Such a strategy may enjoy some success, but any white contribution to a long-term constitutional solution in South Africa will have to be genuinely negotiated rather than imposed. If and when such negotiation does occur, whites will certainly want to place territorial reordering on the agenda, and it is appropriate to conclude a study of imposed separation with a brief consideration of the possible role of territorial reordering in a negotiated settlement.

It must be recognized at the outset that the ANC and mass popular movements within the country will attempt to exclude such an item from the agenda altogether. Their preference for one person–one vote in a unitary state with no special privileges for whites is clear, although the 1955 Freedom Charter does embrace protection for minority groups. But just as genuine negotiation requires official abandonment of Pretoria's often-stated 'non-negotiables', so will a parallel flexibility of approach be necessary from the ANC.

211

Two territorial approaches may be dismissed as non-starters. Confederation or 'constellation', as President Botha has labelled it, based on the present or enlarged and consolidated homelands, would be utterly unacceptable to all groups to the left of the National Party, and to international opinion. It would be seen, rightly, as an extension of the *status quo*, reinforcing vested interests of homeland bureaucracies and prolonging white domination. It would indeed be rejected by those homeland leaders with a genuine popular constituency, such as Chief Buthelezi of KwaZulu and Enos Mabuza of Kangwane.

The most radical territorial arrangement of all, partition, can also be discounted. Stultz (1979) has shown that while South Africa enjoys some of the conditions which have favoured partition elsewhere in the world, such as minority encapsulation, imbalance of communities, bipolarity and political statemate, the international dimensions minimize the chances of partition taking place. The South African problem is too central an issue in world politics, South Africa itself is perceived as strategically important, and international opinion is unsympathetic to white motivations, which are seen to rest on the preservation of material and political privilege rather than self-determination. A fundamental east–west partition of South Africa could theoretically be justified (Maasdorp 1980), but international opinion would certainly support blacks in their rejection of any such scheme. This is perhaps just as well given the unhappy track record of partition in India, Ireland, Palestine and elsewhere.

The one territorial approach which cannot be dismissed out of hand is federalism. An ethnically based federation would too closely resemble current apartheid planning, and would suffer from familiar contradictions in relation to South Africa's economic and population geography (Lemon 1980). Leo Marquard (1971) was the first to advocate a non-racial or geographical federation in southern Africa, and the concept has been explored in some depth by Slabbert & Welsh (1979), who gave intellectual content to official Progressive Federal Party policy. Regional boundaries would be drawn so as to produce ethnically heterogeneous units, not in most cases microcosms of the whole as in the idealized 'symmetrical' model of Tarlton (1965), but cutting across the major recognized cleavages of the society. In doing so they would, it is hoped, serve to minimize inter-group conflict, while the very division of power inherent in federation would help to defuse potential conflict at the centre. The various provinces could be expected to reach different accommodations according to their population composition and the prevalent traditions of their component groups. Such diversity could prove beneficial; one region could benefit from the experience of another, and a party which was excluded from power in one region might win elsewhere, thus helping to avoid its alienation from the wider political system.

To avoid a single province dominating the rest, at least eight or ten provinces would be needed, whilst the division of the Pretoria–Witwatersrand–Vereeniging region, although a functional whole, would probably be necessary. Although several provinces would not include metro-politan areas, it would be essential to draw their boundaries so as to include what Friedman (1966, 39–44) has called 'upward transitional areas': no province could be confined to the periphery of the space-economy, as are most of the present homelands. Provision for the distribution of federal revenue would need to encompass more than the principle of derivation: considerable transfer of wealth between provinces would be necessary.

It will be apparent that such conditions are largely met by the nine regions of the present decentralization strategy. In genuine negotiations this could be a stumbling block: to the extent that federation becomes identified with Nationalist constitutional planning, the concept is unlikely to win popular acceptance. Another major practical problem is the identification of such federal ideas with Chief Buthelezi and the proposals of the KwaZulu Natal Indaba (1986) for a joint KwaNatal administration. Although Buthelezi has himself expressed preference for a unitary state, he has indicated interest in a federal compromise. The ANC views the Indaba proposals as a regional power bid by Buthelezi, whose Inkatha organization it refuses to recognize as a legitimate part of the liberation struggle.

Thus, although there are sound theoretical reasons why geographical, non-racial federation could contribute to a constitutional solution to South Africa's problems, there are also daunting practical difficulties which can only increase if Pretoria does pursue its own version of federation. It must also be recognized that the fundamental political cleavages in South Africa are ethnically expressed, and a genuinely negotiated constitution would have to accommodate the reality of these divisions without in any way prescribing or enforcing their continuance.

Tragically, negotiation is neither imminent nor likely. Existing levels of repression leave the state with considerable untapped reserves of coercion, while opposition movements continue to consolidate their power base by constructing embryonic organs of people's power. Neither reform from above nor revolution from below has significantly shifted the balance of power. Only when Pretoria and the ANC share a common perception of stalemate is genuine negotiation about power-sharing likely. Meanwhile the continuing resistance of the black majority is inevitable if a government which lacks the resources to meet their socio-economic aspirations refuses seriously to discuss their political aspirations.

Note

1 'Black' is used to include the African majority (72 per cent of the population), as well as 'coloureds' (people of mixed race) and Indians, most of whom now regard themselves as blacks. Use of the term 'coloured' does not signify acceptance of this official designation, which has always been rejected by those whom it purports to classify.

References

Adam, H. 1971. *Modernizing racial domination*. Berkeley: University of California Press.

Bell, R. T. 1973. *Industrial decentralisation in South Africa*. Cape Town: Oxford University Press.
Boserup, E. 1965. *The conditions of agricultural growth*. London: Allen & Unwin.

Christopher, A. J. 1983. From Flint to Soweto: reflections on the colonial origins of the apartheid city. *Area* **15**, 145–9.
Christopher, A. J. 1988. 'Divide and rule': the impress of British separation policies. *Area* **20**, 232–40.
Cobbe, H. M. 1986. The land question in South Africa: a preliminary assessment. Paper delivered to conference on The South African Economy After Apartheid. York: Centre for Southern African Studies, University of York.
Cobbett, W. 1987. *Onverwacht* and the emergence of a regional labour market in South Africa. In Tomlinson & Addleson, op.cit., 241–52.
Cobbett, W., D. Glaser, D. Hindson & M. Swilling 1987. South Africa's regional political economy: a critical analysis of reform strategy in the 1980s. In Tomlinson & Addleson, op.cit., 1–27.

Davies, R. J. 1981. The spatial formation of the South African city. *GeoJournal* supplementary issue **2**, 59–81.
de Coning, C., J. Fick & N. Olivier 1986. *Residential settlement patterns: a pilot study of socio-political perceptions in grey areas of Johannesburg*. Johannesburg: Department of Development Studies, Rand Afrikaans University.
de Klerk, W. A. 1975. *The Puritans in Africa: a story of Afrikanerdom*. London: Rex Collings.
de Vos, T. J. 1986. Housing shortages and their bearing on the Group Areas Act. Paper delivered at a seminar at the University of South Africa, Pretoria, 15 May. Cited in *Race Relations Survey 1986*, 359–60. Johannesburg: South African Institute of Race Relations.
du Toit, P. 1988. Regional services councils: control at local government level. In Heymans and Totemeyer, op.cit., 63–76.

Feher, F., A. Heller & G. Markus 1983. *Dictatorship over needs*. Oxford: Basil Blackwell.
Friedman, J. R. 1966. *Regional development policy: a case study of Venezuela*. Cambridge, Mass.: MIT Press.

Giliomee, H. 1985. The changing political functions of the homelands. In *Up against the fences: poverty, passes and privilege in South Africa*, H. Giliomee & L. Schlemmer (eds), 39–56. Cape Town: David Philip.
Giliomee, H. 1987. Apartheid, *verligtheid* and liberalism. In *Democratic liberalism in South Africa: its history and prospect*, J. Butler, R. Elphick & D. Welsh (eds), 362–83. Cape Town: David Philip; Middletown, Conn.: Wesleyan University Press.

Hackland, B. 1980. The economic and political context of the growth of the Progressive Federal Party in South Africa, 1959–1978. *Journal of Southern African Studies* **7**, 1–16.
Hart, D. M. & G. H. Pirie 1984. The sight and soul of Sophiatown. *Geographical Review* **74**, 38–47.
Heunis, C. (Minister of Constitutional Development and Planning) 24 September 1987. Quoted in *Beeld*, Johannesburg.

References

Heymans, C. 1988. The political and constitutional context of local government restructuring. In Heymans & Totemeyer, op.cit., 34–48.

Heymans, C. & G. Totemeyer (eds) 1988. *Government by the people: the politics of local government in South Africa.* Cape Town: Juta.

Hindson, D. 1987. *Pass controls and the urban African proletariat.* Johannesburg: Ravan.

KwaZulu Natal Indaba 1986. *Constitutional proposals.* Durban: privately published.

Lemon, A. 1976. *Apartheid: a geography of separation.* Farnborough: Saxon House.

Lemon, A. 1980. Federalism and plural societies: a critique with special reference to South Africa. *Plural Societies* **11** (2), 3–24.

Lemon, A. 1982. Migrant labour and 'frontier commuters': reorganising South Africa's black labour supply. In D. M. Smith (ed.), op.cit., 64–89.

Lemon, A. 1984. State control over the labor market in South Africa. *International Political Science Review* **5**, 189–208.

Lemon, A. 1987. *Apartheid in transition.* Aldershot: Gower.

Lemon, A. 1989a. Re-designing the apartheid city. *African Urban Quarterly* **4**, 23–50.

Lemon, A. 1989b. What price security? South Africa's white election of 1987 and its aftermath. *Journal of Commonwealth and Comparative Politics* **27** (1), 23–50.

Leys, C. 1975. South African gold mining in 1974: 'the gold of migrant labour'. *African Affairs* **74**, 196–208.

Lipton, M. 1985. *Capitalism and apartheid: South Africa 1910–1986.* Aldershot: Gower.

Maasdorp, G. 1980. Forms of partition. In *Conflict and compromise in South Africa*, R. I. Rotberg & J. Barratt (eds), 107–50. Cape Town: David Philip.

Marquard, L. 1971. *A federation of southern Africa.* London: Oxford University Press.

McCaul, C. 1987. *Satellite in revolt. KwaNdebele: an economic and political profile.* Johannesberg: South African Institute of Race Relations.

Murray, C. 1987. Displaced urbanisation: South Africa's rural slums. *African Affairs* **86**, 311–29.

Peach, Ceri (ed.) 1975. *Urban social segregation.* London: Longman.

Pirie, G. H. 1984a. Ethno-linguistic zoning in black townships. *Area* **16**, 291–8.

Pirie, G. H. 1984b. Race zoning in South Africa: board, court, parliament, public. *Political Geography Quarterly* **3**, 207–21.

Pirie, G. H. 1987. Deconsecrating a 'holy cow': reforming the Group Areas Act. *South African Review Four*, 402–11. Johannesburg: Ravan.

Platzky, L. & C. Walker, 1985. *The surplus people: forced removals in South Africa.* Johannesburg: Ravan.

SAIRR (South African Institute of Race Relations) 1987 and 1988. *Survey of race relations in South Africa 1986* and *1987*. Johannesburg: SAIRR.

Slabbert, F. van Zyl, & D. Welsh 1979. *South Africa's options: strategies for sharing power.* Cape Town: David Philip; London: Rex Collings.

Smith, D. M. (ed.) 1982. *Living under apartheid.* London: Allen & Unwin.

South Africa 1941. *Third report of the industrial and agricultural requirements commission*, UG 40. Pretoria: Government Printer.

South Africa 1943. *Report of the interdepartmental committee on the social, health and economic conditions of urban natives.* Annexure 47.

South Africa 1946. *The native reserves and their place in the economy of the Union of South Africa*, UG 32. Pretoria: Government Printer.

South Africa 1955. *The report of the Commission for the Socio-Economic Development of the Bantu Areas within the Union of South Africa*, UG 61. Pretoria: Government Printer.

South Africa 1985. *Report of the Committee for Constitutional Affairs of the President's Council on an urbanisation strategy for the Republic of South Africa.* Pretoria: Government Printer.

South Africa 1987. *Report of the Committee for Constitutional Affairs of the President's Council on the Report of the Technical Committee*, 1983 and Related Matters, PC 4. Pretoria: Government Printer.

Stultz, N. M. 1979. On partition. *Social Dynamics* **5**, 1–13.

Tarlton, C. D. 1965. Symmetry and asymmetry as elements of federalism: a theoretical speculation. *Journal of Politics* **27**, 861–74.

Todes, A. & V. Watson 1985. Local government reform in South Africa: an interpretation of aspects of the state's current proposals. *South African Geographical Journal* **67**, 201–11.

Tomlinson, R. & M. Addleson 1987. *Regional restructuring under apartheid: urban and regional policies in contemporary South Africa*. Johannesburg: Ravan.

TRAC (Transvaal Rural Action Committee) 1987. *KwaNdebele – the struggle against independence*. Johannesburg: TRAC.

Verwoerd, H. F. 1948. Senate speech on the policy of apartheid, 3 September. *The Senate of South Africa: Debates*, 1st session, 10th Parliament, 5th Senate, 2, 223–58.

Western, J. 1981. *Outcast Cape Town*. London: Allen & Unwin.

Wolpe, H. 1972. Capitalism and cheap labour power in South Africa: from segregation to apartheid. *Economy and Society* **1**, 425–56.

11

Aboriginal Australia: survival by separation

FAY GALE

European settlers moved out of the confined and controlled lands of North-west Europe and the British Isles into the extensive and comparatively sparsely settled lands of Australia, New Zealand, North and South America and South Africa. The trickle of migration beginning in the 17th century became a flood by the 19th century. The ensuing conflicts in one place after another became, primarily, confrontations over land.

In spite of the rhetoric and the wishful thinking, these were not empty lands. They were fully occupied and every piece of land, whether lush river valley or sparsely vegetated desert, belonged to people whose ancestors had lived there for thousands of years. How were the newcomers to deal with this? What were to be the spatial resolutions? Competition for the same areas by vastly different cultural groups with quite opposite views of both land ownership and land use had to be resolved in spatial terms. For all the ideology espoused in political terms or the economic interpretation given by historians these were geographic problems in the classic sense, the use of space.

It scarcely needs stating that Australia is a very large and diversified continent with enormous environmental differences from one part of the country to another. At the time of British settlement Aboriginal people occupied and used all of this vast continent (Gale 1987). Although there was no area unclaimed by Aboriginal groups the size of the social groups and the land they occupied varied enormously from one environment to another. Thus in the central desert area people moved over large tracts of country and had contact with others speaking similar languages many hundreds of kilometres away. However on the fertile coasts or river valleys people speaking a common language (once, inaccurately, defined as a tribe) occupied quite small territories and lived in predominantly permanent and semi-permanent settlements.

Idealism versus reality

The first attempts at accommodation by the British colonizers followed two divergent approaches. One was to encourage, indeed force, the assimilation of the indigenous owners into the social and spatial structure of the newly arrived

217

groups. Missionaries came early to 'civilize' and 'educate' the rightful occupants so that they could be absorbed into the rapidly growing communities of European settlers. The other approach favoured more by the soldiers, but also by many of the settlers, was open warfare. Guns, poison and rape were all used in varying degrees to subjugate the indigenous people and usurp their lands. Over many of the vast territories of the 'New World' this latter approach was far more successful than the former.

A third, unplanned but very successful, method of subjugation was the inadvertent introduction of European diseases and food. The new settlers came from industrializing Europe with its rapidly growing towns which had quickly become incubators of numerous infectious diseases. The immigrants brought these killers with them and quickly transferred them to the indigenous people who had never known such diseases and who had no immunity to them nor knowledge as to how to treat any of them. Smallpox, venereal diseases, measles, whooping cough and a range of respiratory infections wiped out whole populations. In many cases the diseases spread ahead of the settlement frontier so that by the time the colonists came to farm the land the local resistance had already been weakened or destroyed by disease. Usurpation of land under such circumstances was all too easy and required little rationalization of conscience. As a result today there are large areas where virtually no descendants of the original inhabitants now live. Instead those areas are today densely peopled by populations of recent European descent.

The reports of such disastrous side-effects from the settlement of North America fertilized and gave new direction to the growing humanitarian movement in Britain. The colonization of Australia in the latter part of the 18th century coincided with the anti-slavery movement in Britain, and this was to have important implications for the development of reservations for indigenous people throughout the so-called New World. The very month, May 1787, in which the First Fleet sailed from Britain to establish the colony of New South Wales, a meeting was held in London to found the Society for the Abolition of the Slave Trade. Within 50 years the anti-slavery crusade had achieved its goals and its members turned their attention to a new cause, namely the plight of the indigenous inhabitants of all areas of British colonization. They formed the British and Foreign Aborigines Protection Society. They expressed public outcry and horror at the treatment of Indian people in North America and Australian Aborigines in Tasmania and New South Wales. Later colonies established in Australia and New Zealand were given specific decrees ostensibly to ensure that the local inhabitants were treated with humanity and respect.

Thus the proclamation read by Governor Hindmarsh on his arrival with the first settlers to establish the colony of South Australia in 1836 stated:

it is also, at this time, especially my duty to apprise the colonists of my resolution to take every lawful means for extending the same protection to the native population as to the rest of His Majesty's subjects and my firm determination to punish with exemplary severity all acts of violence or injustice which may in any manner be practised or attempted against the natives who are to be considered as much under the safeguard of the law as the colonists themselves, and equally entitled to the privileges of British subjects.

By the 1830s the political influence of the humanitarian movement towards Aboriginal people had become very strong. The Letters Patent establishing South Australia as a colony in 1836 and the Charter establishing New Zealand as a colony separate from Australia in 1840 carry very similar wording concerning the rights of Aboriginal natives and the protection of their lands and livelihood. But how were such goals to be achieved with the arrival of British settlers? What kind of compromise was possible in practical terms to ensure the continued safety of Aboriginal people and assuage the land hunger of the new settlers? The appointment of protectors, the passing of laws, the arrival of missionaries, the establishment of schools, the signing of treaties, all were tried in varying degrees at one place or another but none achieved the impossible compromise of protecting Aboriginal people's right to life and livelihood on their own lands and at the same time providing adequate land for an ever-increasing tide of British settlers.

Reservations: a spatial compromise

Irrespective of the high-flown speeches and the numerous attempts at protect-ion, the same form of solution was resorted to in every colony regardless of its time or nature of settlement. It was a spatial solution used in the last resort. Short of total annihilation, either rapidly through murder, starvation and disease, or more slowly through genetic assimilation, the only possible resolution to totally conflicting goals appeared to be a spatial one. Thus began the establishment of reservations, of using officially decreed, separate space as a means of conflict resolution and the assuaging of conscience.

The first areas set aside were usually termed reservations in North America and New Zealand but were more commonly called reserves in Australia, sited on the edges of European settlement. Then, as the frontier moved inland, the reserves were either left as isolated pockets within areas occupied by Europeans or they were taken over by settlers and the local people were gathered up and moved further out. Each forced movement to new, unknown and very confined territory further weakened and pacified the native people. The forced migration and virtual imprisonment on segregated reserves were little differ-ent from the slave trade that had been so vigorously opposed in previous decades.

Throughout human history spatial isolation has been the one and only means of ethnic and cultural preservation. Only because of this spatial isolation from the rest of the world were Australian Aboriginal people able to develop and retain the numerous distinctive language and culture groups which European arrivals first met and grossly misunderstood during the 18th and 19th centuries. Spatial isolation was again to save these peoples.

Reserves were established from as early as 1815 in New South Wales. They tended to be quite small areas in Australian terms and no use whatsoever as a means of subsistence for people following an Aboriginal way of life. They were much too small for hunting or gathering food, and usually were the leftover pieces of land that settlers had found unsuitable for agriculture. One of the earliest still remaining as an Aboriginal reserve is LaPerouse, typically not given its local name but instead named after a French explorer. Initially this reserve was well on the outskirts of settlement, but now it is a part of suburban Sydney. It is still, however, an Aboriginal community.

In most cases the reserves were crown lands vested in one or other missionary group to run and care for the inhabitants. Not until the land rights movements of the 1960s did Aborigines themselves begin to gain title to any of these lands. Throughout the 19th century missions sprang up wherever British settlers moved, and the need to isolate and ostensibly protect Aborigines was perceived to be necessary. The contemporary view was well expressed by George Arthur, Lieutenant Governor of Van Dieman's land (Tasmania) who wrote in 1828 that he wished

> to settle the Aborigines in some remoter quarter of the island, which should be strictly reserved for them, and to supply them with food and clothing, and afford them protection from injuries by the stock-keepers, on condition of their confining themselves peaceably to certain limits, beyond which, if they pass, they should be made to understand they will cease to be protected (Rowley 1970, 46).

Indeed, all reserves and missions established in the next hundred or so years were intended to remove Aboriginal people from contact with settlers. This was not done only for humanitarian grounds to protect the Aboriginal people, nor for purely religious grounds to Christianize them; it was mainly done to allow the settlers unfettered access to the best Aboriginal land.

After initial friendly approaches Aborigines began to realize in one place after another that these white people were not visitors but enemies who planned to take their land by any means available. As a result they began to fight back, and although outnumbered and lacking guns or horses they did develop and maintain a very effective system of guerrilla warfare which, although not able to prevent settlement, did manage to slow it down and greatly frustrate the new arrivals. As a result, official drives were organized to round up all Aboriginal people and take them away from contact with settlers and on to newly declared reserves. For Tasmanian Aborigines this eventually meant complete removal from their homelands on the main island and, in 1832, virtual imprisonment on the smaller rugged unwanted Flinders Island in Bass Strait. Yet from the few remnant people taken there to die out of sight and away from any public conscience there grew up today's Tasmanian Aboriginal descendants numbering some 6500 people. Hard and cruel as it was at the time, separation had saved them. Indeed, but for such forced isolation it is doubtful if any people would now be able to identify as descendants of the original Tasmanians.

During the early phases of settlement in South Australia the Overlanders drove sheep and cattle from New South Wales to the new pastoral lands. There were numerous skirmishes with Aboriginal groups along the Murray river and eventually virtual war was declared. Those Aboriginal people who were not killed were rounded up and taken to specially declared reserves where they were protected and issued with regular rations of food. One such reserve, Moorundie, on the central reaches of the lower Murray, was administered by the government sub-protector, Edward John Eyre. His diaries provide valuable insights into Aboriginal culture of the day.

The majority of reserves were run by missionaries who very soon built churches and schools. The separate mission schools for Aboriginal children were viewed as the only means of preparing them for eventual assimilation into European society, but, in effect, they achieved the opposite. Their isolation ensured the growth of quite separate people in many ways distinctive both physically and culturally from either their Aboriginal forebears or the Europeans they were meant to emulate. There are now substantial numbers of Aboriginal people descended from those who were confined to mission settlements last century. Usually where there were no reserves or missions no Aboriginal people remain. Thus, as appalling as it was for the people concerned, the reservation system saved those in much of southern and eastern Australia from complete extermination – a fate which befell much of the flora and fauna of the country.

The protective function of environmental isolation

When the settlers from Europe arrived they perceived the Australian continent through very different cultural eyes. To them much of it was thought to be uninhabitable, even if Aborigines successfully inhabited all of the continent. To the British settlers vast tracts were seen as useless desert or tropical forest. In those areas Aboriginal people were left alone until well into the 20th century. Here again it was initially spatial separation which saved them, but it was isolation determined by perceived environmental conditions not legislative decrees. In these seemingly remote areas, with large tracts of their homeland relatively untouched by Europeans, the local people were able to survive and maintain much of their language and culture. It is only in these so called waste and marginal lands that 'full–blood' Aborigines still live, and only in such areas are there large groups of people speaking their own languages.

Today's descendants of the people living in southern and eastern Australia, initially protected by reserves and missionaries, are all of mixed European and Aboriginal ancestry and only a few of the older people have retained any knowledge of their traditional language. But virtually all have a very strong Aboriginal identity and proudly manifest their origins even within a totally Europeanized urban lifestyle.

It is only since the mid–1950s that these southern people have been free to move off the reserves where they and their parents and grandparents were born. It is only since the mid–1960s and later that restrictive legislation, forcing them to remain on reserves unless they were granted and carried with them exemption certificates, has been removed. These pieces of paper entitled them to move into white society but in doing so limited their connections with their relatives on the reserves. It is no wonder the feeling of today's Aboriginal people is strongly identified with their reserve background and their clear categorization as Aboriginal, no matter how fair skinned they might be or how urbanized in their lifestyle. Even those younger people, born in a town or city away from the reserve, have parents born in a controlled segregated place and have relatives still living on those reserves, although now most reserves are Aboriginal–owned or –controlled and no rules prevent the free movement of residents.

Thus, broadly speaking, and not taking into account the enormous regional differences both in traditional times and now, there are two groups of Aboriginal people in Australia both owing their survival and central identity as Aboriginal Australians to geographic separation determined for different reasons by the British settlers who slowly took over the continent from 1788 onwards. Over much of central and northern Australia there are groups of traditionally oriented 'full blood' people living on the land of their ancestors and able to do so because it was land not wanted by the British settlers. Only recently, with the growth of mining and tourism in the 'outback', have these people faced real competition for their land and livelihod. The isolation that protected them has now been broken by four wheel drive vehicles, tourist buses and mining companies.

The other broad group of Aboriginal people, westernized and in varying degrees 'white', see themselves, and are seen, as Aborigines because of generations of forced separation on small reserves, usually not even on their traditional lands, within the confines of European settlements. They have survived only as isolated small groups on pockets of land set aside for them as the settlement frontier engulfed them and usurped their land.

The current situation of these two groups is vastly different and within each there are substantial variations from one place to another. Their positions have also changed dramatically since the 1960s. A federal referendum in 1967 changed the constitution of Australia to allow all Aboriginal people to be counted as Australian and to have full citizenship rights. This merely consolidated legislatively at a Commonwealth level what had been taking place in some southern states since the early 1950s. It forced changes in other states, such as Queensland, which had been slower to recognize the rights of people of Aboriginal descent.

Land rights

While in many ways the past experience of these two groups has been very different their present situations are much more closely linked. All are now caught up in what is usually termed the land rights movement. From whatever their backgrounds, Aboriginal people now seek land rights, the actual legal ownership and title of all lands and reserves on which they live and the further acquisition of lands still held by the crown. In doing so they are seeking to consolidate spatial separation as a means of ethnic and cultural survival. Even within cities they are seeking separate areas including separate schools. In Australia the move toward segregation, once inflicted upon them by whites, is now being actively sought by the Aboriginal people themselves. And this now is often quite vehemently fought against by non-Aborigines who oppose on grounds of equality any granting of separate space or conditions for Aboriginal people. The tables have been turned. Those who once were forced into separation by their conquerors are now fighting for such separation against the current wishes of the white majority society.

Land rights became a unifying theme for Aboriginal people across Australia in the 1960s and gathered momentum rapidly in the early 1970s when Gough Whitlam became Prime Minister and guaranteed land ownership. The Commonwealth government could not, under the federal constitution, give such directive to the states, so it was only in the Northern Territory that the Commonwealth was directly able to grant land rights.

The first legislative move to give Aboriginal people separate title to land took place in South Australia when in 1966 an Aboriginal Lands Trust was created. Under the Act the title of all lands, which up to this time had been declared reserves, was vested in the Aboriginal Lands Trust. Many of the reserves established last century had long since been resumed by the crown and sold or leased to Europeans. However, some 43 separate areas scattered in small pockets across the state, in addition to the very large Central Desert Reserve in the northwest of the state, were still dedicated as reserves. The title to these 43 smaller reserves was gradually vested in the Lands Trust and 11 of these, where substantial Aboriginal communities still resided as separate social entities, were then leased back to those resident communities. These 11 settlements had mainly come into being as missions, and most southern South Australian Aborigines had been born on one or other. But this was the first time they had been given ownership or control of either the land or their own lives. The change to self-management was fraught with difficulty for people who had lived under tight controls. For many the freedom to decide their own future was a drastic contrast from living forever under the watchful eye of the white, all powerful superintendent. This first legislative return of land title to Aboriginal people heralded a whole movement towards land rights and personal freedom. In South Australia the move was a culmination of years of agitation by largely urbanized Aborigines spurred on by white intelligentsia and radicals meeting the favourable response of a reformist Labour government.

In the Northern Territory, the push for land rights took place at much the same time as that in South Australia but it took a completely different form. The South Australian leaders of the movement were Europeanized people who had grown up on the segregated reserves on the south. They had been 'assimilated' into the mainstream English language and culture but forced to live in separate areas. They had no doubt about their Aboriginality irrespective of how fair skinned or lacking in any traditional knowledge they might be. They had been educated separately as a group apart from Australian society at large. They had been socially and economically marginalized. If they were to be treated as distinctive and indeed as 'second class' then they believed they at least had a right to the title to the lands on which their forebears had been segregated and forced to live for several generations.

The move for title in the north, however, came from traditionally oriented 'full-blood' people who could speak little English and who were living on land with which they had strong spiritual ties. Their isolation by environmental forces meant that, unlike the people of the south who had been rounded up and taken to new country, these northerners were still living on land that, both in physical and spiritual terms, they believed was rightly theirs.

This struggle for land rights (acknowledgement of legal title to traditional lands) became publicly recognized in August 1966 when the Gurindji people walked off Lord Vestey's Wave Hill station in the Northern Territory. The strike was ostensibly for proper wages but the basic issue was land. Why should they work for a pittance, usually hand-outs of flour, sugar and tea, on land that was traditionally theirs but where they felt themselves to be treated as virtual slaves by an owner who did not even live in Australia? The Gurindji walk-off created enormous ripples in the whole Australian land ownership system. Both the government and the cattle industry at large supported Lord Vestey and refused to recognize the land claims for fear this would spread across Australia. The persistence of the Gurindji is now legendary. The problem did not go away. They stayed out on strike for nearly ten years until public opinion had been aroused and the government attitude changed.

The Gurindji persistence took on almost epic proportions over time. Many songs, poems and stories have emerged commemorating this and other battles for equality and land ownership. The first verse of one such song, 'Gurindji Blues' by Ted Egan, is quoted as an example of the evocative messages increasingly becoming popular across Australia during the 1960s and 1970s.

> Poor bugger me Gurindji
> Me bin sit down this country
> Long time before the Lord Vestey
> Allabout land belongin' to we
> Oh poor bugger me, Gurindji
> Long time work no wages, we,
> Work for the good Lord Vestey
> Little bit flour, sugar and tea
> For the Gurindji, from Lord Vestey
> Oh poor bugger, me.

The government of the day had good reasons to fear the publicity and support the Gurindji struggle was attracting. In December 1968 the Yirrkala people of the Gove Peninsula in Arnhem Land sought land title through the Supreme Court of the Northern Territory. The disquiet, the strong sense of injustice, the pressure for change was spreading. Yirrkala land was not cattle country. It was reserve land held as a church mission to which the Nabalco Mining Company had been granted a lease to mine bauxite by the Australian government. Being legally crown land the government was able to lease out Aboriginal reserves or missions without necessarily even consulting the local inhabitants or determining compensation. The understandably angry Yirrkala people gained widespread publicity with the presentation of a petition in the form of a bark painting sent to the United Nations. They lost their case at that time before the Supreme Court of the Northern Territory but they did not give up, and across the country other groups began to take political action.

In 1973 the Commonwealth government, which still had legislative and administrative control of the Northern Territory, appointed the first Aboriginal land rights commissioner to report on appropriate means to recognize Aboriginal title. In line with South Australia he recommended that all current Aboriginal reserves and missions be transferred to Aboriginal ownership. The Aboriginal Land Rights (Northern Territory) Act 1976 came into being, and under this Act quite extensive areas of lands have reverted to Aboriginal title. In some cases their claims were heard and agreed to relatively quickly because there was little contention over the land sought, but in other cases there have been long drawn out legal battles with mining and pastoral companies.

Kakadu National Park, now acknowledged on the World Heritage List, owes its existence to a compromise agreement over Aboriginal land and mining. The Gadjudu people, from which the name Kakadu comes, were given title to their land in western Arnhem Land on condition that they allowed sections to be excised or exempted to allow mining and that they lease the remaining area back to the Australian National Parks and Wildlife Service. As a result the people are granted royalties from the uranium mines within their territory and are consulted about tourist development in the park. It was on this same model that, after many years of negotiation with the Northern

Territory government and tourist groups, the Pitjantjatjara people were eventually (in 1988) given the title to Uluru (Ayres Rock) National Park on condition that it be leased back as a park open to all visitors.

Over the last decade or so Aboriginal groups have gradually won claims to title for just over one-third of the Northern Territory. While much of this was mission, reserve or crown land, unwanted and unclaimed by pastoral companies, more recent claims have been made for land already being used. Aboriginal groups have won title to some cattle stations which they are now operating themselves as viable economic ventures. Ironically, however, it was the very land, unwanted by settlers or even by large-scale pastoralists, that in some cases has become the most contentious. The poor soils, inedible vegetation, desert or tropical savannah and rainforest, were not attractive even to cattlemen. But these are the very areas which have in recent years been found to be rich in minerals – uranium, bauxite, gold, diamonds, oil – in fact almost everything. They are also the remote rugged areas, left relatively untouched in ecological terms, that are now attractive to tourists. Visitors from all over the world are being encouraged by all kinds of glossy advertising to experience the Australian 'wilderness' in these regions.

The end of protective isolation

Thus Aboriginal people and their lands, once protected by isolation, are no longer secure. The very environment which saved them, their culture, their language and their land, is the same environment which is now attracting ever-increasing numbers of visitors. To protect both themselves and their land, which is the essential force of their culture, they believe they must own title and maintain separation from non-Aboriginal society.

Most groups do not feel greatly threatened by mining companies. These multi-national companies tend to operate in small confined areas, and are very sensitive to public opinion. They are well aware of the economic need to avoid politically caused delays. Thus Aborigines now find it possible to negotiate with most mining companies and, as one Aboriginal leader said, they just make a big hole in the ground for a few years and then go away later. It is the burgeoning tourist industry that most threatens Aboriginal livelihood and their future existence. Tourists, like cattle, destroy whole areas of territory and do not respect the environment or other people. It is to protect themselves and their land from tourists especially that Aborigines are increasingly seeking separation in areas where they can control the presence of white visitors.

The need to be separate has spread throughout Australia. The development of a land rights flag, now used everywhere as the Aboriginal national emblem, heralded the commonality of the belief in separation as a survival measure. And the historic evidence is all on their side. This is segregation, not forced upon them as it once was, but actively sought by them as a weapon for dealing with an otherwise inequitable situation in which they have no chance of surviving.

The states of southeastern Australia, namely New South Wales, Victoria and Tasmania, have all followed the South Australian model by one means or another. They have established, through legislation, an administrative structure to enable the transfer of mission and Aboriginal reserve lands to local Aboriginal councils. The actual administrative structures vary from place to place but by and large, Aboriginal people now have control of those reserve lands which were originally set aside for them under mission or government control. In 1983 the New South Wales parliament passed the Aboriginal Land Rights Act, which allocated for 15 years 7.5 per cent of the annual state land tax collection to fund the establishment of regional land councils with subsidiary local land councils. This aimed to give not only reserve land back to the people but to add to this and also to give Aboriginal people a voice on the general use of land where Aboriginal sacred or significant sites existed.

While in these southern areas the transfer of title to small remnant groups of people isolated and marginalized for generations is not seen as economically very significant, most Aboriginal people feel it to be at least a recognition of their rightful ownership of the country. But although they have gained some small financial benefits, and certainly a greater control over their day-to-day lives, most people realize that in real terms this is 'too little too late'. In fact such transfer of reserve ownership may actually encourage people to remain on the segregated reserves because they now have legal and administrative authority, albeit over lands which have little or no economic value. Almost without exception a viable economic base is impossible in most areas. The only opportunity for earning income from their land is the spin-off from tourists or from mining. However, while mining developments benefit people in the Northern Territory they are unlikely to advantage southerners. Most mining potential in the south and east has already been developed and Aborigines have long since lost control of such land.

Queensland and Western Australia, the two largest states, have been slower to recognize Aboriginal land rights. Both states have populations in the settled areas that have become, perforce, urbanized and have lost traditional ties. Both states also have large populations in their northern and inland areas that are still traditionally oriented and culturally related to their land. Partly because of the enormous variations in these two states, but mainly because of the various conflicting arguments from different interest groups, neither state has given title to Aboriginal people in the sense that it has been done in all other states and territories. Queensland has established legislation which enables Aboriginal communities to manage their lands under what is called 'a deed of grant in trust'. It is a halfway measure towards recognition of Aboriginal occupation and ownership. Figure 11.1 showing Aboriginal lands in Australia illustrates the differences from one state to another as well as depicting the extent of area now legally owned by Aboriginal people in South and Northern Australia.

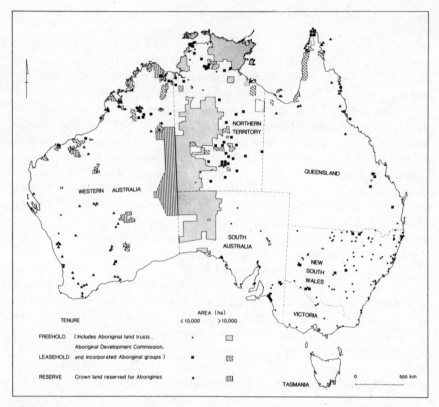

Figure 11.1 Aboriginal lands, 1986, illustrating different forms of land title and the degree of acknowledgement of Aboriginal ownership from one state to another.

The South Australian government realized that the westernized southern people and the traditionally oriented people of the desert could not be dealt with by the same legislation. Thus following the 1966 Lands Trust Act former mission and reserve land was ceded to local people but two separate and independently negotiated Acts, the Pitjantjatjara Land Rights Act of 1981 and the Maralinga-Tjarutja Land Rights Act of 1984, gave comprehensive rights to people in the desert areas. In Figure 11.1 these adjacent areas are shown as an extensive block in the western sector of South Australia.

In Western Australia the pressure to recognize Aboriginal rights has taken a different form. In 1986 the state government passed an Act enabling Aboriginal groups to acquire the land they occupied on 99 year leases but did not give title and, most important, did not give any rights in relation to mineral exploration. This very important area of political voice and financial compensation has been denied to them.

228

A varied population

Thus in Australia today the situation is complex and varied with enormous differences evident from one part of the country to another. According to the 1986 census approximately one quarter of Australian Aboriginal people now live in the major cities. While a few of these have become relatively well-off, middle-class public servants or professionals, the majority are poor and live in conditions comparable to the poor of the mainstream population, heavily dependent on welfare payments and subsidized housing. Although they identify as Aboriginal, usually with strong links to the rural Aboriginal reserve communities from which they came, to the outsider they are scarcely distinguishable from the general poor of the city.

Whereas the majority of white Australians live in the major cities most Aboriginal people are to be found either in country towns, small rural settlements or on reserves (Table 11.1). Their population distribution is thus quite the reverse of that of the non-Aboriginal population even 200 years after the first arrival of British settlers.

Although there has been an increasing migration of Aboriginal people to the cities, the majority live virtually separate lives in northern and central Australia, the tropical and desert regions which Australians of European origin were not able to utilize intensively. The significance of the past environmental separation is still abundantly clear in the census figures.

Table 11.1 shows that the highest proportion of Aboriginal people now live in country towns. The definition of 'other urban' is a population of between 1000 and 100 000. It is in these relatively small communities scattered across rural Australia that many Aboriginal people can be found. Usually they remain as marginal people even within small towns. Once such people were called 'fringe dwellers' because they lived, or rather stayed, in makeshift camps, just outside the town boundaries. Usually they had nowhere else to go. They had been driven or taken off their traditional lands and gradually they had drifted to the edges of the developing towns where they were tolerated, or ignored, but where casual work and food were available.

Initially they were given rations, a set quota of food issued regularly by a government officer, who in most towns was a policeman. The resultant control over their lives is obvious. Today they depend primarily on welfare payments and live in houses built within the town boundaries by Aboriginal housing organizations. They are no longer fringe people in spatial terms living on the outskirts of such towns but the location of their houses often means that they are grouped together and separated from most white people. Approximately one-third of Australian Aboriginal people live in rural areas largely on reserves, to which they now have title or a lease or trust arrangement. Survival by spatial separation is thus still the dominant factor in Aboriginal Australia.

Policy-makers in the 19th century saw segregation as partly a humane compromise and partly a useful rationalization of 'out of sight out of mind'.

Table 11.1   Aboriginal population of Australia, 30 June 1986.

	Metropolitan city	Other urban	Rural	Total
New South Wales	21 416	27 352	10 243	59 011
Victoria	5986	5224	1401	12 611
Queensland	11 091	28 788	21 389	61 268
South Australia	5696	4580	4015	14 291
Western Australia	8949	15 775	13 065	37 789
Northern Territory	–	10 700	24 039	34 739
Tasmania	1351	3460	1905	6716
Australian Capital Territory	1048	–	172	1220
TOTAL	55 537	95 879	76 229	227 645

That was where the majority of Australia's Aboriginal people remained until well into the 1960s. Today official policies use terms such as self-management and self-determination. These words are more acceptable than the earlier policies of segregation, assimilation or integration and are thought to represent more accurately and more sensitively the situation of people who are seeking to break away from the bureaucratic domination of their past lives and to have a greater say in their own futures. The whole land rights movement has been essentially about Aborigines regaining control of their lives. It is a search for political power by people who have been frustrated by their extreme powerlessness. The high rate of Aboriginal suicide while in police custody, the subject of a Royal Commission inquiry, is the end of the road for a people consumed by their own absolute powerlessness.

Separation by request

The land rights movement has thus become the organizing force, the virtual religious drive of all Aboriginal people today, irrespective of their past or their present cultural or economic situations. It is ownership of separate land which they see as the only means of establishing any economic base or of gaining any kind of social or political power. The people still living on traditional lands also have a deep sense of spiritual need to care for the land in ways that have held strong ceremonial significance over thousands of years. It is not unusual to hear older Aboriginal people explain this tie in terms like 'you white fellow say you own the land; we blackfellow know the land owns us'. This philosophy holds, of course, an essential ecological truth which has attracted many conservationally minded people to support the land rights movement. The return of land title has in many areas enabled people once removed from their lands to return to them. Across central and northern Australia people have been drifting back from the large mission settlements to decentralized outstations or homelands. In the Northern Territory, the government prefers to call them outstations to distinguish them from South African homelands. But the Aboriginal people who voluntary return to these traditional lands tend to speak of them as homelands. Figure 11.2 shows the homelands of the Pitjantjatjara people of central Australia. It illustrates how people have moved out from larger settlements to locations of more traditional meaning. It also shows the extensive use of areas thought by Europeans to be uninhabitable desert. The map illustrates the importance of land rights in enabling people to decentralize and return to more traditionally oriented social groupings. On these homelands families have been able to supplement their food from local sources, and this has not only led to an improvement in their diet but has also enabled them to teach young people some of their bush skills. There has also been a conspicuous decline in the very high infant mortality rates experienced in towns and on the larger settlements. 'Our babies don't die any more' was how an Aboriginal woman expressed the importance of land ownership and the return to their homelands.

However, whether they are traditionally oriented people living in remote small communities or sophisticated urban Aborigines living in capital cities, the common Aboriginal identity, maintained by a common cause, the fight for independent land title, has unified an otherwise extremely diverse people. In the cities and larger country towns the call for distinctive Aboriginal title tends to take the form of increasingly active movements towards the establishment of separate Aboriginal schools, housing organizations, clubs, medical and legal services. Thus even within cities many Aboriginal people mix only with other Aboriginal people and spend their lives virtually separated from other Australians. But in so doing they feel more in control of their lives and less discriminated against. In Alice Springs, for example, the Yipirinya school was established in 1978 to teach children living in Aboriginal housing around the town. The children felt discriminated against in the general school, were intimidated by the large classroom method of teaching and often stayed away. Between absenteeism and alienation they fell increasingly further behind other children in their general school performance and less able to achieve the standards that would enable them to be employed later in life. Such disadvantage has been the pattern of Aboriginal education in most integrated schools across the country. The introduction of separate schools has attempted to overcome these problems, but also to introduce local, relevant Aboriginal cultural material into the curriculum to encourage children to develop self-respect and to maintain a pride in their own backgrounds. In these schools the separation is achieving both conflict control in social terms and the maintenance of cultural pride and identity.

There are strong economic as well as social forces driving the increasing move towards separation. Aboriginal cultural items, especially paintings, are becoming increasingly popular with tourists, and the market overseas as well

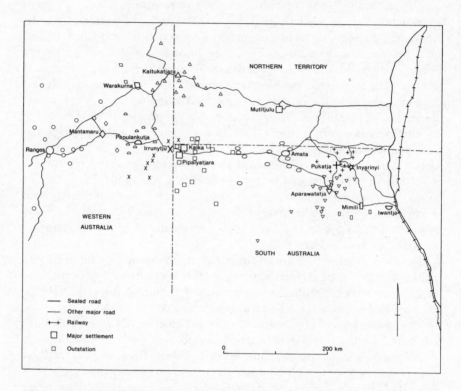

Figure 11.2 Central Australia showing core settlements and the smaller homelands or outstations which have grown up in association with each centre. Each major settlement with related outstations is shown by a different symbol. In each case, the large symbol represents the major settlement and the smaller symbol the connected outstations.

as locally is rapidly expanding. There are therefore very sound reasons for encouraging a return to traditional craft styles and teaching young people the necessary skills. The tourist industry increasingly has other monetary spin-offs with job opportunities as guides, rangers and shop assistants. Compensation from mining and other uses goes only to people who own their land and can demonstrate distinctive Aboriginal roots. When separation is at last beginning to pay, why become integrated into the lowest socio-economic level of a white society that is still fundamentally racist and discriminating? Furthermore, the social advantages of limiting alcohol consumption can only be gained if people live separately in areas they can control. Most important, however, political power, and with it increased services and provisions, has been developed only by group action of people able to maintain close communication ties. There

232

can be little doubt that spatial separation, albeit now in a voluntary form, does enable the maintenance of culture and identity, and indeed nowadays has social and economic advantages as well. But will this always be so in the face of an increasing white backlash? Whether, in the long term, it will bring equality is yet to be seen. Australia's present multi-cultural euphoria adheres to a philosophy of equal but different. There is no evidence from the past to give encouragement to this view. Separate and different may have made survival possible but there is little to encourage a belief that such approaches will also lead to equality in the long term.

What is abundantly clear is that however the Australian Aboriginal situation is portrayed in social, political or humanitarian guises it is fundamentally a geographic question of the uses and misuses of space.

References

Barsh, Russell L. 1984. Aboriginal rights, human rights, and international law. *Australian Aboriginal Studies* **2**, 2–11.

Cribbin, J. 1984. *The killing times*. Sydney: Fontana.

Dutton, F. 1846. *South Australia and its mines*. London: Boone.

Egan, Ted 1987. *The Aboriginals song book*, Faces of Australia Series. Richmond, Australia: Greenhouse Publications.

Gale, Fay (ed.) 1982. *We are bosses ourselves: the status and role of Aboriginal women today*. Canberra: Australian Institute of Aboriginal Studies.

Gale, Fay 1987. Aborigines and Europeans. In *Australia, a geography: space and society*, D. N. Jeans (ed.), 129–43. Sydney: Sydney University Press.

Gray, A. & L. R. Smith 1983. The size of the Aboriginal population. *Australian Aboriginal Studies* **1**, 2–9.

Griffin, Trevor & Murray McCaskill 1986. *Atlas of South Australia*. Adelaide: Government Printer and Wakefield Press.

Hallam, Sylvia J. 1983. A view from the other side of the western frontier: or 'I met a man who wasn't there . . .'. *Aboriginal History* **7** (2), 134–56.

Layton, R. 1986. *Uluru: an Aboriginal history of Ayres Rock*. Canberra: Australian Institute of Aboriginal Studies Press.

Long, J. P. M. 1970. *Aboriginal settlements: A survey of institutional communities in Eastern Australia*. Canberra: Australian National University Press.

Maddock, Kenneth 1983. *Your land is our land: Aboriginal land rights*. Ringwood, Victoria: Penguin.

Mattingley, Christobel & Ken Hampton (eds) 1988. *Survival in our own land: 'Aboriginal' experiences in 'South Australia' since 1836*. Adelaide: Wakefield Press.

Miller, James 1985. *Koori: A will to win*. London: Angus & Robertson.

Natham, Pam & Dick. L. Japanangka 1983. *Settle down country*. Malmsbury, Victoria: Kibble.

Peterson, Nicholas & Marcia Langton (eds) 1983. *Aborigines, land and land rights*. Canberra: Australian Institute of Aboriginal Studies.

Peterson, N. (ed.) 1981. *Aboriginal land rights, a handbook*. Canberra: Australian Institute of Aboriginal Studies.

Read, Peter 1984. 'Breaking up these camps entirely': the dispersal policy in the Wiradjuri country 1909–1929. *Aboriginal History* **8** (1), 45–55.

Reynolds, Henry 1981. *The other side of the frontier*. Townsville: James Cook University Press.

Reynolds, Henry 1987. *The law of the land*. Ringwood, Victoria: Penguin.

Rosser, Billo 1978. *This is Palm Island*. Canberra: Australian Institute of Aboriginal Studies.

Rowley, C. D. 1970. *The destruction of Aboriginal society: Aboriginal policy and practice*, Vol. 1. Canberra: Australian National University Press.

Rowley, C. D. 1978. *A matter of justice*. Canberra: Australian National University Press.

Rowley, C. D. 1986. *Recovery: the politics of Aboriginal reform*. Ringwood, Victoria: Penguin.

Toyne, Phillip & Daniel Vachon 1984. *Growing up in the country: the Pitjantjatjara struggle for their land*. Fitzroy, Victoria: McPhee Gribble/Penguin.

Williams, Nancy M. 1987. *Two laws: managing disputes in a contemporary Aboriginal community*. Canberra: Australian Institute of Aboriginal Studies.

12

Making Europe: towards a geography of European integration

ROGER LEE

Qu'est ce que l'Europe? Une forme contradictoire, á la fois stricte et incertaine . . . une pensée qui ne se contente jamais (Paul Hazard, quoted in Barraclough 1963).

One thing seems to be certain: that the actual physical area of Europe, in geographical terms, is a changing quantity . . . For this reason it is generally agreed that any merely geographical definition of Europe is unsatisfactory, and does not correspond fully or accurately to the notions which the word Europe awakens in our minds (Barraclough 1963, 4).

To take time into account is imperative, for . . . the flow of history in Europe . . . has not been interrupted by a major break for at least two thousand years. This continuity of development has contributed to the originality of Europe (Gottmann 1969, 2).

Europe and European integration: 'historic or a dead bore?' If one of the major difficulties facing anyone enquiring into the nature of Europe is its geographical constitution (whether, for example, it includes Russia and what that implies about the USSR, an issue given added piquancy in the nationalist response to *perestroika* and *glasnost'* in the Soviet Union – see Graham Smith, this volume), a further question concerns the basis of unity within the appropriately defined region. Is it merely a unity imposed by external threat emanating from within or beyond 'geographical Europe'; a nebulous and thinly spread idea of a common culture or civilization; a deeper cultural response related to the day-to-day experience and practice of the mass of Europeans; an institutional creature of international treaties (see, for example, Blacksell 1981); or a product of the 'annihilation of space by time' (Marx 1973, 524) which accompanied the transformation of the role of geography in economic life following the emergence of capitalist social relations (Lee 1989a)?

Geographical unity and identity are, as Jean Gottmann (1969, 4) reminds us, socially constructed: 'It has taken long centuries of continued effort to produce most of the regions of Europe'. They are the products of human labour and have created their own historical geographies during a continuous European history of over 2000 years (Thompson 1962). The construction of Europe cannot, therefore, be reduced either to the dynamics of even the most well developed of institutions like the European Communities (EC), to timeless structures such as the physical environment (e.g. East 1961) or to a given culture (e.g. Jordan 1973). This essay attempts to outline the processes involved in the making of this geography and history and so to demonstrate the complexity of Europe and of European integration.

The major thrust of the argument is far from novel: European integration – the making of Europe – is a geographical process based upon the establishment of a set of social relations capable of operating at a European scale and of involving the whole population of Europe. The question then arises as to how the various projects for European integration, the most highly developed of which is the European Community, scarcely a third of a century old, derive their own momentum from this ongoing historical geography? This is the question with which this essay is concerned. In this context, it is worth recalling Sidney Pollard's (1981a) periodization of the European economy, which begins with the phase of economic integration (from the 18th century to the 1870s), followed by the phase of *dis*integration (from the 1870s until the late 1940s) and reaches the present with a phase of *re*integration into two Europes ('East' and 'West') after the Second World War. The creation of the European Community is heavily implicated in this phase of reintegration, but the longer historical perspective and the wider sense of what economic development involves demonstrate that there is rather more to the making of Europe than the late-20th-century development of international institutions.

However, such a perspective is rare in discussions of European integration, and Andrew Shonfield (1973, 9) was the exception that proved the rule when he asked his audience at the Reith Lectures, delivered on the eve of the United Kingdom's accession to the European Community, 'Well, which is it? Feeble or powerful? Historic or a dead bore?' His question was directed specifically at the EC but it raises some rather more general and profound issues: what is the significance and place of institutional integration (i.e. the formal creation of international institutions such as the EC which operate under an agreed set of rules and administration) in the dynamics of contemporary society, and how do they relate to past and present tendencies towards integration or disintegration? The meaning and significance of the EC, for example, go well beyond its institutional appearances and practices and its emergence raises a range of complex questions (Lee & Ogden 1976). These include the geographical meaning of Europe and the significance of divisions *within* European space, the alternative meanings which may be given to integration (Lee 1976), the relationship between changes in European economic geography and the uneven transformation of European culture, society and politics, and the sources of the drive towards European integration. Above all, the debate surrounding the EC is concerned with the question, what is Europe? The non-congruence of European geography, society and state remains a major motor of European history in which the contemporary quest for a Europe constituted by institutions is a very recent manifestation. But such issues are rarely incorporated into discussions of European integration. Even the most effective account of the economics of integration in the EEC (Swann 1988) has only a very brief historical introduction limited to institutional moves towards integration, and makes no mention of the socio-geographic evolution of Europe or its role in the making of the EC. The meaning of Europe itself then becomes 'a dead bore' or perhaps even a non-issue.

European integration: a skeletal historical geography

L'effrondement d'un empire et la naissance d'une Europe (Calmette 1941).

The disjunction between these processes continued in later centuries: the breakthrough towards merchant capitalism produced a world network of economic transactions and undermined political and cultural boundaries, while on the other hand the emergence of strong states tended to mark off clear boundaries and to accentuate territorial identity and citizenship. This is the great paradox of western European developments (Rokkan & Urwin 1983, 25).

The distinction drawn by Immanuel Wallerstein (1974) between world empires and world economy may help elucidate the apparently paradoxical interpretation of Europe as a post-imperial or, perhaps more accurately, a non-imperial entity. Wallerstein (1974, 15) sees '[P]olitical empires' as 'a primitive means of economic domination' and Geoffrey Barraclough's (1963, 13) account suggests that 'the richness and diversity' of European peoples present imperial integration with what have historically been insurmountable problems. He argues that Europe has never been constituted as an empire: the Roman empire was Mediterranean; the Carolingian empire – an incomplete Europe – involved not unity but a dichotomy with the Roman empire in the East and, in equating Christianity with its own limits, was instrumental in the splitting of the Orthodox and Catholic churches. In the post-Carolingian period diversity broke through and 'European unity could henceforward only mean the articulation – not the suppression – of ingrained regional diversity'. (ibid., 13)

This point stems from his argument that the history of European unity since the Renaissance and the Reformation starts from 'the hard fact of existing nation states' (ibid., 26). A concept of European unity based upon the notion of a republic of sovereign powers articulated by a balance of power maintained by diplomatic means was one response, but the partition of Poland at the end of the 18th century undermined this notion. And yet the combined effects of the belief in nationalism – intensified by the French Revolution – and of European imperialism served to render almost unthinkable any alternative notion of integration despite the implications of the rise and fall of Napoleonic Europe. One reason for this lies in the process of European state-making during the 19th century (see Williams 1986, Connor 1981). The state system was dramatically consolidated into a smaller and smaller set of larger and larger states (Tilly 1979). The 50 or so European states on the eve of the French Revolution were reduced by French conquest to about 25 in 1800 and 20 in 1812. Following the defeat of the French, the number increased to about 35 before a new consolidation process which, according to Williams (1986, 204), involved 'the wholesale dismantling of multinational empires in central and eastern Europe under the impulse of nationalism', and led to 25 by the First World War. There is, therefore, sufficient geopolitical experience of the significance of conflict and warfare in the shaping of national territories to back Barraclough's description of the 19th-century belief in the ideals of nationalism as specious. Faced with the implications of the rising superpowers and the emergence of Japan, nationalism led to the attempts in two world wars to create a Europe under the hegemony of one national power. This in turn promoted postwar attempts once more to think of a Europe based upon some credible concept of 'real unity'.

But this is a view of European integration as an essentially political process imposed from above. By contrast, others have given greater priority to *la longue durée* – the slow and geographically sensitive unfolding of social and economic rhythms over a long period of time – and in the process are able to construct a historical geography of integration in Europe rather more responsive to what Fernand Braudel (1985) sees as a triple division of the world into the structures of everyday life, the workings of the market, and the circulation of capital. Strangely, although Barraclough is ready to acknowledge both the supra-national role of the church and the pan-European dimensions of feudalism in a unity of culture and civilization in medieval Europe, his discussion of the European question in modern and postwar history does not refer to what Wallerstein calls the European world economy, based upon capitalist social relations of exchange, which emerged in the late 15th and early 16th centuries. In this sense, then, his is a history which gives priority to political dynamics and institutions. Stein Rokkan & Derek Urwin follow Barraclough's notions of the simultaneous operation of integration and reactive disintegration. They identify 'three distinct elements' (Rokkan & Urwin 1983, 14) of integration and resistance: military-administrative, economic, and cultural. It is the economic which is largely absent from Barraclough's account. Nevertheless, Rokkan and Urwin point, like Barraclough, to the post-Roman rise of feudalism and, like him, they stress the emergent social diversity of the European territory in the medieval period based on the 'multitude of waves of migration, conquest and occupation' that 'has layered the European landscape since the early Iron Age' (ibid., 22).

Nevertheless, their account stresses the emergence of the formative structures of everyday life in the making of Europe: 'it was the alphabet and the city that ultimately decided the fate' of the 'extra-ordinary tangle of territorial structures' (ibid., 30) in Europe. They postulate a North–South and an East–West axis to explain the geography of territorial structuring that ensued. The alphabet facilitated the development of vernacular languages, while the invention of printing permitted mass communication within vernacular boundaries, strengthened as a result of the Reformation. This led not only to the theological break with Rome but to the closer integration of church and emergent state and so to the intensification of nationalism in the North. And printing was also the means for the making of a written and therefore a more permanent geography and history through which, for Benedict Anderson (1984), the imagination of increasingly distinct national communities was stimulated.

The fulcrum of the East–West axis was the string of trading cities from Florence to Hamburg. The competitive relations between these cities inhibited the development of states in central Europe. Political fragmentation in this region contrasted markedly with the formal unification of nations to the West, the consequence, according to Williams (1986, 198) of 'the superior capacity of the local bourgeoisie and state apparatus to control and influence internal economic arrangements while also pursuing vigorous foreign trade and revenue campaigns'. The Elbe river became an increasingly significant marker. Longstanding differences in the social structure of agricultural production on either side of the Elbe (Anderson 1974), ruled in the East by feudal empires and constantly disrupted by the Turkish and Mongol-Tartar invasions of the late Middle Ages (Wallerstein 1974), came to be crucially exacerbated during what Robin Okey (1982, 17) calls the 'sixteenth century turning point ... that made Eastern Europe thereafter a land apart, ... remote from West European experience'. This separation was the product of a process of combined and uneven development: the fragmentary dissolution of feudalism and rise of capitalism in the West contrasted with and exacerbated the limitations, imposed by feudal empires, of the development of industrialization and an urban bourgeoisie in the East.

This continental geography of unevenness provided the context for what were, according to Eric Hobsbawm (1962), the most formative influences upon present-day Europe: the revolutionary changes of the 18th and 19th centuries. Consider the implied transformation of Europe contained within the following commentaries:

pre-industrial, pre-Revolutionary Europe was a conglomeration of small, semi-autarkic markets (Landes 1969, 133).

Europe at the end of eighteenth century was very far from being an economic unit (Ashworth 1974, 296).

The highly commercialized cities and regions, looking to all the known world for trade, aroused great admiration and exerted much economic influence; but they were too few and too small to be able to bind Europe into a closely interdependent economy (ibid., 293–4).

Since 1815, the assimilation of modes of life of European nations into one great common pattern has gone far enough for it to be necessary to treat Europe and the United Kingdom integrally if their recent history is to be understood at all (Thompson 1962, viii).

the whole of Europe ... one single macro-development area (Pollard 1973, 639).

the industrialization of nineteenth century Europe was a single process and had an economic logic of its own (ibid., 647).

Transformation was, it seems, dramatic:

the Englishman of 1750 was closer in material things to Caesar's legionnaires than to his own great grand–children. (Landes 1969, 5).

In fact, the drama was even more intense as the transformation of Europe was highly uneven. We could, for example, substitute the Germany of 1840 for the England of 1750. There is, of course, room for chronological controversy here (see, for example, Tilly 1979, Dodgshon 1987). But, as Robert Dodgshon (1987, 349) points out 'we must avoid the mistake of confusing the achievement of interconnectedness with the more advanced state of interdependence'. Clearly Europe was interconnected well before the 19th century but, as Ashworth (1974) insists, the connections were few and narrowly based (see, for example, Fig. 12.1) until the release of industrial capital across the region enabled a deeper and more broadly based interdependence. Thenceforward, the process of uneven development was precisely a process of the achievement of interdependence.

And the immediate cause of this rapid change? It lay, according to many observers, in 'the nature of production ... if the binding of Europe into a more homogeneous whole came to depend more on economic activities, it was the developments of the 19th century that did most to accomplish the change' (Ashworth 1974, 296 and 292). Put simply, a 'society based on agriculture [had] been replaced by one based on industry and commerce' (Milward & Saul 1973, 19). But this is too simple, for Europe had experienced 'probably the most important event in world history' (Hobsbawm 1962, 29): it had

Figure 12.1 Mozart's Europe, 1756–91. The map shows the principal places visited by Mozart during his extensive European tours undertaken from the age of six. It demonstrates both the limited nature of this geography of European culture connections at this time (see pp. 240) and picks out the largely pre-industrial trading cities in central Europe as crucial to Rokkan & Urwin's geography of European integration.

experienced the industrial revolution and, in the experience, it is argued, a genuinely interdependent Europe was made.

According to this line of argument, Europe was made from the ground up. The uneven spread of capitalist social relations and methods of production, unevenly orchestrated in time, generated profound quantitative and qualitative changes in the geography of economic development (Hall & Preston 1988, Lee 1989a & b). And, from the start, this process was firmly rooted in a geography which had little regard for Barraclough's 'hard fact of existing nation states'; it was, rather, both regional and international and it was, as Pollard (1973, 1981b) had been at pains to stress, a process of uneven development, of integration and disintegration. It could not be otherwise under a form of social organization based upon capitalist social relations which, above all, are based on the 'freedom' of both labour and capital from social and hence geographical constraints upon their relationship. The emergence of productive capitalism in Europe was a geographical and social process far more complex than models of 'modernization' would allow: certainly it offers support for Dodgshon's (1987, 1) view that 'the unfolding human landscape records the successive imprint of different systems of spatial order', and for Tilly's (1979, 39) conclusion that 'the analysis of capitalism and of state making offers a far more adequate basis for the understanding of change'. It was a socially-structured material process demonstrating that 'societal formations are not devised by society in isolation from the practical problems of living in the world, as an exercise in pure idealism, but develop out of the material conditions of existence' (Dodgshon 1987, 2).

Integration and uneven development in Europe

> We are indeed inclined to go so far as to claim that the question of the geographical anatomy of industrial capitalism is likely to become of major theoretical significance throughout the social sciences at large (Scott & Storper 1986, 311).

The geography of development is a crucial component of development itself; it is part and parcel of the wider social relationships of particular forms of society which are always constituted in geographical space. The stress on geographical anatomy highlights a crucial element of development which has been given only sporadic consideration in the past because of the use of spaceless models and the acceptance of containers like nation–states as unproblematic definitions of economies. Michael Dunford (1988), for example, shows that all the differentiated activities involved in the economic development of capitalist societies have geographical requirements and that the conditions to satisfy those requirements are themselves geographically uneven in their occurrence. Furthermore, the extreme flexibility implied by the capital–labour relation in capitalism permits and demands a continual redefinition of both spatial requirements and geographical conditions so that spatial structure is both a dynamic and an exploitable element of production.

Sidney Pollard's (1973, 1981b) critique of the industrial revolution in Europe as a series of national events takes this line of argument further. He shows that the industrialization of Europe between 1760 and the present was shaped not only by regional variations in the endowment of preconditions attractive to industrial investment, or by the regional traditions of technology, styles of industrial organization and labour relations, structures of migration and labour flows, provision of capital and the raising and spending of taxes, but by what he calls 'the differential of contemporaneousness' (1981b, 184). By this is meant that development is shaped not by a mere chronology but by geographical synchronism in that the nature of development in any one place reflects not only the timing of development but the geography of its relationships with other regions. In effect, Pollard's account is a very large-scale case study of the arguments presented in Doreen Massey's (1984) *Spatial divisions of labour*, and so it is not surprising that it has already entered the field of contemporary human geography (Lee 1982, Knox 1984). Pollard sees industrialization in Europe as a temporally and geographically uneven process – 'a process ... of regions, operating in a European context ... an outgrowth of a single root' (ibid., vi, v) – in which the early industrializers entered into complex relations with regions that followed their lead. The industrial revolution 'jumped, as it were, from one industrial region to another, though in a general direction outward from the North-West, while the country in between remained to be industrialised ... much later, if at all'. National frontiers 'still had relatively little influence on economic growth' (ibid., 141) and, while 'the regions of Europe differed ... greatly in their preparedness for change' (ibid., 45), 'industrial growth was essentially a local affair' within the 'single economic community' (ibid., 41, quoting Wrigley 1962) of Western Europe. Of course, the implication here is not that nation-states were of little consequence to the emergence of industrialization in Europe. There were quite clear reciprocal relations between the emergent powers of the state and capitalist industrialization (see, for example, Held 1983), but the point made by Pollard is that industrialization was simultaneously a regional and a Europe-wide process of geographically uneven development and not a series of national processes.

The spread of industrialization gained much of its momentum from the emergent but geographically selective Europe-wide circulation of capital in its various forms. This is an important point, for too much has been made (by, for example, Langton & Hoppe 1983) of Pollard's stress upon the region in industrial development. Pollard's argument stressed the *interrelations* of a pan-European circuit of capital orchestrated by transfers of technology, and flows of labour, capital and trade on the one hand, and the regional constraints upon the conditions of existence and expanded reproduction of the circuit on the other. The result by the late 19th century was an integrated Europe – 'the world's first and greatest industrial region' (Ashworth 1974, 309): Europe 'had a bigger share of [international] trade than all the rest of the world together' (ibid., 307), most of which was intra-European. People, technology and forms of industrial organization flowed across the region. A 'single world-wide system of multilateral trade and payments was in existence, with its centre in London and its most important subordinate activities in a few other European cities' (ibid., 305).

The economic geography of Europe, which was both cause and consequence of this process, has remained remarkably influential, as a sequence of analyses from Delaisi (1929), Clarke, Wilson & Bradley (1969), Seers (1979) and Keeble, Owens & Thompson (1982) asserts. For Rokkan & Urwin (1983,

48), the 'major conclusion is that the European economy is structured around one nodal region, the space of the lower Rhine'. Keeble, Owens & Thompson concur, finding that the region with the highest index of economic potential is Rhineland-Pfalz at the centre of a 'golden triangle' of economic potential in the northeast of the EC with outlying secondary peaks around Paris, London and West Berlin. Their conclusion that 'this basic pattern reflects historic processes of industrialisation, urbanisation and investment in fixed capital which have been operating for at least two centuries' (1982, 430) also points to the relative permanence of the broad outlines of the geography of the European economy. Indeed, Pollard (1973, 638) argues that today, 'after two world wars, the relative level of industrialization and of incomes across Europe still has basically the same pattern' as that achieved by 1914.

Nevertheless, this apparently simple outcome is the product of a complex historical geography. The decisive role was played by capital but not as a simple, mechanical unfolding of some structural logic (Hudson 1988). The very social relations of capitalism themselves are the product of the need for flexibility in the process of accumulation (Lee 1989a). Alternatives are always available but none may be implemented without the engagement with labour and the involvement of the state. And the outcome is not as simple as the necessarily aggregate and macro-scale analyses of economic potential may imply. At a slightly finer spatial scale, Hall & Hay (1980) find that although economic and population growth in the European megalopolis during the 1950s and 1960s was concentrated primarily within an extended triangle (North Holland–Madrid–Rome), it was taking place outside the older industrial areas and the large cities in the North. The exception here is Paris but both London and the eastern Randstad conform to the general rule. Most growth was concentrated in medium-sized cities whilst in southern Europe, by contrast, growth was concentrated in the large cities associated with rural–urban migration.

The incorporation of southern Europe has been a marked feature of postwar development in Europe (see, for example, Dunford 1988, Hadjimichalis 1987, Hudson & Lewis 1985, Williams 1984). The further incorporation of eastern Europe also looks to be increasingly possible as a result both of opportunities for investment and trade now and in the future and of the provision of aid and inter-state co-operation between East and West with the reform of the internal social and political structure of countries such as Poland and Hungary. But this process will be highly complex. It must involve not only divergent social systems, the articulation of which requires new models of social change, but unevenly developed economies – the product, some would say, of distinct world systems (see, for example, the debate in Chase-Dunn 1982), and it may be complicated further by the possible re-emergence of *Mitteleuropa* as the conditions which have maintained a divided Germany and a separate eastern Europe begin to be transformed.

The future of the geography of European capitalism is, like its past, unpredictable. The intersection of the sectoral, technical and organizational dynamics of capital and its changed requirements, the relations between labour and capital and the associated development of what Peter Dicken (1986) calls enabling technologies, will combine in ways which create puzzling new processes of development and puzzling new geographies (see Allen & Massey 1988 for a case study of the extent of those puzzles for the UK economy). Ray Hudson (1988, 494) is only slightly less confused: 'the only reasonable scenario is one of a growing concentration of control functions in a few world cities alongside an increasing variety of forms of organisation of production over space, a simultaneous co-existence of a wide variety of spatial forms of organisation'.

Such a spatial division of labour is driven in part by the increased interpenetration of capitals *within* the advanced economies which, as Amin & Smith (1988, 44) correctly observe, is 'one of the most significant developments in the world capitalist economy in the last two decades'. Taken together, these developments suggest that Europe is being transcended as a space for production (Lee 1985). They give renewed impetus to the moves towards the formal integration of national economies within Western Europe and to the suggestion that a geographically wider notion of Europe than that characteristic of the major international institutions in contemporary Europe might be pursued.

Institutional integration in Europe: a skeletal history

The European Economic Community ... represents an attempt to overcome, within the context of capitalism, one of its major 'contradictions', namely the constantly more marked obsolescence of the nation state as the basic unit of international life (Miliband 1973, 15).

The problem as it presents itself today is how to secure the public interest through the control and sometimes through the active mobilization of enterprises and groups of people which straddle national frontiers (Shonfield 1973, 13–14).

But the Rome Treaty was itself a classic statement of 'negative' integration, or the assumption that the free working of the market – if properly policed – would, in the long run, promote harmony and balance in the structural, social and regional distribution of resources (Holland 1975, 320).

To consider the relationship between economics and politics, or between public and private, is not the same as considering the relationship between capital and state. From this perspective, the EC – even if it is conceived of as an institution – is hardly a 'dead bore'. Its emergence raises a whole series of issues which concern the relationship between the scale of and control over the structure and dynamics of the contemporary economic geography of Europe. It poses anew questions about the existence and nature of Europe, the role of the state in contemporary society and the contemporary significance of the nation-state.

Indeed, the very genesis of postwar institutional integration in Europe was itself a complex consequence of idealism and uneven development within and between the major capitalist and socialist powers of Europe. In 1947 the United Nations (UN) Economic Commission for Europe (ECE) was established with headquarters in Geneva. Its objective was 'to create an instrument of cooperation between all the states of Europe – Eastern, Central and Western' (Swann 1988, 2). It had grown out of the UN Relief and Rehabilitation Association (UNRRA) which had been especially active in Central and Eastern Europe – Italy, Austria, Yugoslavia, Greece, Czechoslovakia, Poland and the Ukraine. But already it was out of touch with reality: the division of Europe between the spheres of the postwar superpowers of the USA and the USSR was founded along the ancient frontier between East and West (see p. 239 above). With the emergence of the World Bank and the IMF under American tutelage, the USA was able to integrate the capitalist world under its leadership as well as limiting the spread of communism within western countries like France and Italy, so encouraging the development of Western Europe as a defence against the East and maintaining access to colonial territories. On the other side of the 'Iron Curtain' it is easy to describe the Soviet-led communization of Eastern Europe either as a 'cynical subversion of democracy by Moscow and its local agents, a manifestation of the Soviet lust for world dominion' or as a 'legitimate response of the Soviets to American imperialism's schemes of military and economic encirclement' (Okey 1982, 188). Events on the ground were rather more complex:

> only the interrelation of local circumstances and international events can fully explain the communization of Eastern Europe ... The search for new directions imposed by the tasks of reconstruction, the energy and ambitions of local communists and disunity and miscalculation of their opponents, the fatalism and opportunism induced by the experiences of war all combined to facilitate the path towards communism that geopolitical realities foreboded. (ibid., 196–7).

And material realities were crucial too. The loss of over 20 million Soviet citizens (about 10 per cent of the total population), 6 million Poles (about 20 per cent) and nearly 2 million Hungarians (about 20 per cent) gives a chilling reminder of the extent of wartime devastation in the East which, combined with the experience of the Allies' strategy with respect to the eastern front during the war, the dropping of the atomic bomb by the Americans in 1945 and, in the same year, the stopping of aid by UNRRA to the Soviet Union, helps towards an understanding of the international context in which, three years after the ceasefire, every state in Eastern Europe was under communist rule.

The Marshall Plan of 1947, under which the USA offered economic aid to the war-devastated European countries (including those in the East – they refused the offer), provided dollars to import goods from the USA as well as providing the material means of restoring the hegemony of capitalist social relations west of the Iron Curtain. The body established to administer the Marshall Plan, the Organization of European Economic Cooperation (OEEC, later to become the Organization for Economic Co-operation and Development – OECD) and the North Atlantic Treaty Organization (NATO) 'dominated the whole pattern of political integration in the years after 1945' (Blacksell 1981, 34). To the extent that this view of European integration forced from without is true, it applies not only in Western Europe. The Council for Mutual Economic Assistance (COMECON) was established in 1949 as a Soviet-led counterpoint to the OEEC, while the Warsaw Pact was formed in 1955 after West Germany joined NATO (Short 1982).

For Pollard, the significance of such instruments of superpower geopolitics for European integration was profound. Writing (1981a, 85 and 86) of the Marshall Plan, he notes its 'success ... which must have astonished even its authors' and points out that:

> its motivation was anti-Russian and anti-communist and it set out to achieve its aims directly by grouping the countries of Western Europe firmly in an anti-Soviet alliance, and indirectly because it was sustained by the belief that poverty would favour communism and prosperity would diminish its impact. Since Eastern Europe was by that time firmly in the hands of communist governments friendly to the Soviet Union, what emerged was that the 'unification' of what is often inaccurately referred to as 'Europe' was achieved only by splitting Europe in two, deliberately and irreversibly, at least for years to come.

But it is as mistaken to interpret the postwar process of European integration as being imposed from above as it is to consider the longer history of European integration as a product of the will of superpowers. Robin Okey (1982), for example, stresses the alternative possibilities that were open to Eastern Europe after 1945 and argues (ibid., 198) that, in the case of Czechoslovakia for example, faced with the realization that 'the west would not fight for Eastern Europe and that the East European states could not cooperate against a mighty neighbour', a further reason for the communist takeover was 'the desire to find a broader solidarity, both between nations and classes'. East European resistance leaders had been involved in drawing up the Geneva Declaration of 1944 (see Pollard 1981a), which proposed a federal Europe including the eastern half of the continent and, as early as October 1957, Adam Rapacki, the Foreign Minister of Poland, was proposing a demilitarized zone in Central Europe. Such an initiative was taken up later by Greece and some neighbouring East European states, and provides a *leitmotif* of the concept of a 'common European home' (see p. 254 below) which was given further substance in the 'Bonn Declaration' signed in June 1989 by President Gorbachev and Chancellor Kohl.

European integration was not, therefore, simply willed as part of a global strategy. Gordon Smith (1972, 305) argues that there were three motives for integration after the Second World War: political, idealistic and economic. Given the new balance of power, some Europeans 'saw that their main hope of self-assertion, even survival, lay in making collective approaches'. For the idealists there was 'the vision of a united Europe' giving 'expression to the "European idea", the institutional realization of a common European culture'. By contrast, the 'realists' argued 'that the needs of advanced capitalism made the old political boundaries outmoded'. None of these orientations favours the nation-state as 'a suitable vehicle for development' and at 'different times each of these diverse motives has preserved the ... momentum'. What is also the case is that West European integration has been prompted as much by national self-interest as by wider European objectives. The smaller countries of Western Europe, Belgium, the Netherlands and Luxembourg – all heavily dependent upon external trade – agreed as early as 1944 to form a Customs Union (Benelux) which came into effect in 1948. The United Kingdom has tended to abhor the concept of supra-nationalism in Europe, turning the Council of Europe, for example, into little more than a debating society and precipitating the resignation in 1951 of Paul Henri-Spaak, its president, who went on to chair the Messina Conference of 1955, established by the foreign ministers of Benelux, France, West Germany and Italy to explore the possibilities for, and to draw up a draft treaty to establish, a European common market and atomic energy organization. For France the problem was the resurgence of industry in the Ruhr. Given that West German industry was vital to the development of the European economy, the 'fundamental question was how the German economy in the sectors of iron, steel and coal (the basic materials of a war effort) could be allowed to regain its former powerful position without endangering the future peace of Europe' (Swann 1988, 6). The answer was the plan, elaborated by Jean Monnet and promoted by Robert Schumann, the Foreign Minister of France, in May 1950. The Schumann Plan brought the European Coal and Steel Community (ECSC) into existence in 1951. Federalists like Altiero Spinelli (1972), for example, found the limitations linked to its sectoral specializations more significant than its achievement of a high authority which was, for him, fundamentally restricted by national rather than European considerations. National interests also prevailed in the abortive attempts to establish European defence and European political communities during the early 1950s and, faced with these political failures, the Benelux countries were instrumental in calling for the establishment of a common market. The United Kingdom withdrew from the negotiations in November 1955 but the Treaties establishing both the EEC and the European Atomic Energy Community (EURATOM) were signed in Rome on 25 March 1957 in, appropriately enough, the *Palazzo dei Conservatori* built at the end of the 16th century to the asymmetrical designs of Michelangelo and in sight only of the rear of the overpowering monument to Victor Emmanuel II and Italian unification located in the *Piazza Venezia*.

A political economy of integration in Western Europe

Positive and negative integration

The economic integration of more or less separate national economies involves, it is said (Pinder 1969, Tinbergen 1954), both negative and positive integration (Lee 1976). The former involves the removal of national barriers to international integration. Three types of negative integration are often recognized: free trade area, customs union and common market. The commitment to create the single European market (an example of a 'common market') by the last day of 1992 was contained in the Single European Act (Cmnd 9758) of 1987 which reaffirms and extends the scope of qualified majority voting within the Council of Ministers of the EC to expedite the passage of the proposals contained in the Commission's White Paper, *Completing the internal market* (1985). This development served to re-establish the drive towards negative integration contained in the Treaty of Rome signed 30 years earlier. In essence (see Pelkmans & Winters 1988 for a more detailed discussion), completing the internal market involves the removal of physical, technical (including barriers to the free movement of labour across national frontiers) and fiscal non-tariff barriers to integration. The intention is to regenerate both static (the removal of costly barriers) and dynamic (the promotion of competition) growth effects within the economy of the EC.

The Commission of the EC (1988) estimates that the static effects of the removal of barriers will amount to between 2.2 per cent and 2.7 per cent of community GDP, while the dynamic effects will range from 3.6 to 3.7 per cent of GDP. Both effects will tend to increase the internal integration of the EC's market and to reduce its accessibility to the rest of the world. The largest micro-economic effects from integration are likely to be experienced within the manufacturing sector, especially in the electrical goods, motor vehicles, chemicals and mechanical engineering industries. Thus, capital goods industries are likely to be most affected and so might be expected to show the most dramatic spatial adjustments, with highly uneven consequences for the future technological base of European regions. By contrast, service industries will be rather less affected by the completion of the internal market, with only sea and air transport, the credit and predominantly nationally organized insurance business and the communications sectors showing significant increases in output as a result of the static and dynamic effects of integration. At the macro-economic level, the major effects of integration (over a period of six years) will be to increase GDP by 4.5 per cent and reduce consumer prices and inflation by over 6 per cent. The effects on employment growth are estimated to be far smaller at around 1.5 per cent.

Positive integration involves moves towards the design and implementation of a unified common policy to regulate the newly integrated economic area. Like negative integration, positive integration can take a number of forms. Distinctions between the integration of particular sectors of the economy (as in, for example, the ECSC) or means of economic management, like exchange-rate policy, on the one hand, and economic and monetary union (EMU) and political integration on the other, are common. Some would argue (see, e.g. the debate in Hodges 1972) that these forms of integration are stages in that the achievement of one provides the preconditions for the achievement of the next.

International integration and the nation-state

Negative integration conforms to the ideology of the liberal state anxious to increase the level of competition within an economic system and responding to the making of European economic geography by removing barriers to interaction across national frontiers. Positive integration involves both an acceptance of state intervention and a belief that supra-national intervention is necessary in an increasingly integrated industrial region which straddles many national frontiers and which is dynamized by circuits of capital operating at a supra-national scale. Under these circumstances, Shonfield argues, a national state has a choice of three options:

> It could insist … on its exclusive national sovereignty and inflict … constraints and controls on the people that it governs; or it could opt out of any kind of public power over these private interests; or it could enter a Community of nations, aiming to exercise such public power jointly (1973, 14).

For Shonfield (ibid., 15) the EC represents the last option: it is 'a group of nations aiming at the joint exercise of public power'. The assumptions underlying this conclusion are that states do indeed have autonomous power to exercise public power and that there is an unambiguous public interest. This conforms to what Richard Scase (1980) calls the 'liberal-democratic' conception of the state and it is, of course, problematic. Robin Murray places his discussion in the context of an international economic geography and raises one difficulty with Shonfield's position:

Liberal models of the international economy, as of international relations in general, still spring from an early utilitarianism. The nation state is treated as the basic category in the world: the atom of the system. States are assumed to be rational, self-conscious, self-determining units, analogies of economic man [*sic*] . . . In contrast . . . Marxist writers have tended to see the international economy, not as an aggregation of national economies, but as a total system in which nations are subordinate structures (Murray 1975, 107, 108).

Thus, for Ernest Mandel, for example,

if there is a tendency towards interpenetration of capital ownership in Europe, the nation state ceases to be an effective means of defending this increasingly international capital. From then on a new form of state will be needed which conforms more closely to the new socio-economic situation (1970, 55).

In this view, the EC is a straightforward supra-national response to the geographical logic of capital accumulation.

But this is just too simple. Clearly, nations are not autonomous but neither are they subordinate. One reason for this is that the nation-state cannot be regarded merely as an economic entity. The nation is, in Hugh Seton-Watson's phrase, 'a community of people whose members are bound together by a sense of solidarity, a common culture, a national consciousness' (1977, 1). And national consciousness is, as we have seen, highly developed in Europe. It is, to use Johnston, Knight & Kofman's qualification, a 'political product of a particular set of circumstances' (in the case of Europe, of the long and continuous history of the continent) 'and hence contingent' (1988, 11). Much of Europe consists, according to Seton-Watson, of 'old nations' – those that had 'acquired national identity or national consciousness before the formulation of the doctrine of nationalism'. The old nations of Europe in 1789 were 'the English, Scots, French, Dutch, Castillians and Portuguese in the west; the Danes and Swedes in the north and the Hungarians, Poles and Russians in the east'. The violence which has attended the development of modern Germany, modern Italy and modern Spain, and which continues in Ireland, testifies that national consciousness is highly developed in 'new' states too.

Thus, in arguing that the nation-state is 'an economic, territorial, linguistic, symbolico-ideological unit linked with "tradition"' Nicos Poulantzas (1974, 172) implies both that the state is dominantly national and that it is legitimated by its concern with all aspects of political and social life and not just the economic. Thus, far from the EC representing what Tom Nairn called 'Europe's newest "constitutional régime"' (1973, 156), overriding the outdated and inadequate nation-states, it remains merely a *delegation in the exercise*' of those functions necessary to sustain society as a whole (Poulantzas

1974, 173). Such a conclusion would be endorsed by the pronounced national (rather than European) bias in the structure and processes of the EC (see, for example, Lee 1976).

Recent developments in European integration

The recent history of European integration, however, begins to question such a judgement. The emergent proposals for positive integration within the EC in the shape of economic and monetary union (EMU) have potentially far-reaching consequences for the geography of the European economy. The achievement of EMU would reduce if not remove national economic sovereignty of a purely formal kind (the ability, for example, to set exchange rates) and replace it – or so its advocates aver – with greater real sovereignty stemming from an increased control over international economic interaction. A crucial feature of EMU is the removal of exchange rate adjustments as a means of national economic policy to cope with problems such as trade imbalances, currency speculation, uneven development in national or regional conditions of production, and inflation. Such adjustments have the effect of dividing a shared economic space and disrupting the flow of capital in its various forms across the boundaries of national economies, thereby disrupting the process of integration (narrowly defined by Harvey 1982, 375 as 'the linking of commodity production in different locations through exchange').

In many ways, then, the move towards EMU simply intensifies negative integration, although the need for institutions like a European System of Central Banks (ESCB) and common policies for dealing with regional and structural adjustment in EMU clearly involve positive integration and could have pronounced geographical consequences. The establishment of a European central banking system would, no doubt, increase the level of inter-urban competition for the operating arm of such an institution. A well-established financial centre such as London could prove attractive as a location, thereby increasing London's primacy within the European circuit of finance capital even if the headquarters of the ESCB were to be located close to the centre of administration of the EC. Such a geographical division of labour would parallel that between Washington (location of the Federal Reserve Board) and New York (where the Federal Reserve Bank is located). But this possibility would be dependent on the participation of the United Kingdom in EMU. It may, in any case, be offset by the already intensifying inter-urban competition within Europe for financial transactions on the international and global markets, and it could be overridden by the claims of, for example, the Bundesbank located in Frankfurt. And outside EMU it is unlikely that London could maintain a role as the major offshore centre for the members of the union, despite its current primacy in many financial sectors.

A further consequence of EMU would be to punish geographical immobility. Whereas unemployment, for example, could be controlled to a certain extent by the sealing effect of currency devaluation, the removal of such an option of policy implies the enforced mobility of labour and capital in the face of geographically uneven development. Indeed, one feature which helps define the geographically optimal extent of an EMU is the mobility of labour and capital. But capital assumes different forms around the circuit of capital (Lee 1989a), and so is inherently far more mobile than labour, whilst the cost of mobility for finance capital tends to zero. Fixed capital also gains, because fluctuations in its exchange value (and hence, given the central significance of profitability as the index of success or failure in capitalist societies, its use value) will be dampened as a result of increased levels of currency stability.

Furthermore, costs of production will fall as markets become less fractured – so facilitating economies of scale, the reduction of transaction costs and the removal of the need to hedge against future variations in sales resulting from currency fluctuations. The removal of barriers to trade will have similar effects upon costs as technical specifications are harmonized. As a result, an effective EMU is likely to increase Europe's attractiveness for inward investment. By contrast, labour faces the increased likelihood of becoming unemployed as its physical form is unitary and its attachment to place far deeper, more complex and indeed crucial for its own reproduction than that of capital. It is far less able to realize its exchange value in geographically distant markets except at great personal, social and economic cost. Hence the need, if EMU is to be politically sustainable, both for a mechanism to generate automatic fiscal transfers in response to shocks affecting particular regions and for statutory rights for all workers.

Alongside the moves towards EMU are the suggestions for making the formally integrated Europe conform more closely to its geographical definition which, in the process, might lead to a greater overlap between the idea of Europe and its physical extent. In 1984, the members of the European Free Trade Area (EFTA) – Sweden, Norway, Iceland, Finland, Portugal, Switzerland and Austria – along with the members of the EC committed themselves in the Luxembourg Declaration to the creation of 'a European economic space' covering the 18 democratic nations of Europe. According to Xavier Pintado *et al.* (1988, 1), the European economic space (EES) is 'a linking arrangement between the EC and EFTA countries designed to limit trade diversion and foster trade creation within Western Europe, while maintaining essential elements of national autonomy' (see Hodder & Lee 1974, ch. 7 for a discussion of trade creation and diversion). Physical border controls will continue to exist within each EFTA country to enable the regulation of relations with third countries but not to limit trade in industrial goods within the EES. Free-trade arrangements within the EES will be extended to non-tariff barriers and quotas and will extend to trade in services.

The Luxembourg Declaration was reaffirmed at the Oslo summit of EFTA in March 1989, when the communiqué spoke of 'the fullest possible realisation of the free movement of goods, services, capital and persons, with the aim of

253

creating a dynamic and homogeneous European economic space' (*Financial Times*, 16 March 1989). (Homogeneity refers here to the reduction of international inequality in formal economic mechanisms and policies rather than the inevitable increase in the sameness of European cities and regions in the face of increased flows of capital at an international scale.) On the same day, Jacques Delors, the President of the European Commission, was addressing the European Parliament in Strasbourg and declared that 'we are not interested only in EFTA but also in the whole of Europe'. Moving even closer to the merger of the idea of Europe and its geography is President Gorbachev's 'common European home' which relates more to an acceptance of the end of the Cold War (including the Soviet recognition of national sovereignty in Eastern Europe) and political initiatives on, for example, the environment, defence and economic co-operation, than to moves towards the formal integration of East and West – despite the Soviet concern for the possibilities of a 'fortress' Europe from 1993. Nevertheless, there is, in the step-by-step approach to rewriting East–West relations, a possibility similar to that pointed up by neofunctionalist theorists of political integration (see Hodges 1972) in the West. The removal of, or reduction in, the significance of defence issues, for example, may change the terms on which East and West may discuss a common future. Nevertheless, the possibilities for more concrete moves towards integration remain uncertain and, as indicated earlier, extremely complex. Of course, none of these developments imply an emergence of Europe from within; they might perhaps be more readily viewed as a strategic response to threats from without (Lee 1985), a response which, as Barraclough (1963) makes clear, has run through much of the history of the purely formal attempts to share a divided space. Certainly, NATO and the Warsaw Pact look likely to remain significant for years to come as supra-European means of intra-European stabilization.

Indeed, the history of integration in post-Carolingian Europe leads Barraclough (ibid., 54–5) to distinguish between European integration as 'a real unity of all the peoples of Europe without exception' and 'common action between such governments as have certain interests in common, within the limits of those interests'. He goes on to question whether 'Europe really constitutes a unity' and points to 'a root problem which has dogged the question of European unity throughout its history: namely the difficulty of making a convincing case for it' (ibid., 56–7).

On geographical integration and regional distinction

VEHICLE EXHAUST PLANS MAY SPLIT NORTH AND SOUTH EUROPE
... the Commission's plan to move to even stricter standards [of controls on car pollution by 1993] will split the EC between the environmentally sensitive north, including West Germany, Denmark, the Netherlands and

Belgium and the volume car producers of the south, Italy, France and Spain (*Financial Times*, 10 April 1989).

EC CURBS ON CAR POLLUTION AGREED
The European Community yesterday agreed far-reaching measures to curb car pollution ... The final package was ... 'greener' ... than the Commission proposal on the table ... This was due to the determination of a key group of countries, led by West Germany and the Netherlands ... Although alliances shifted in the ... negotiations, this lobby was strongly resisted by other member states, notably Britain (*Financial Times*, 10 June 1989).

Much of what is written above is impersonal and concerned with the operation of large-scale processes. It could easily give the impression that we are made by our history and geography rather than that we are responsible for their making. And yet, the point about international integration is not that it implies an increasing homogeneity but that it involves a set of social relations which may be shared. Indeed, geographically uneven development within capitalist society is a component of its dynamism: regional distinct- iveness both influences and is incorporated into the wider framework of capitalist development. International integration and regional distinctiveness are, then, powerful reminders that, in sharing distinction, we are presented with alternatives; it reminds us too that we are heirs *and* creators of geography and history, and that alternatives are always possible if we choose to engage with eyes wide open to the lessons that sharing with distinctive regions may bring.

Such conclusions resonate closely with those of Denis Cosgrove on the significance of landscape. Landscape, Cosgrove argues, 'reminds us of our position in the scheme of nature ... reminds us that only through human consciousness and reason is that scheme known to us, and only through technique can we participate as humans in it' (1989, 122). But, more than this, landscape is 'a constant source of beauty and ugliness, of right and wrong and joy and suffering, as much as it is of profit and loss'. Landscape and region can, in short, enliven us and make us aware of the landscapes and regions that we are capable of constructing. And no matter how uneven the sweep of economics and politics, the *geography* of integration in Europe is more subtle still. More subtle and more profound as its lessons are those of construction: of the ways in which historical geographies have been made over the centuries of European settlement and of how they might be made.

The so-called third Italy (Bagnasco 1977) is a region currently much discussed (see, e.g. Piore & Sabel 1984) as a model for the future development of flexible accumulation in capitalist society. Largely excluded from 19th- and early 20th-century investment in large-scale systems of production more typical of the north of the country, its landscape is characterized by small, craft-oriented, owner-operated agricultural and industrial enterprises, quite distinct from the remoteness of ownership in much of the agricultural and industrial economy of the *Mezzogiorno* (see Dunford 1988). But the region is far more than this; set within the immense achievements of the Renaissance and with traces of earlier Etruscan culture, it evokes in its participants and observers not merely an economic future but a way of understanding the nature of past and present as its own shapes and rhythms – heavily influenced, no doubt, by its form of economic organization – synchronize only in part with those brought in from outside:

> The procession trudged up out of the town. It was easy to recognise what it was but comprehension of its meaning and, more especially, its provenance was something else. Nevertheless, it was a chance encounter of an ordinary event made extra-ordinary for the outside observer. It was fascinating.
>
> At the head the priest walking with a dignity both practised and born of long-standing local acquaintance. Behind him the coffin borne on a hand cart followed by the widow and her relatives, grieving openly. Then more distant relatives, friends and acquaintances, their involvement in the passing seemingly inversely correlated with their distance from the body. All familiar enough except for the openness of a journey not contained behind glass and steel.
>
> But much more remarkable were the bit parts in this drama. There must have been well over two hundred of them – one in forty of the total population of the town. And they followed this death with an acceptance and continuance of life. They had left their shops, offices, fields, factories, houses and workshops in the middle of the day – the sun was bright and the sky deep blue – and talked of what they had left behind. Some were engaged in serious business, others in gossip and badinage. This, for them, was a natural part of the living day, hardly a disruption or a special event. These are the people who make the region work, who collect in the square of an evening to talk and display, to banter and haggle at the Saturday market and to engage on a Sunday in religious worship with an informality which extends, for the older men, to entering the church only for the *Hostias* and leaving immediately afterwards. The requirements of communion satisfied in as conformable a way as possible. They did not enter the cemetery beyond which the road goes unmetalled but returned in much the same way as they had arrived.
>
> Remarkable too for this was an event which allowed the outsider to share in a moment of intense exclusion and so to glimpse a little more deeply into the making and remaking of this place and its people.
>
> Ten minutes later, in the queue (or more accurately its opposite) in the renowned but still tiny butcher's shop (the *Antica Macelleria Falorni*, established in the 1840s, and the exporter of wild boar sausages and

prosciutto all over Europe) the talk is of cycling, meat, football, the new fangled weighing and pricing machines, youth, cooking. And the seat – occupied until this year by the grandmother who accepted payment whilst the grandsons served and wrapped the purchases – is empty. (An Italian summer, Roger Lee, Greve-in-Chianti 1985).

References

Allen, J. & D. Massey (eds) 1988. *The economy in question*. London: Sage.

Amin, A. & I. Smith (eds) 1986. The internationalization of production and its implications for the UK. Chapter 2 in *Technological change, industrial restructuring and regional development*, A. Amin & J. Goddard (eds), 41–76. London: Unwin Hyman.

Anderson, B. 1983. *Imagined communities*. London: Verso.

Anderson, P. 1974a. *Passages from antiquity to feudalism*. London: New Left Books.

Ashworth, W. 1974. Industrialization and the economic integration of nineteenth-century Europe. *European Studies Review* **4**, 291–315.

Bagnasco, A. 1977. *Tre Italie. La problematica territoriale dello sviluppo Italiano*. Bologna: Il Mulino.

Barraclough, G. 1963. *European unity in thought and action*. Oxford: Basil Blackwell.

Blacksell, M. 1981. *Post-war Europe*. London: Hutchinson.

Braudel, F. 1985. *Civilization and capitalism, 15th–18th centuries*. Vol. 1: *The structures of everyday life: the limits of the possible*. London: Fontana.

Calmette, J. 1941. *L'effrondement d'un empire et la naissance d'une Europe. IXe-Xe siècles*. Paris: Aubier, Editions Montaigne.

Chase-Dunn, C. (ed.) 1982. *Socialist states in the world system*. Beverly Hills: Sage.

Clark, C., F. Wilson & J. Bradley 1969. Industrial location and economic potential in Western Europe. *Regional Studies* **3**, 197–212.

Commission of the European Communities 1988. The economics of 1992. *European Economy* **35**.

Connor, W. 1981. Nationalism and political illegitimacy. *Canadian Review of Studies in Nationalism* **8**, 201–28.

Cosgrove, D. 1989. Geography is everywhere: culture and symbolism in human landscapes. Chapter 2.2 in *Horizons in human geography*, D. Gregory & R. Walford (eds), 118–35. London: Macmillan.

Delaisi, R. 1929. *Les deux Europes*. Paris: Payot.

Dicken, P. 1986. *Global shift. Industrial change in a turbulent world*. New York: Harper & Row.

Dodgshon, R. A. 1987. *The European past. Social evolution and spatial order*. London: Macmillan.

Dunford, M. 1988. *Capital, the state, and regional development*. London: Pion.

East, W. G. 1961. Europe – a geographical expression. In *A geography of Europe*, 2nd edn, G. W. Hoffman (ed.), 3–13. London: Methuen.

Gottmann, J. 1969. *A geography of Europe*. New York: Holt Rinehart & Winston.

Hadjimichalis, M. 1987. *Uneven development and regionalism: state, territory and class in southern Europe*. London: Croom Helm.

Hall, P. and D. Hay 1980. *Growth centres in the European urban system*. London: Heinemann.

Hall, P. and P. Preston 1988. *The carrier wave*. London: Unwin Hyman.

Held, D. (ed.) 1983. *States and societies*. Oxford: Martin Robertson.

Hobsbawm, E. J. 1962. *The age of revolution: Europe 1789–1848*. London: Weidenfeld & Nicolson.

Hodder, B. W. and R. Lee 1974. *Economic geography*. London: Methuen.

Hodges, M. (ed.) 1972. *European integration*. Harmondsworth: Penguin.

Holland, S. 1975. *The socialist challenge*. London: Quartet.

Hudson, R. 1988. Uneven development in capitalist societies: changing spatial division of labour, forms of spatial organization of production and service provision, and their impacts on localities. *Transactions of the Institute of British Geographers* **13**(4), 484–96.

Hudson, R. and J. Lewis (eds) 1985. *Uneven development in southern Europe*. London: Methuen.

Johnston, R. J., D. B. Knight & E. Kofman (eds) 1988. *Nationalism, self-determination and political geography*. London: Croom Helm.

Jordan, T. 1973. *The European culture area*. New York: Harper & Row.

Keeble, D., P. L. Owens & C. Thompson 1982. Regional accessibility and economic potential in the European Community. *Regional Studies* **16**(6), 419–32.

Knox, P. 1984. *The geography of Western Europe*. Beckenham: Croom Helm.

Landes, D. 1969. *The unbound Prometheus*. Cambridge: Cambridge University Press.

Langton, J. and G. Hoppe 1983. *Town and country in the development of early modern western Europe*. Historical Geography Research Series No. 11.

Lee, R. 1976. Integration, spatial structure and the capitalist mode of production in the EEC. Chapter 2 in *Economy and society in the EEC: spatial perspectives*, R. Lee & P. E. Ogden (eds), 11–37. Farnborough: Saxon House.

Lee, R. 1982. What should we think of when we think of Europe? In *Fresh perspectives in geography: papers presented to the QMC sixth form conference 1981*, M. Gray & R. Lee (eds), Special Publication No. 3. London: Department of Geography, Queen Mary College.

Lee, R. 1985. The future of the region: regional geography as education for transformation. Chapter 5 in *Geographical futures*, R. King (ed.), 77–91. Sheffield: Geographical Association.

Lee, R. 1989a. Social relations and the geography of material life. Chapter 2.4 in *Horizons in human geography*, D. Gregory & R. Walford (eds), 152–69. London: Macmillan.

Lee, R. 1989b. Urban transformation. In *Social problems and the city*, D. Herbert & D. M. Smith (eds). Oxford: Oxford University Press.

Lee, R. & P. E. Ogden 1976. Introduction. Chapter 1 in *Economy and society in the EEC: spatial perspectives*, R. Lee & P. E. Ogden (eds), 1–7. Farnborough: Saxon House.

Mandel, E. 1970. *Europe vs America*. London: New Left Books.

Marx, K. 1973. *Grundrisse*. Harmondsworth: Penguin.

Massey, D. 1984. *Spatial divisions of labour*. London: Macmillan.

Miliband, R. 1973. *The state in capitalist society*. London: Quartet.

Milward, A. S. & S. B. Saul 1973. *The economic development of continental Europe 1780–1850*. London: Allen & Unwin.

Murray, R. 1975. The internationalization of capital and the nation state. Chapter 5 in *International firms and modern imperialism*, H. Radice (ed.), 107–34. Harmondsworth: Penguin.

Nairn, T. 1973. *The left against Europe?* Harmondsworth: Penguin.

References

Okey, R. 1982. *Eastern Europe 1740–1980*. London: Hutchinson.

Pelkmans, J. & A. Winters 1988. *Europe's domestic market*. London: Routledge.

Pinder, J. 1969. Problems of European integration. In *Economic integration in Europe*, G. R. Denton (ed.), 143–70. London: Weidenfeld & Nicolson.

Pintado, X., T. Suselainen, T. Wieser, P. M. Wijman & J. M. von Wurtemburg 1988. *Economic aspects of the European economic space*, Occasional Paper No. 25. Geneva: Economic Affairs Department, European Free Trade Association.

Piore, M. J. & C. F. Sabel 1984. *The second industrial divide. Possibilities for prosperity.* New York: Basic Books.

Pollard, S. 1973. Industrialization and the European economy. *Economic History Review* **26**, 636–48.

Pollard, S. 1981a. *The integration of the European economy since 1815*. London: Allen & Unwin.

Pollard, S. 1981b. *Peaceful conquest*. Oxford: Oxford University Press.

Poulantzas, N. 1974. Internationalization of capital relations and the nation state. *Economy and Society* **3**, 145–79.

Rokkan, S. & D. Urwin 1983. *Economy, territory, identity*. London: Sage.

Scase, R. 1980. *The state in western Europe*. London: Croom Helm.

Scott, A. J. & M. Storper 1986. *Production, work, territory*. London: Allen & Unwin.

Seers, D. 1979. The periphery of Europe. In *Underdeveloped Europe*, D. Seers, B. Schaeffer and M. L. Kiljunen (eds), 1–35. Brighton: Harvester.

Seton-Watson, H. 1977. *Nations and states: an enquiry into the origins of nations and the politics of nationalism*. London: Methuen.

Shonfield, A. 1973. *Europe: journey to an unknown destination*. Harmondsworth: Penguin.

Short, J. R. 1982. *An introduction to political geography*. London: Routledge & Kegan Paul.

Smith, G. 1972. *Politics in Western Europe*. London: Heinemann.

Spinelli, A. 1972. The growth of the European movement since the Second World War. Chapter 2 in *European integration*, M. Hodges (ed.), 43–68. Harmondsworth: Penguin.

Swann, D. 1988. *The economics of the Common Market*, 6th ed. Harmondsworth: Penguin.

Thompson, D. 1962. *Europe since Napoleon*. London: Hutchinson.

Tilly, C. 1979. Did the cake of custom break? in *Consciousness and class experience in nineteenth century Europe*, J. Merriman (ed.), 17–44. New York: Holmes & Meier.

Tinbergen, J. 1954. *International economic integration*. Amsterdam: Elsevier.

Wallerstein, I. 1974. *The modern world system*. London: Academic Press.

Williams, A. M. (ed.) 1984. *Southern Europe transformed*. New York: Harper & Row.

Williams, C. H. 1986. The question of national congruence. Chapter 9 in *A world in crisis?*, R. J. Johnston & P. J. Taylor (eds), 196–230. Oxford: Basil Blackwell.

Wrigley, E. A. 1962. *Industrial growth and population change*. Cambridge: Cambridge University Press.

Index

260

DATE DUE

DEC 1 1 1991	JUN 1 5 1997
NOV 21	JAN 2 7 1998
MAY 1 4 1992	MAR 1 8 1998
MAY 1 1 1992	MAR 1 8 1998
JUN 0 3 1992	OCT 1 9 1998
MY 16 '92 4	March 1, 1999
OCT 0 2 1992	4/28/99
SEP 1 6 1993	OCT 2 7 1999
	MAR 0 7 2003
APR 2 2 1996	
MAY 1 3 1996	
JUN 0 5 1996 W	
JAN 2 8 1997	
MAY 0 6 1997	
MAY 2 1 1997	
JUN 11, 1997	

DEMCO 38-297